Give Me Irish Heroes

15 Reasons to be Happy

By

Ian Mc Keever

Donations from sales to Gaisce – the President's Award
and other charities

Publisher
Ian Mc Keever

Front Cover Design
Andrew Dawson

Layout & Proofing
Michelle Thomas
&
Genevieve Farrell

ISBN 978-0-9564042-0-6

© Ian Mc Keever, 2009

Printed by
OBrien Printing, Dublin 10. Tel [0]1 6266722

Contents

Acknowledgements

First and foremost, the greatest thank you goes to the 15 'heroes' about whom this book is written. I wish to thank each and every one of you for sharing your stories, for your courage and support and continued positivity...

In addition:
- The entire rowing team that attempted to cross the South Atlantic Ocean. Thank you all for your wise and considered reflections. To Matt's wife, Helen, for her support and advice
- To Gertie and the entire Mc Donnell family and also to Dr Clare O' Leary. Thank you all so much for your time and support. It was a genuine privilege to be allowed to share this remarkable story of Ger's
- To Niamh Power. Thank you so much for your advice and wisdom on your mother's remarkable journey
- To Matt Porter for your wonderful illuminations on Elaine's journey in Africa. To Grainne Bagnall and all at the Dublin Rotary Club for your support
- To Emma and her family and to Dr Tony Bates. Thank you all so much for helping me in the sharing of Emma's incredible story
- To Tish Durack for the painstaking hours of research and the support in the telling of Seamus's epic roller coaster journey to date
- To Jim Barry and family for your wonderful support in helping me to share Orla's courageous story
- To fellow colleagues, friends and family of Dr Austin O' Carroll for your invaluable help in telling Austin's story
- To fellow colleagues, friends and family of Gary Keegan, in particular Dr Johnston Mc Evoy, Dr Jim Ryan, Billy Walsh and Daragh Sheridan
- To the staff and pupils at Post Primary School Maynooth and in particular to the family of Dave Campbell
- To the entire Sheahan family for your help and support and to Barry O' Donovan from the Irish Red Cross in contribution to 'Ma's' remarkable story
- To Breffny and the Morgan family for allowing me to share Richard's inspiring story

- To Alison Maguire. A very special thank you. We invited public nominations for one 'publicly nominated hero' and this is her inspiring story about her husband Alex
- To the Hughes family and in particular to 'Laz' for his tireless efforts in the telling of Dave's courageous story
- To the Roche family and in particular to Miriam Farrelly and colleagues in the Chernobyl Children's Project for their invaluable support in telling Adi's wonderful story

- To the Staff and Management of the Louis Fitzgerald Group and the Heritage Hotel in Portlaoise.

Donations from the sales of this book will go to Gaisce – The President's Awards, The Chernobyl Children's Project, The Irish Red Cross and 'Operation Smile' – Changing lives one smile at a time, and towards the setting up of a permanent museum for the Dublin Fire Brigade, which will be on view to the public.

In helping to make all of this possible, I would like to thank you, the reader, Hughes & Hughes Booksellers, Tesco Ireland Limited, The Independent Book Shops of Ireland and participating secondary and primary schools across the country.

I want to pay special tribute to Michelle, Genevieve and to Anne Swanton for their work behind the scenes in all the edits and corrections – your support and patience meant a great deal.

When we are *'up against it'*, and we need to have remarkable people in our corner to help us through, I was very privileged to have two of the very best people, one could ever wish to have, supporting me... To Tracy Swanton and to Maura Dolan, I owe you both a debt of gratitude that I may never be able to repay. Your kind and selfless actions made it possible for me to be able to finish this book, when really I didn't think I could...

Dedication
This book is dedicated to all of those unsung heroes who are all around us...

In memory of Ger Mc Donnell

Message from
The President of Ireland
Mary McAleese

It gives me great pleasure to add my voice to those of the fifteen people featured in *'Give Me Irish Heroes'*. This has been a difficult year for Ireland and for Irish people, faced with worries about the economic situation, unemployment and a host of related challenges. It would be easy to lose hope and to give in to the counsel of despair. Yet it is precisely in these dark times that we can most benefit from the stories of inspiration and hope brought to us by the fifteen heroes featured in this book. Some are people whose stories I know personally, some are people who I have never met, yet they are all people who have faced challenges and overcame these through hard work, self-belief and a wonderful sense of hope. Some were pushing the boundaries that they faced due to disability or illness, some set their own challenges for personal fulfilment or to support a cause in which they believed. They range in age from children to the elderly and include every point in between. Their courage and ambition inspirational and give us cause to hope in these challenging times. Standing behind the heroes celebrated in this book are the families, friends and professionals who supported them on their individual journeys and this book is also a tribute to their encouragement and backing.

These modern Irish heroes are an inspiration to us all. They can teach us how to overcome adversity and harsh times and they have shown us the power of never giving up. I am delighted that their remarkable spirit can also be found in the countless volunteers and community workers around the country who, in ever increasing numbers, give of their time and skills and effort to make a difference to the people around them. *'Give Me Irish Heroes'* is a celebration of the wonderful Irish capacity to tackle challenges head-on and to make a difference in situations of hardship. I thank these fifteen wonderful people for sharing their stories and I wish them all well in continuing to make a positive impact on their own lives and the lives of their communities.

Mary McAleese

MARY McALEESE
PRESIDENT OF IRELAND

Message from
P.G. Callaghan
Gaisce

Is onóir mór dom cúpla focal a rá maidir leis an leabhar seo. I am honoured to make a contribution to this worthy endeavour. Ralph Waldo Emerson told us that *nothing great was ever achieved without enthusiasm.* Ian McKeever has approached this work, as he always does, with great enthusiasm. It is clear from the people that Ian has interviewed that they all felt a level of dissatisfaction in themselves to want to change things about themselves, their communities and the world they live in. Their stories will energise and inspire all who read this book.

In Gaisce we are continually exposed to people of all ages who are dissatisfied with sitting back and who live heroic lives on a daily basis nurturing and supporting their fellow human beings. Helen Keller said that *one can never consent to creep when one feels an impulse to soar.* The people whose stories are contained in this book will provide an impetus and inspiration to its readers to change themselves and to change the world we live in.

Comhghairdeachas agus mile buíochas do chuile dhuine atá páirteach leis an obair ghaisciúil seo.

P. G. Callaghan (Barney)
Chief Executive
Gaisce – The President's Award

October 2009

Prologue

Dictionary definitions of a 'Hero'

A man or woman of distinguished courage or ability, admired for his or her brave deeds and noble qualities.

A person who, in the opinion of others, has 'heroic' qualities or has performed a heroic act and is regarded as a model or ideal: *He was a local hero when he saved the drowning child...*

Beginnings....

It was a beautiful spring afternoon in 2008. On that memorable day, I sat mesmerised in Donnybrook. I had never been to a *'school boy'* rugby game before. On the pitch, two schools, Belvedere and Terenure College, were contesting the first round of The Leinster Schools Senior Cup; the most coveted prize in school boy rugby. Nothing means more to these lads than being picked for their respective teams and playing for seventy minutes with passion and honour.

Despite giving away almost 17lbs a man, and starting the game as the clear underdogs, the 15 players on the Terenure team were filled with belief, belief in each other and belief in themselves. Thanks to a coach, Padraig Forde, who had tasted All Ireland glory back in 1995 as a GAA player with Kilmacud Crokes, these boys realised that the only thing they had to worry about was what **they** did on the pitch, how **they** reacted when things went wrong and how much responsibility **they** were prepared to take for their own actions.

At half-time, leading by the narrowest of margins, despite not having the ball for large portions of the half, Padraig informed the team that they were only approaching the *'summit'* and that they still had to come off this mountain safely if they were going to achieve one of the greatest upsets in the recent history of school boy rugby.

For 35 more minutes, the boys in purple and black, the lads from the *'Nure'* as they were better known, put their bodies on the line; tackling furiously, defending doggedly, supporting each other, man for man, encouraging each other, fighting for every inch of the pitch as they clawed their way into their opponents' half, time and time again, defending their precious two point lead.

In the end, Belvedere needed five and a half minutes of extra time to finally breach their opponents' line and in so doing with the final play of the game, try finally secured, they had finally broken their opponents' resistance… In a way, it was heartbreaking to watch. Everyone in the packed stands knew they had witnessed something very special, something that surpassed ego and glory, and something that was far nobler indeed.

I had never seen anything like it. Though I had played on wonderful teams in my own school days, I had simply never seen a group of lads ever try harder than they had done on that day.

I felt very privileged, in some small way, to have been given the opportunity to be part of the Terenure setup, to have been given the opportunity to address the boys in purple and black and offer some words of encouragement before the game.

I knew that those lads were made of the *'right stuff'* and that they would go on to great things not only on the pitch but, moreover, in life. I knew too that many of these lads would be returning as sixth years and would get a second chance in 2009.

Their time would come; they would yet achieve their moment … After the match, I approached Padraig to see if we could work with some of the lads going forward, off the rugby pitch, to give one or two of them the opportunity to grow as individuals and team leaders… the chance to work outside their comfort zones. *"What have you got in mind?"* he asked. *"I have a godson, Sean, who needs an exceptional mentor for a very exceptional challenge"* I replied, smiling.

****

At approximately 8am, on the 5th of May 2008, Sean McSharry made a little bit of history in becoming the youngest European to stand on the summit of Africa's highest peak. The *'Broccoli Kid'* as he had become affectionately known, who had switched his diet, trained diligently for 3 months and put up with having to take orders from his godfather, had shown the world what was truly possible when you believe in yourself and what life can feel like when your glass is perceived as half full… There are no words, nor will there ever be, to describe the immense pride I felt standing there beside him that day.

The admiration I felt too for his mother, Noeleen, for having the courage to let him try in the first place. Sean's achievement aside, his <u>actions</u> were heroic to me. He had, unbeknownst to himself, set in motion a chain of events that would have a profound effect on a great many more people back home in Ireland; kids and adults alike who dared to dream of what might be possible in life. In 2009, a group of 62 climbers from all walks of life would take their place on *'Uhuru'* peak, Africa's highest point, in support of the Irish Red Cross, thanks in no small part to what one brave, modest little ten-year-old had managed one year previously.

One story that didn't make the headlines from Sean's great achievement was the selfless actions of one 5th year student from Terenure College who had volunteered to help train and mentor Sean in both his preparation and on the actual trip to Kilimanjaro.

One young man, a brilliant and talented winger for the Terenure Senior Cup Team who, despite never having climbed himself before, was willing to make whatever sacrifices were necessary for no obvious return other than what the experience might do to enrich his own life.

What nobody knows, in fact, is that on that mountain, Harry Moore, aged 17, struggled desperately to cope with the altitude. He was sick every day up to and including summit day.

On the actual summit night, he crawled on his hands and his knees to make sure that he could be there for Sean as his mentor when he reached the summit point, never complaining once, never shirking his responsibility … Without this unsung hero there might not have been a summit that morning, there might not have been that surge of hope that others would feel back home and, most of all, there might not have been the true inspiration for this book.

****

Ask any 17-year-old today to name the greatest speech they have ever heard or seen and most of them will automatically hand you their iPods and play you back the words of Tony D'Amato, the character played by Al Pacino so memorably in *'Any Given Sunday'*.

To paraphrase, if I may, the inspiration and the heroes, like the inches we seek, are all around us. *"They are the six inches in front of our face…"*

I hope that these stories may help, in some small way, to give you all the *'inches'* that you seek in life… They represent 15 reasons to be happy. Enjoy!

1

A Life of Giving

Hannah Sheahan

'A handful of pine-seed will cover mountains with the green majesty of forests. I too will set my face to the wind and throw my handful of seed on high.'

Fiona Mac Leod

The trip to Mallow that afternoon was a strange experience. I was coming from Limerick on *'All Ireland'* Sunday into the heart of Cork County. The streets were awash with colour. As I left the parts of Limerick County, bordering with the Kingdom, the colours spectrum slowly changed from a bright flurry of gold and green to a very distinctive sea of red. Anticipation was in the air... Yet I felt strangely detached, unable to take in the revelry. As I approached the town of Buttevant, my mind turned the clock back to the only two other previous occasions I had been in this quaint place, formerly a medieval town incorporated by charter by Edward the Third.

The first time was a sad affair, the funeral of a friend of mine who had been killed in a head-on car crash. The second was equally sombre. I was attending a meeting in Charleville when I passed through the town just before lunch on August the 1st 2005... the place was eerily silent. There was a minute's silence and the town stood still in memory of those who had tragically and needlessly lost their lives in the horrific Buttevant train crash. That day marked the 25th anniversary of one of the worst train derailments to ever occur in the Republic of Ireland...

At 12:45, a CIE express train coming from Dublin bound for Cork, entered Buttevant station at 115km/h carrying some 230 Bank Holiday passengers. It careered into a siding and smashed into a stationary ballast train. The carriages immediately behind the engine and goods wagon jackknifed and were thrown across four sets of rail-line. Two coaches and the dining car were totally demolished by the impact. It resulted in the deaths of 18 people and over 70 people being injured. The passengers who were most severely injured or killed were seated in coaches with wooden frames! This structure was wholly incapable of surviving a high speed crash and did not come near to the safety standards provided by modern (post 1950's) metal bodied coaches. The expert bodies that reviewed that accident discovered that the old timber-frame carriage bodies mounted on a steel frame were totally inadequate as they were prone to complete collapse (creating what's known as the '*accordion*' effect) under the enormous compression forces of a high speed collision. While the steel underbody remained structurally intact, other carriages could '*mount*' the frame, completely compress, and destroy the wooden frame body....

The aftermath of this tragedy is significant for two reasons. Firstly, the travelling Irish public was provided with a modernised fleet - one that ensured the rapid elimination of the wooden-based coaches that had previously formed part of the train. Equally significantly, were it not for the actions of the woman I was en route to visit in Mallow and her hard working colleagues in the Mallow branch of the Irish Red Cross, more people would have certainly died that Bank Holiday afternoon...

****

Hannah Sheahan had the dinner on that afternoon when the phone rang at three minutes past one. The caller, a local councillor, asked if Mrs Sheahan of the Irish Red Cross was anywhere nearby. "*You're speaking to her*", Hannah responded. She knew there was trouble ahead. She had taken similar calls in the past many times... Before you could blink an eye, she was off that call and making a host of others.

First up a call to Dermot, her son-in-law. They needed a crane to remove various obstacles on the main Cork Road, (which was being built at the time) but his wasn't big enough. Without hesitation it was on to one of the main crane suppliers in the Cork area, William O' Brien who, following his call, downed tools and was soon on his way. Next, she rounded up her fellow volunteer colleagues from the Mallow branch of the Irish Red Cross: Mike Murphy, Pat Mc Auliffe, Donal Cullity and Gerard Hartnett. She put in a call to the then Area Chairman, Tom Mills, who in turn contacted Liam Ware, another colleague working in CIE. She then called the sugar factory, draperies, and all the workplaces where the Red Cross volunteers worked, and asked them to go to Buttevant as soon as possible. "*Employers were good in those days,*" she remarked, and they realised the importance of the voluntary work these men did in their spare time, and so the men were all released and headed immediately to the site of the accident.

With her calls made, Hannah Sheahan put on her familiar white coat and ran out the door. It was a baking hot day. The councillor had simply informed her that they would be dealing with anything up to 400 passengers but made no reference to the numbers injured or fatalities.

They left her home in the Red Cross ambulance that was parked in her driveway behind the house and headed for the station in Buttevant, uncertain of what lay ahead ... With the crew all assembled at the scene of the accident, and Hannah being the only woman, they began to pull the trapped victims out from under the carriages and shuttle patients to Mallow Hospital in the ambulance. At the hospital, Hannah was asked to clear the wards of visitors so that the nurses and doctors could work more effectively.

Back at the devastating scene, Hannah's colleagues, along with other members from the emergency services, placed yellow plastic sheets over the dead, and walked with them on stretchers to the makeshift morgue on site. They would then re-use the sheets on the other dead bodies that were taken back to the morgue. Later in the day, the Red Cross ambulance was used to take the fatally injured to the Cork Regional Hospital for inquest. Hannah and her team stayed providing support until midnight that night, helping in the search for any more victims who may have been trapped, and returned early the next morning again to continue the search under other carriages...

****

When I arrived in Mallow my spirits began to rise. I was en route to meet a true living legend. Some of us make our way through life, stumbling and teetering along the way, feeling sorry for ourselves as we continue to see the glass of life as always being half empty. Some even delight in the idea of bad news, find cynical pleasure in being negative about anything and anyone to anyone and everyone that will naively give them the time of day. Such people drain us. They suck us dry of our positivity, our energy and our spirits...

'*Ma*' Sheahan, as she is affectionately known throughout the length and breath of Cork city and county, is the complete antithesis - a human dynamo whose ability to always turn a pending disaster into an undiscovered opportunity, is not only refreshing but a godsend! An octogenarian with the spirit of a twenty-year-old and energy of a woman less than half her age, we agree to meet at the family home which is just a short few miles north of Mallow town.

"*You'll be eating before we get started, I assume?*" She greets me warmly and escorts me into the dining room - news of my massive appetite for food must have spread south! As I sit down to eat, I pass a picture of herself and the Secretary General, John Roycroft, that sits proudly on the mantle piece. "*I was catching flies that day,*" she says laughing in reference to the wide grin on her face. I inform her that, as part of the 70th anniversary celebrations, the picture is included on a massive banner outside the Head Office of the Irish Red Cross on Merrion Square. Ma had a kind face, whose smile could light up any occasion. I'm sure many people's moods have been lifted in Dublin city from looking at the happy picture of her and John as they pass the IRC office on their way to or from work.

Before we get down to business, curious, I ask her to show me the blazer she's pictured wearing in the photograph with John. It's neatly hung away, but Ma is happy to indulge my inquisitive nature… I'd heard the stories of the various stripes emblazoned on the famous Red Cross blazer. I asked her about the stripes and what they signify. "*Well there are five there at the moment*"… She smiles at me. "*There will be a sixth in place in 2011!*" Each stripe, as Ma explains, signifies 10 years' voluntary service.

10 years of voluntary service. It's hard to fully comprehend this woman has given almost sixty years of her life, voluntarily, very happily, to an organisation she cares about passionately. Interestingly, Ma Sheahan is the first to acknowledge that being a volunteer means you get back as much as you give; how refreshing to hear someone acknowledge that, I think to myself. Ma is, not surprisingly, the longest serving member of the IRC. Modestly she comments, "*It gives me immense pride and joy to be still involved'.'*

Two of the biggest recent movie remakes, '*Scrooge*', which starred the irrepressible Bill Murray and '*The Day the Earth Stood Still*', featuring a rather wooden Keanu Reaves as the alien sent to earth to warn the human population to change its ways or face extermination, were both based on original films that came out in 1951. In fact, both films were in the top five grossing back in the year in question. One might argue, in fact, that 1951 was a particularly good year for cinema goers with a host of wonderful films released, which included two of my all times favourites: '*The African Queen*', which brought Bogart and Hepburn's chemistry nicely to the boil and '*Strangers on a Train*', the brilliant, if sometimes forgotten, quintessential Hitchcock thriller that tells the tale of '*Two men, a problem, and a crime*'- an old theme, but the list of works that exploit it perfectly is a short one. '*Strangers on a Train*' I would argue, belongs on it. When I ask Ma's opinions, she laughs out loud. Ironically was it not for this lady's complete distaste in cinema-going, we might not have been sitting together that All Ireland afternoon.

You see Ma's husband at the time, Patrick, was an avid cinema goer and, realising quickly his wife was never going to be become an ardent lover of the silver screen, he encouraged her to take up another hobby for herself, an outlet that would provide her with the means to channel her zest for life... Their local parish priest informed her that Mrs Tom Barry, who was Chairperson of the Irish Red Cross, was coming to Mallow to form a local branch. There had been a branch during the emergency years (the euphemism given by the Irish Government to the years of the 2nd World War during which Ireland remained neutral but nevertheless declared an official *'State of Emergency'*) but it had died out. *"Mrs Barry thought that men and women were so good during that period that they should try and do something to bring the branch back together."* The notion seemed reasonable enough... So on the 6th of October 1951, along with 103 other people who gathered together in the local parish hall that night, Ma became a founding member of the new Mallow branch of which she remains the only active member.

****

"The perfect husband is born once in a lifetime," Ma reflects to me, when I ask after her own one, Patrick.

It's a line I suspect she's used many times in the past, having to explain to curious folk why she chose never to marry again. Patrick died of stomach cancer in Christmas 1962 leaving Ma with five kids, the youngest of which was only five months old at the time. She shows me a photograph of him.

He's tall in stature with a kind and handsome face. *"I wonder why he picked such a small woman,"* she says smiling modestly. They had been married 16 years when he sadly passed away. She had heard a lot about this man with the *'trashing machine'* that managed his uncle's farm at the time and lived in a small village called Drispy. Ma was living in Donoughmore at the time. *"All the girls had said how gentlemanly he was and what a lovely person he was to be around."*

When they met he asked her out and they moved to Mallow, whereupon he took over managing the Ballyclough Co-op. This would later become Dairy Gold following the merger with Mitchelstown Dairies in 1990. *"He had come from the country and didn't know that much about Mallow at first. It was quite a progressive town with lots of small industries."* Little did Ma realise she would go on to give First Aid courses in all of them!

Ma had married young. She was only 20, in fact, at the time. It was tough going at the time for a widow trying to make ends meet. Perhaps it was pride, perhaps her iron will, but despite the difficulties one can only imagine - in trying to raise 5 children ranging in ages from 6 months to 15 years, Ma Sheahan never took a penny in supplementary allowance income. *"In the years after Paddy's death we became very close, more like sisters in fact"* she says, referring to the special bond that grew between herself and her daughters. She had some limited savings but the bulk of what she would earn incomewise came from a four acre field which was behind the family home. With the help of her kids, they completed the regular chores required to make the pennies stretch: fattening the pigs and raising poultry for market and milking the cows for supplying the local creamery.

'Ma' never put pressure on her kids where their school work was concerned. But the strong work ethic and the need to pull together when the chips were down seemed to instil a natural desire in all of her kids to want to give their very best in all that they did. Indeed the local priest, Fr. Denis O' Connor, used to pass the house, often likening it to Cork airport with all the lights on... Each of the children inherited a number of Ma's qualities: her passion to work hard, her love of all things to do with the Red Cross and a keen sense of humour.

Ma had always wanted to do nursing herself bur her own mother wasn't too keen on the idea. One of the proudest days in her own life was to see two of her own daughters, Mary and Imelda, becoming nurses themselves. Mary now teaches on the pre-nursing curriculum while Imelda works as a cardio vascular nurse for the HSE. Her son, John, who went to college to do accountancy, now runs a successful practice in Mallow and Coachford as a chartered accountant. One of her other daughters, Kathleen, became the secretary of the Mallow Mart. One day her other daughter, Patricia, was on her way to the bank when she met a group of her male friends who were gathered around. *"Where are you all off to?"* she asked. They informed her they were applying to be guards. She decided to join them. The Sergeant assured her she had the height and so off to Templemore she went. *"At first she was quite homesick,"* but Ma encouraged her to stay till Christmas. Patricia, to her credit, did and never looked back. She's now stationed in Adree in Co Louth where she lives with her husband.

Looking back on those years Ma is philosophical about the entire period. *"Will power gets you through that"* as she points out and *"five kids that were all very good and got stuck in to help when it was needed most."* In the early days the siblings would all come together to look after the baby of the family, Patricia, on certain evenings when Ma was out doing duties for the Red Cross.

Since that time, Ma has taken a range of First Aid courses and she is still a First Aid instructor today. Did you know that over 6,000 people die of *"out of hospital cardiac arrest"* every year? A startling statistic – that's 18 people every day. One of the first questions Ma and others often ask is, *"if you were the first person on the scene of one of the cardiac arrests, would you know what to do?"* *"More and more companies are beginning to see the benefits associated with being able to make an immediate difference and the importance of learning First Aid today,"* Ma observes.

The Red Cross is, in fact, the world's largest provider of First Aid training. The courses they provide are of the highest standard and delivered by high quality, experienced instructors. One of the most amazing things that always struck me about this organisation, whose famous logo of the Red Cross on a white background is arguably better known throughout the world than any other, is the fact that the Irish people know so little about what the Irish Red Cross does here on the ground in this country. I ask Ma's opinion. *"Certainly we are synonymous with overseas disasters. One only has to think back to the Tsunami disasters years ago,"* she comments. But what of the Irish side of their operation? *"We have a fleet of over 90 vehicles. These include ambulances, 4 wheel drive ambulances and minibuses. The Irish Red Cross provides First Aid cover at numerous events around the country every week."* It's perhaps worth taking a moment to think about those various events... from certain events in the recent Special Olympics to the great battles at Thomond Park. None of these things in truth could happen without the support of these Irish Red Cross people on the ground. Ma goes on to explain the great wealth of services they provide elsewhere. Who comes to your aid, for example, if you get lost in the Wicklow Mountains? (So many do every single day) - the mountain rescue service is Red Cross supported.

One of my personal favourites, is the International Tracing and Family Communication Service, which primarily helps to reunite family members that have lost contact through war or disaster. The Irish Red Cross also has a nationwide, vibrant youth service, provides skin camouflage for those with markings or disfigurements, hand care for the elderly; the list goes on... The organisation is truly unique; operating a dual mandate - providing vital services at home and abroad, yet, as Ma points out, *"remains one of the country's best kept secrets"* - a real shame.

Having *'lectured in every factory in North Cork'*, Ma would go on to found new Red Cross branches in Kanturk and Charleville. Those who have come to know and love this marvellous woman call her *'Ma Sheahan'*, a name she received from her very first trainer, George Slocum - being in her twenties with a husband and new baby, she stood out from the younger contingent who had also joined at that time all those years ago back in 1951.

Yet nevertheless, Hannah remained active in the Red Cross and subsequently all her children joined too. She served on the overall governing body of the Irish Red Cross, the Central Council for 12 years, and also on two of the leading boards, the National Executive Committee and the Overseas Committee. Furthermore, with the late Col. Jim Croake (RIP), she was on the interviewing board of the Overseas Committee. She is also one of the founding members of the St Patrick's Day Parade Committee for the past twenty one years and still remains its Treasurer to this day.

****

One of the most endearing qualities that this very special lady has is her wonderful sense of humour. As we sit and shoot the breeze together, she shares a few precious memories with me. She recalls a gentleman, Patsy Quinlan (since deceased) "*a very jovial man and extremely nice guy!*". Patsy worked in the Irish Rail offices many years ago. His wife used to drive them everywhere and Patsy at the time was more associated with being spotted everywhere on his old black bike. One night for a dare, (he'd been threatening to do this for years), he said he would bring Ma down the town on the bar of his bike. "*He was only supposed to bring me down a small bit of the way, mind!*" Ma's legs were dangling in the air as they free-wheeled all the way that night down to the clock tower in Mallow - she loved it!

Many years ago Ma drove an Anglia car. For those unfamiliar, it was related to the old Ford Escort and then the later Ford Popular. The Anglia name was applied to four models of car that came out between 1939 and 1967.

The car was her pride and joy. As part of their training, the Mallow branch of the Irish Red Cross was one of the first groups to use a Resucianne (the dummy used in CPR). One day Ma was loading the dummy up into her Ford Anglia to take it to a branch meeting. "*The dummy was almost longer than the car itself. I'd never seen anything like it!*" she tells me. It was a gorgeous sunny afternoon and so for a bit of devilment Ma decided to roll down the passenger window and leave the dummy's long arms hanging out the window. As she approached the traffic lights, half of Mallow stood open-mouthed in amazement at this figure beside Ma that looked like it had passed out! "*They had never seen anything like that before in all the 35 years,*" she chuckles.

To really appreciate Ma and her '*glass half full*' attitude to life we must consider this woman's childhood for a moment ... Growing up, she moved to Dunamore, which is about 15 miles from Mallow. Her dad was a farmer.

"We made the best of everything in those days." It's Ma's reflections about her school days that are most telling however.

In the primary school that she went to, she recalls vividly how her two teachers, one being her principal Conor O' Driscoll, who hailed from Skibbereen and his wife, Eileen Crimmin, from Blarney portioned the classroom, which was effectively one long room, into two sections. The 103 enrolled in the school were split into two groups. *"The master pointing in one direction took the 3rd up to 7th class, while his wife all those below third class."* Remarkably, during those years, 'Ma' learned everything from Shakespeare's *'Merchant of Venice'* to learning to cook. *"We were taught every stitch of sewing ever invented!"* The cooking lessons were facilitated using the old boilers. Ma remembers the boys bringing in the kindling for fires in the morning with two fires being lit in the winter time, one for each group of kids. The washing of the floors was taken in turn by the boys supervised by the Master himself. Inspired by such great teachers from such an early age, it isn't hard to see where this woman's dogged resilience in the face of all adversity springs from.

Over the past almost sixty years, this lady has encountered many situations that have required her vast knowledge and range of skills learned first hand in the Irish Red Cross. A select few spring to her mind: In 1956, the Irish Red Cross was called upon to look after 528 Hungarian refugees who had just arrived from Hungary to seek refuge in Ireland. Hannah was present at church-gate collections from morning 'till noon. One day, (she remembers it being the first night she wore her newly purchased Red Cross uniform), she proceeded to raise IR£500 for these displaced people; an equivalent figure in today's economy would be € 12,236.93 – and all in one day!

In the early 1970s, Hanna was also on the committee involved in the setting up of the *'meals-on-wheels'* service that was dedicated to the provision of food to the elderly and isolated folk living on the outskirts of the town of Mallow, a service which saw Hannah not only organise and help to set up, but also deliver the meals herself.

About twelve years ago, Hannah and her team were returning from the Red Cross Novice competition in Drogheda where they had taken 1st place, when a Garda car stopped the ambulance they were driving and asked them if they would tend to a crash that had occurred near Monasterevin.

A car with four passengers, two young girls and their parents, had crashed into the back of a jeep that was carrying two older ladies and a younger girl. The man in the driver's seat was sitting upright with both hands on the steering wheel but when Hannah got closer, she realised that he was, in fact, dead. The mother was also dead, and the two children were concussed and had sustained various fractures, cuts and bruises.

After comforting and reassuring the girls, Ma tended to their injuries while another Red Cross member was looking after the victims in the Jeep. They then took the patients to Portlaoise Hospital under instruction from the Gardai, where they made a full recovery. On the way to the hospital, they passed the health board ambulance heading toward the site of the crash. Only for their excellent first aid skills, and close proximity to the crash site, the outcome could have been a lot worse.

But her personal favourite, and most gratifying moment, came 20 years ago. She was travelling with a group from Mallow to a novice All-Ireland competition in Dublin when the group stopped to eat in Portlaoise. A man at the top table in the restaurant began to choke, and he had gone blue. Ma got up to console the woman who was crying, thinking this must be the person who had fainted. "*Are you ok?*" she enquired. "*My brother's dying.*" He had turned blue and only had a matter of minutes to live. *"He has a heart condition. Please help, he's had a heart attack and fallen down,"* the woman pleaded. Ma got down on her knees to perform CPR on the man. She opened his mouth, pulled out his dentures and handed them to the nephew who was a priest. She took the fork and opened his mouth, "*I was worried that his tongue had rolled back.*" To straighten the tongue she put in her forefinger to check that it was in place when she felt the object, then put in her thumb. "*The doc arrived in and informed me to keep going. He only has a matter of seconds to live*", he said! To everyone's amazement, (including her own) she pulled out a piece of steak, two inches long which had been cooked rare!

When the colour finally came back to his face, "*it was the greatest moment of all!*" Before long, the priest who hailed from Silvermines in Co. Tipperary, en route back from his brother's funeral in Galway, was sitting upright enjoying his food once again.

***

Most recently, almost seven years ago, Ma Sheahan was one of the founding members of the Mallow Day Care Centre that looks after the elderly of the community, and she remains actively involved in raising money for the Irish Red Cross through every possible means, from social dances to flag days. On her wall sit a few modest accolades: for her activities with the Mallow Branch, she has been commended by the Irish Red Cross and the Mallow Chamber of Commerce. In 2002, she was granted a Civic Reception by Mallow Town Council and a presentation was made by the Mayor of Mallow, Mr. Dan Joe Fitzgerald, in recognition of 50 years of service to the community and the Irish Red Cross.

And in March 2006, she was inducted into the Mallow Hall of Fame. Next year, in 2010, when the RTE judges are considering their nominees for the People of the Year awards, perhaps they might remember Mallow, Co Cork, and consider a woman whose dignity and heart, whose caring attitude and positivity to life itself, not only inspires those around her, but also an organisation to which she has belonged for almost 60 years and, in truth, an entire nation... a nation that owes Ma Sheahan an eternal debt of gratitude.

As I leave her home, I decide to travel back the Limerick road and back through Buttevant, my heart now lightened once more...

2

The Flying Doctor

Austin O'Carroll

'You have to learn the rules of the game and then play better than anyone else.'

Einstein

I come, in part, from a pharmaceutical background. Over the five or so years that I worked directly or indirectly as a Communications Consultant in that area, I was privileged first hand to witness just how the advancement of certain drugs can make a real difference in people's lives, be they antibiotics or vaccines, in reducing and eliminating the risks associated with infections, or other medicines that help to prolong life, slow down or even prevent disease. Unquestionably, the ethical use of such drugs operating in a regulated environment can help to improve the quality of life and make a real difference.

But sometimes things can and do go very seriously wrong. Sometimes it's with the drugs themselves - associated lethal side effects that only become known when the drug is in wider circulation – a certain drug that was prescribed, for example, in the treatment of diabetes that could cause liver or heart failure, drugs that were prescribed in the treatment of arthritis which could cause strokes and diseases of the skin, or other drugs associated with the treatment of obesity which can induce heart valve failure in certain patients. The list I'm afraid goes on…

Thankfully we have watchdog bodies such as the FDA in the States that can monitor and ban such drugs and have them removed from wider circulation. But what of countries, for example, where there is no system in place to monitor the harmful side effects of certain drugs? Countries such as India, where, despite reports of widespread serious adverse side effects in children and associated chronic liver toxicity levels, a certain anti-inflammatory drug used in the treatment of pain relief and fever-like symptoms continues to be as readily available as 'Smarties' sold on the streets.

One drug that has raised a number of eyebrows worldwide, in its reintroduction, is Thalidomide, which was reapproved in 1998 for the treatment of 'erythema nodosum leprosum', or skin lesions associated with leprosy. In fact, research is ongoing for other possible treatments associated with the potent drug including HIV, mouth related ulcers, inflammatory diseases and even certain forms of cancer.

Many in this country will shudder with understandable concern when the word Thalidomide is mentioned. Produced by a German pharmaceutical company, the initial synthesis of the drug was in 1954. Following the typically associated marketing activity several years later, its widespread impact spread to many countries in Europe, Asia, Australia, America and Africa.

Nobody, not least the unsuspecting mothers in Ireland, could have foreseen the worldwide epidemic that would ensue; horrific malformations of limbs, particularly arms and legs and of the ears, often accompanied by malformations of the internal organs...

The drug Thalidomide is sadly infamous for the deformities it caused in thousands of children. In some countries, for example, Belgium, Brazil, Canada, Italy and Japan, Thalidomide shockingly continued to be sold for several months (after the eventual withdrawal of the drug from West German and British markets).

Dr Austin O'Carroll remembers, as a child, his doctor looking intently at him from the end of his bed... He spoke rather abruptly into his dictaphone: *"amputation would be a good option to consider!"* Austin was in the National Rehabilitation Hospital in Dublin, brought there, along with a number of other Irish children whose mothers had been prescribed the drug, Thalidomide, for morning sickness in pregnancy in the late 1950s and early 1960s. Born with shortened legs, like the majority of the other 31 cases living with the condition in Ireland today, his health continues to deteriorate. On the question of whether the drug should be allowed to retain a wider remit, such as in the treatment of leprosy, he remains entirely open minded and philosophical as he is about a great many things. His positivity to life and people is quite remarkable.

We agree to meet in the Merrion Inn, a handy half-way point en route from his home in Phibsboro, Dublin, and his mother, whom he's en route to collect in Stillorgan. *"Have you seen Virginia Wolfe?"* he pipes up enthusiastically. The multi Oscar-winning film which starred Richard

Burton and Elizabeth Taylor at the height of their powers, directed by an up-and-coming Mike Nicholls, was, thankfully for my sake, one of my all time favourites. The plot centres on an aging couple who, through the use of alcohol, manipulate a younger couple to fuel anguish and contempt on each other. For Austin, the film is one that he uses frequently in his use of narrative-based medicine in helping to treat his own patients or in working with his medical students. "*Narrative-based medicine is just one of several patient-centred approaches to the practice of medicine that can give us docs access to the lived experience of our patients.*" If we consider the process to be a more elaborate way to gather patient history, narrative approaches can be very helpful in assisting a doctor to formulate the most appropriate diagnostic and treatment options as well as even improving doctor-patient relationships.

"*But how does it actually work?*" I ask fascinated. "*We all construct stories out of life circumstances. Our real life events do not have plots, obviously, but it is a common human experience for us to construct meaning from otherwise seemingly disparate life events,*" he explains patiently. These constructions he refers to as stories, we tell ourselves and others that provide coherence for our lived experiences. These stories are not fixed but rather change with time as new events occur or new insights arise.

From a GP's perspective, '*narrative*' events imposed by the experience of sickness and disease, be they chronic or acute, can have a tremendous impact, of course, on patients, families and communities. Illnesses therefore do not occur, as Austin explains, in some sort of an isolated vacuum, but are situated in real day-to-day experiences. How well we might all do to remember that, I think to myself.

The point is simple really. We all have to be aware that there's more to the patient than the simple presentation of symptoms. Where does this man find the time to do all that he does? I wonder to myself.

Among other things Austin was a relationship counsellor for 5 years. '*We can't do counselling in general practice, we can use the skills to help elicit the patient's issues but we do not have enough time to explore deeply! Doctors are under too much pressure and there's the constant fear of time*'. I'm tempted to seek some advice of my own but something tells me he already knows that!

Two of his early influences included James Mc Cormick, who taught him in Trinity College, one of his own personal heroes, in fact, who made him look at evidence-based medicine in a whole new light.

"*His book, 'The Doctor – Father Figure or Plumber' influenced me greatly.*" In the book, Mc Cormick questions the extent to which doctors as professionals have neglected their ethical responsibility to mankind as a whole and suggests that the profession is in danger of losing its special place within society. Austin believes that danger remains as great today. *"We need to come off our pedestals. We need to be able to offer our patients real reassurance and support. Medicine goes beyond being a job!"* he points out passionately.

The second key influencer, a gifted lecturer and well known in medical circles at the time, Petr Skrabenek, hailed from the Czech Republic. He recalls the Czech's famous saying, *"Leave your mind open but not so open that your brain falls out"*. Skrabenek read medical papers. A true skeptic by nature, he would often criticise popular medical thinking at the time, questioning for example whether mental illness should be viewed as a disease or not? *"He made me go beyond the book cover in seeking answers."* Ironically, Austin would become more holistic in his thinking as a result.

But what about when it comes to breaking bad news, I ask? *"How should a doctor do that?"* In a wonderful moment of self-parody, he looks down at his shortened legs, and then looks across at me, smiles, and in a neutral voicesays, *"When I was 12, my mother told me I had a great personality. I knew I was screwed!"* He laughs out loud - we both do.

****

Dr Austin O' Carroll was born in 1962 in Blackrock, Co Dublin. His mother, a powerful woman, *"and still is"* he reminds me, came from Limerick. His father, a true blue Dub, was born in the North Strand. Interestingly, like a great many others I suspect at the time, his father was faced with a telling dilemma upon leaving school - the civil service or university?

He chose the civil service – a job which would enable him to support his sister, his mum having died at birth - hence the encouragement for Austin himself to choose college when he was older. That same encouragement was given to each of Austin's three sisters and two brothers. Medical regulation was poor at best in 1962. It was typical at the time that free samples of Thalidomide were given out back then to pregnant women who were suffering with nausea. Not surprisingly, his own mother remained very sick for weeks.

At the end of 1962, Erskine Childers, our Taoiseach at the time, made an important announcement banning the use of the drug in Ireland. The fact was, according to Austin, that they had known nine months previously of the devastating effects of Thalidomide and, though they removed it from pharmacy shelves, they did not want to go public in case they caused distress to pregnant women. Unfortunately, during those nine months, some mothers took free samples of the drug and their children were damaged, a tragedy that could and should in Austin's case, have been averted.

Austin's mother was a very pragmatic lady... He would be treated as normal from the start. He was in and out of hospital like an unsuspecting yo-yo. Dr. Brady, his physician, had him walking by the age of five, but an accident in which he fell down the stairs and broke both his legs had consequences. *"One of the legs wasn't straight. They told me not to play footie."* Big mistake. His leg was reset a further four times. Sometimes his mother walked by him on the way home from school with some kid kicking three shades of crap out of her son. *"Fight back"* she would shout at him. As he approached his teens he put the calipers he was using down to the fact that his legs had been simply broken. Schooling wise, his early primary education began at Carysfort National and then it was on to Oatlands College like most other normal kids.

He remembers going to be assessed with other Thalidomides and feeling very strange. *"I had lived such a normal existence. I just couldn't comprehend what was going on."*

As teenagers we naturally become more concerned about our body images. It happens to the best of us. Austin reflects back on that very notion *"because you can't sell yourself as a sexual person, you sell yourself as a fun person, a nice person - the jolly, happy person playing the disabled clown".* As he grew into his teens he learned rapidly. *"Having Thalidomide affects how you perceive yourself and how other people see you."* *"After that,"* he says smiling defiantly, *"you simply learn to get on with it."*

He describes his mother Maureen as *"a strong woman."* *"Great fun"* he points out, *"but a real fighter".* His dad like so many, struggled to say the words *"I love you"* but showed his tremendous support in a variety of other ways including joining various school committees. His dad would often turn to Austin and ask *"Are you ok son? Do you need money for anything?"* His mum would show she cared for Austin by always encouraging him to do things for himself but not through the expression of physical love. The support was always pragmatic in nature.

His early memories include waking up at the age of five and seeing there was Taylor Keith lemonade and sweets at the end of the bed on the side locker. He remembers feeling very upset wondering if his parents had gone away.

I suspect the memories of syringes and kids crying loudly never leave a person. He was brought to Lourdes on three occasions. He used to love playing hide and seek with his sister, Clare, with whom he shared a special bond. One time, in fact, he hid so well, the police were called to a campsite in San Sebastian in Spain where the O'Carrolls were holidaying.

He remembers his mum telling him sternly that he was being placed in a room on his own in the hospital because he had told the other kids in the room with him to '*fuck off*'. Young Austin, it would be fair to say, was a rather lively child!

In the scouts, one of his major early influences, he was made camp on his own by his mother who promoted a strong sense of independence in her son. His two older sisters, Catherine and Mary, were highly protective of their little brother. "*Mary is a GP too in the UK and a highly conscientious person*" and, as Austin proudly points out, a wonderful doctor.

In terms of sheer honesty, Catherine, the other twin, was very black and white. He admires this clear ethical position. "*Honesty with patients and ethics is underestimated*" he points out. "*Every time we make a decision with a patient, for example, how much information to give them, - that's an ethical decision. If you undercut your time then that's an ethical judgment too. If you're being grey you need to examine why.*"

Of his other siblings he smiles. "*Liam was wild. Now look at him!* he says laughing "*He's now this responsible guy working in the bank scene.*" When it comes to a crisis, however, he cites Liam as the man to take over, "*whether you want him to or not*", he says winking at me. Two of Liam's sons have made tremendous strides in the world of GAA. Ross made the Dublin hurling team while Rory famously stuck by his guns earlier this year taking time off to go away on holidays and ignored radio criticism from Dublin fans. "*That boy knows his own mind.*" Austin informs me with a certain pride. Austin has a very strong bond with all his family. He is very proud of all his nephews, (Bill, Oisin, Jack, Simon and Andrew) and his only niece and godchild, Madeleine.

Johnny, his other brother, is the most logically-minded of the three. "*He's a guard, a real reflector by nature. He can be a real dog in the bone when it comes to relinquishing his point of view mind you!*" Often the family would gather to have debates and sometimes, just for the hell of it, they would sometimes change their respective views just to make the debate last longer, or take their mother's side just to look at her way of seeing things. Although his brother Johnny would go on to become an accountant, Austin remains convinced he would have made a brilliant social worker instead. "*Johnny's very blunt. Tells you exactly what he thinks always!*" I begin to laugh, thinking about the social workers I know personally.

Both his parents were actively involved in voluntary work, with his dad working with Sr. Stan in Focus Ireland. Those influences marked the beginning of Austin's concern for the less fortunate in our society.

When Austin was in Oatlands College he couldn't play regular sports so he debated instead and played table tennis. "*Colm Slevin was on the Irish team and in my school, so that was encouraging,*"he points out. But throughout school, his love of the scouts grew and grew. In time, he became a scout leader and was able to harness these skills in the wider community. He came top in the school in his Inter Cert exams. Encouraged naturally, he went on to get an excellent Leaving Cert, but was initially put off the idea of trying to do medicine – originally he got advice that, because he had non functioning or rudimentary thumbs he would have problems taking a blood line for example, so assuming the worst, he opted for Law in Trinity instead.

There can't be too many people who can say they were tutored by two Presidents back to back. In his first year, he was tutored by the very brilliant Mary Robinson and the following year he came under the tutelage of the woman whom he cites and credits as the major reason he was able to finally make it into medicine, Mary McAleese. *"I was two years into a degree that I knew wasn't really for me. I found law too dispassionate."* He remembers being on holiday in Italy in the summer of 1982 and chatting to this particular girl that he fancied. *"I told her about working in the youth club scene and the connections that I'd been making with people around me."* He missed that... That September, he came home to chat it through with the President. *"Go for it,"* she told him smiling. She pushed his case and got him an appointment with the Board.

The interview was tough going he recalls. They had queries and questions but in the end his passion won the day and he was accepted into the School of Medicine.

Reflecting back on his days in Trinity, which he loved immensely, his own reservations centre on the teaching methodology. *"We used the traditional building blocks of teaching medicine. In our system you get to meet the patients after five years having gone through the things they think you need to know first."* Those things included all of the knowledge associated with the human body from anatomy to pathology.

However, Austin believes that in countries like Canada, for example, in the McMaster University of Ontario, where the undergraduate meets patients after their first year, their interpersonal skills are greatly improved, the whole experience becomes more holistic (not to mention their bedside manner improves one suspects). *"The stuffing isn't knocked out of you and you haven't lost your passion for the things that really matter - namely people, regardless of the specialism you might go on to choose"*...

During his student years he was involved in various youth projects, which often included organising local hikes to the Wicklow Mountains. *"We ran our youth projects in the likes of Sean Mc Dermott Street, Ballyfermot and Pearse St. "They were wild summers"* he says laughing. Many of the kids he worked with would go on to become his patients today…His love of the inner city and the youth were copper-fastened during those seven wonderful years in Trinity.

He met his partner Dorothy when he became involved with the disability movement in the 1980s. The time helped him to refine his own perception of having a disability. *"You learned to see things in context. Having a disability was a condition, plain and simple,"* not as Austin himself refers *'an entity'*. Equality of access, where open and equal access was available for all, became a significant mandate that he would help to fight passionately for. He was involved in the campaign for setting up the Commission on the *'Status of People with Disabilities'* in this country between the years 1992 and 1994 and was an advisor to that commission. He worked with the *'Forum of People with Disabilities'*. They were sharing a room at the time with *'Special Arts'* for which former US Ambassador, Jean Kennedy Smith, had provided funding. This was where Dorothy was working. *"She was rightly pissed off that she had to share. We both had partners at the time,"* he recalls. It took them both five years to sort things through, to learn perhaps to get on properly, but eventually as with most things they finally got it together.

"Dorothy came from an artistic background. She's a real fun person, sexy and vibrant." Dorothy seemed to compliment Austin; she wasn't a planner and was more laid back in nature. Perhaps more importantly than anything else this woman has freed space up in Austin's life. Just as well he reckons, because otherwise being able to share in his two children's upbringing might have been curtailed... It's very obvious, just how much he loves his children. His face beams with delight when he talks about them. *"Hannah is eight, so very talented and full of chat. She's a real school teacher!"* Their son, Naoise, is six. *"We named him after the son of Oisin, as in 'Ti r na n'Óg'.*" Oisin, he describes as wholly affectionate. Not quite as independent as his big sister, but very loving. The family doesn't do *'Sky TV'*. They sit and chat and play together, inventing games and being happy in each other's company. Dorothy has helped to ensure that Austin has discovered a work life balance. He can now share his passions equally between those who have and those who have not.

The day that Austin and I meet coincides with an announcement from the housing agency, Focus Ireland, telling us that the figures are, in fact, twice as bad as the ones that the Government is apparently hiding behind. According to the latest statistics from the housing needs assessment, the figures suggest that there are 1,394 homeless households. Focus, as with Sophia Housing and others, believe that figure is closer to 3,000.

Austin nods to me in agreement. We see the issue of homelessness in the same light… *"It's about a lack of security, lack of belonging, lack of privacy and lack of safety."* People sleeping out in doorways, parks, in derelict sites and in abandoned cars experience and represent the most extreme form of homelessness. *"On any given night, there are up to 100 people sleeping rough in the Dublin area. But this is just the tip of the iceberg,"* he points out. The *'invisible'* homeless, people who live in emergency accommodation: in shelters, hostels, refuges, in B&Bs or double share with friends and relatives, make up about 20 times the number of people sleeping rough. They are also in need and equally without a home.

Dr Austin O' Carroll should know better than most. Nobody in medicine has done more to assist the homeless in this country. Among other things he's contemplating is a further Doctorate in Health not for the glory of more qualifications but rather because he recognises the value of research. The burning issue for this man and others like him who care enough is how do we engage homeless people into the services and grant them equal access to services? Together with several colleagues, including Philip Crowley, Fiona Reilly and David Whitford, they set about assessing the actual health needs of homeless people in Dublin's inner city. The results made startling reading: 1:2 had HIV, 1:3 had Hepatitis C and 1:2 had severe depression. They looked at the idea of providing intermediate care centre facilities for people who were too sick to be on the streets but not sick enough to be in hospitals. They currently have a site but no funding.

It all began back in 2002 when Austin had been working with asylum seekers, non nationals mostly, which earned him an award for his work from the African Regue Network. The HSE had just started to place nurses into hostels for the homeless. He got a call one day. *"It was Denise, one of the nurses, who told me that one of the patients had become psychotic and there was no GP to admit him."*

From there he was running weekly clinics; seeking more funding from the HSE to fund more positions... his work was just beginning in earnest. In 2006, he put in a suggestion to the HSE that they set up a *'safety net'* for the homeless; a common set of guidelines and protocols which would allow for the sharing of information amongst medical professionals about members of the homeless community. An agreement was reached with the HSE to help those who had no access to medical cards and so the train to *'Wellville'* was slowly put into motion. In places like the Mater Hospital, Austin was able to persuade colleagues like John McInerney to provide cover and in Cork they linked up with guys like Dr Don Coffey.

I ask about the swine flu. *"The homeless weren't going to be a priority, I'm afraid, though they should be! The research is there to back their needs up."* So instead the *'safety net'* team (consisting now of 9 docs/7-8 nurses) will set about providing up to 1,200 consultations to homeless people.

So enthused to help, another colleague, Dr Dermot Power in the Mater

Hospital rang him recently to say they had a spare bus to help with the Outreach Programme that Austin has planned to provide for sexual screening (cervical and health type checks) to the homeless in inner city Dublin. He'll find the volunteer medical students to help out. "*They can begin with painting the bus!*" he says jokingly.

Dr Austin O'Carroll has finally made health care accessible for homeless people in this county. But it's just the beginning and he knows it. "*If we really want to do something to help, then we need to provide housing support, not to be going to casualty so that they can score up on heroin. They should be given methadone in the queues.*" As Austin points out, they really need to be linked up with the relevant agencies, Simon, Cedar House, Sophia Housing and the likes.

If ever I met a person who could turn a negative into a positive then it has to be this incredibly humble and selfless man sitting beside me. Walking abnormally puts undue pressure on Austin's joints. He suffers from osteoarthritis in his ankles, which makes walking long distances impossible. Covering as little as 500 metres can be excruciatingly painful. Today, cycling is his preferred mode of transport - he can comfortably cycle up to 70 miles. He cycles everywhere. I've decided his new nickname will be "*The Flying Doctor*"! In certain ways he believes his condition has helped him, although he naturally misses not being able to walk with Dorothy and the kids. Sometimes his wisdom and personal empathy with pain management can offer great comfort to those patients he sees in his clinic who are in a great deal of pain with conditions like osteoporosis. Above all else, he retains an incredible sense of humour. Only yesterday, he saw a woman who was born in the heart of Dublin where she had lived all her life. She had a problem but was afraid to share where exactly. Eventually after much coaxing, she eventually leaned across the table, and said "*Doctor, it's in my gentleman's entrance.*"

****

This year marks the 50th anniversary of the introduction of Thalidomide which resulted in deformities in up to 12,000 infants worldwide. Dr Austin O'Carroll continues to fight for those who were affected even today. Thalidomide is known to be hereditary in laboratory animals; however, it is yet to be determined whether it can be passed on in humans. "*When we had children, I was waiting for the scan at 18 weeks when you could be reassured; the fear was definitely there,*" he says.

In hindsight, Dr Austin O'Carroll agrees with the doctor who reviewed him as a child and advised a double amputation below the knee. However, as we walk out of the Merrion Inn, he says, *"it probably wasn't a good thing to dictate at the end of a patient's bed"*.

I smile to myself and wonder if perhaps all persons considering taking medicine simply because of the associated prestige or pressure placed at home where points are concerned, should rather, in fact, form a queue and take just five minutes to speak with the *'Flying Doctor'* to see if their interpersonal skills and attitude to life are up to scratch first.

3

Behind The Scenes

Adi Roche

'Is ar scáth a chéile a mhairean na daoine.'
'It is in the shadow of each other that we survive.'

As I stand at the entrance to No 82 Merrion Square, waiting for the great doors to open of this historic, most cherished and protected building in which WB Yeats himself once lived, a great many thoughts fill my mind. A plethora of dates suddenly go flashing through my congested brain...

First, 1953 and the date that changed the world of climbing forever. Of course I wasn't even alive when the great rock stars of the climbing fraternity, finally knocked, as Hillary so appropriately put it, "*the great bastard off*".

After Everest came another unthinkable. Within 12 months, one English man dared to dream that he could go under 4 minutes for the mile. Hillary and Bannister had opened the floodgates. Man's imagination would know no bounds and these respective dates would be etched forever in our minds. Ten years later, we would ask ourselves where we were when the wasteful assassination of JFK would shake the world to its very foundations. Course, I still wasn't born. I missed the Beatles too. I was even too young to recall Watergate. But over the course of the next two decades, I would be around to witness a number of life changing moments, moments that would change my own perspective on life forever.

Could any of us ever forget how the tragedy of one young lady's life, which was played out on the world stage like a dark and macabre Shakespearian play, would impact on all of us so profoundly? The outpouring of human emotion around the world on the night that Princess Diana died will forever strike a chord. Juxtaposing such emotions, the moment we witnessed the release of one man who dared to defy a notion and in the end, a nation. We all give thanks for the day Mandela walked free. Somewhere in there among the mix was the day that taught me that a collective conscience can make a difference. It was the day that Sir Bob made Live Aid a reality and Phil Collins, took advantage of Concord's supersonic capabilities, and caught the world's imagination, by playing in both the UK and the US concerts...

As the door finally opens a friendly voice ushers me in: "*Welcome to my humble abode*", she says smiling her magnetic smile and greets me warmly. As we meander up the magnificent stairs in the direction of the boardroom, I think to myself as I try to recall one final date... The date that, were it not for the person in front of me, would have been consigned to the annals of history without remorse and without redemption. The date was the 26th of April 1986. "*Where were you on this date, Ian?*" I probe my mind to possibly recall... Ironically, 12 years later I would learn first hand just how important this woman's work was.

***

Adi Roche is literally just back from the glitz and glam of the Rose of Tralee, where, along with one of Ireland's other glamorous fifty somethings, Mary Kennedy, she was a judge. "*From the wellies to the make-up room!*" she says laughing out loud. She proceeds to share the priceless story of the dress that was designed on loan for her appearance on the show by esteemed dress designer, Marion Murphy Cooney. "*Well, I was in Kerry and I asked Sean* (the hubbie, soon to be nominated for canonisation!) *to measure me. I'd agreed to do the show and I didn't know my own measurements!*" Now I know some of you are thinking that's impossible. Believe me, for Adi Roche such matters are wholly inconsequential. "*So out he pops with a builder's tape.*" "*Eh, isn't that a rather difficult method to get an accurate measurement with?*" I enquire, perplexed as to the use of a builder's tape on the human body. "*Jeez, you can chalk it down!*" she admits. When Marion rings politely to get the measurements, Adi duly informs her she's a size ten.

An hour later the phone rings again. Marion informs Adi that the measurements she'd taken with the builder's tape were, in fact, those of a size 16!

Funny isn't it, how perceptions are so important? For Adi, the chance to show the world that she's, in fact, a very humorous '*Walter Mitty*' like character comes as a welcome relief. "*People think I'm so serious all of the time.*"

She giggles. "*It was nice to be able to show a lighter side – that I'm not one-dimensional.*" Daithí Ó Sé was a scream I'm told. The women loved him. Women of all ages too. So they all had a blast in Kerry. The highlight for Adi, apart from getting to really know the girls taking part, was meeting Tom Crean's last remaining living daughter, Mary. My own eyes light up as Adi tells me about this great character who "*could regale you with her wit and humour*". The event is, however, tinged with a little sadness as Adi receives a call to tell her that the funding had been cut for the project's life-saving Cardiac Programme operations that so many of the children depend on for survival. "*My God that's another € 150k to be found,*" she winces as she drives from Kerry to Dublin contemplating the same question she's been contemplating undoubtedly for over 20 years. Where will the money come from? And so it goes.

For over three decades this human dynamo has been grappling firstly with her work on peace and justice and then the reins of the Chernobyl Children's Project, desperately trying to make a difference in the lives of so many.

Adi Roche has literally spent her entire life, since 1977, campaigning for, and publicly active in issues relating to the environment, peace and justice. Having worked for a number of years in the Irish national airline, Aer Lingus, Adi took redundancy to work full-time as a volunteer for the Irish Campaign for nuclear disarmament. She devised a Peace Education Programme and delivered it in over fifty schools throughout Ireland.

In 1990, she became the first Irish woman elected to the Board of Directors of the International Peace Bureau in Geneva and, in 1991, filled with compassion and zeal to contribute, established the Chernobyl Children's Project International.

Since the explosion in Belarus, Adi has worked tirelessly as a volunteer for the past 23 years to provide humanitarian aid to the 3-4 million children who the United Nations recognises as affected by the world's worst nuclear disaster in Belarus, Western Russia and the Ukraine. But what actually drives this extraordinary woman?

Under her personal leadership, Chernobyl Children's Project International has initiated an incredible 16 aid programmes and has delivered direct and indirect medical and humanitarian aid valued, incredibly, at over €80m to the areas most affected by the Chernobyl nuclear disaster.

Her super-human efforts on behalf of these children and her thorough understanding of the Chernobyl accident aftermath have brought her unquestionable international recognition.

For her commitment, passion, selflessness and energy Adi was awarded European Person of the Year and Irish Person of the Year in 1996, Cork Person of the Year 2002 for the many years service to the children of Chernobyl and the Paul Harris Fellowship Award for exceptional service to the community by the Rotary of Ireland. She was presented with the highly prestigious European Woman Laureate Award, which is a permanent title, awarded each year by European countries to the individual they feel is worthy of European-wide recognition for their achievements. Adi also holds an Honorary Doctorate of Laws from the University of Alberta, Canada. In 2002, she was awarded a Joint Doctorate of Laws with the project's patron, Ali Hewson, for their ongoing humanitarian work, by the National University of Ireland, Galway. In February 2005, Adi was presented with the Humanitarian Award at the Meteor Ireland Music Awards and in May 2005 she was presented with the Jim Larkin Justice and Peace Award in Tralee at the Labour Party Annual Conference. In April 2006, Adi was presented with Gradam an Phiarsaigh, as she best exemplifies the ideals of Pearse in the fields of education, art, literature, civil liberties, the media or among the community. The Chernobyl Children's Project International has received official charitable status in Ireland, the United Kingdom, Belarus and in the United States. The nominations are, in fact, simply too many to include here and too embarrassing for Adi to continue to have to share. Rather than accept any plaudits herself, Adi prefers to deflect any attention she may receive to the countless CCPI volunteers in Ireland and abroad. This is not about a singular person. *"It is about the power and spirit of the volunteers behind me. They are the ones who make us strong."*

But has any of this changed her? What of the woman behind the awards, behind the person we see and hear so much about in the media?

What of the woman who stood defiantly to become our President, despite a blatant smear attack that nearly robbed her of her sanity and almost destroyed her family?

****

Born on the 11th of July 1955, one of Adi Roche's abiding memories growing up as a kid was giving the hair of her grandmother, Ellen Harrington, 100 brush strokes each night in return for impassioned stories of the famine, the origins of the Republic and the wild and infamous '*Galtee Boy*', Adi's ancestor, John Sarsfield Casey, also known as '*a Fenian Champion of the Tenant Farmers' Rights*'. He wrote in the Fenian paper '*The Irish People*' under the pseudonym '*The Galtee Boy*'. In a round-up of Fenians in 1865, he was arrested and sentenced to five years of penal servitude, and in 1867, along with other republican prisoners, was placed on board a convict ship bound for Australia. On his eventual return to Mitchelstown he took up the cause of tenant farmers who were brutally oppressed by the local landlords. He was successful in his campaigns and later was appointed county coroner for Limerick, despite refusing to swear allegiance to the British sovereign. He believed in non-violence and used his voice, the power of the larynx, to effect change.

These early examples of active citizenship and volunteerism had a profound effect on the young Miss Roche growing up. The Galtee Boy's plight was captured in song by Christy Moore. Her mum, Chris, born on Christmas day 1916 was also a keen activist and local volunteer. From an early age, it was instilled in Adi to play a part in her local community. Theirs was a staunch Fenian household and a bastion of Fianna Fail support. Often, De Valera would come to visit when he was in the vicinity of the local Hibernian Hotel. Her aunt would gather up the local children to come and lend their support to the great man. An incredibly strong sense of 'teanga' and Irish traditions were instilled in Adi from birth. She remains the only one on the family, however, who doesn't go under the preferred Irish name 'De Róiste'.

From that very early gestation period, where a young Adi soaked up stories of adventure and activism, her own parents led by actions, not words. They didn't talk to Adi about what should be done but, rather simply, got on with the business of serving their local community as if it were something that was innate in them, fuelling their need to behave this way. Adi would often accompany her father on his 'Meals on Wheels' rounds, or on his call-outs for the local St Vincent De Paul. Adi had a superb upbringing and wanted for nothing in the middle class Ireland she had become accustomed to. The images of seeing those around her struggle without electricity or running water, the poverty etched on the faces of those who depended on fuel vouchers and who hadn't the means to make ends meet, still burn brightly today. "*It all felt so hopeless and I felt I was living inside a cocoon protected from this other world around me,*" she recalls.

Her parents offered refuge to members of the travelling communities frequently. Adi couldn't understand why these people were so misunderstood. "*They were an indigenous group living on the outside of Irish society, misunderstood and feared for the most part. Why?*" she questioned. "*Because, they were culturally different?*" It broke her heart to see such divisions and from the get-go she was determined that one day, she might be able to make people understand.

One of the biggest influences on Adi's early life was her ballet teacher

Joan Denise Moriarty. Her mother encouraged her to become a dancer and to take up ballet and Irish dancing. She started her ballet lessons at the age of 5. "*Once a week, Joan Denise Moriarty would come to Clonmel to provide us with lessons.*" She smiles when she remembers how they were encouraged to express themselves freely and openly. "*Now ladies, I want you all to be like little babbling brooks,*" she would tell them. Ms. Moriarty would bring her ballet company to small towns across Munster and was, in fact, responsible for setting up the National Irish Ballet Company which boasted renowned International dancers in their ranks. Eventually young Adi would go on to represent the Cork Ballet Company. "*I even got to do Tchaikovsky's 'Scheherazade' in the Cork Opera House!*" she tells me proudly. It isn't difficult to see where Adi Roche gets her poise and elegance from.

Growing up into her teens, much of Adi's time was spent on a virtual island on the River Suir which was reached by crossing over on a slender timber bridge.

Her *'Island'* , where she and her friends would spend many happy summers, was home to tennis courts, local shops, dances and boys, she readily admits. Although the young Ms Roche would eventually row bow and also occupy the No 3 spot on the Clonmel rowing team, rowing internationally in the triangular games, her primary motivation lay in the pursuit of the opposite sex. "*The lepping hormones took over in me!*" She winks over at me, as she recalls those warm heady summer days.

"*When you're out at sea or rowing on the river, you see Ireland differently,*" she suggests. As she looked back at Clonmel, she saw this garrisoned, planted town that housed some of the most beautiful homes in the country. Whatever the views, and regardless of the motivations, Adi Roche was highly competitive in and out of the rowing boat.

She laid out her goals from the start and set clear and smart objectives for herself. "*I got it from dad,*" she admits. Both of her parents pushed all of the children to be the best that they could be. Her father, a respected technical engineer, and her mum, a former teacher, had high expectations for their four kids. Eventually, Adi and her parents would clash fiercely about where those mutual expectations, in fact, lay.

Adi's interest in school was lacklustre at best. For her, it was primarily a means to an end. That said, her *'Grá'* and passion for languages, debating, the classics and drama were fostered from a very early stage. "*Sr. Alphonsus was such a passionate teacher,*" she says. The woman who taught in the Presentation Sisters in Clonmel, gave her a deep love of English. Adi would enter all of the local *'feiseanna'* where she got the chance to participate in productions for herself.

"I'd get the 'scetimíní' (butterflies) but loved performing. I also loved the chance to speak 'as Gaeilge'," something she got from her parents who were both staunch *'gaelgeoirs'*. Her father's close alliances with the Fianna Fail party had continued under Lemass.

The relationship with Adi and her parents as she began to grow up could be best described as complex. Although it did eventually improve with time, many hurdles would have to be first overcome. She explains, *"Because they set such high standards, you felt when you were younger like you were being set up for a fall inside your own mind. I sensed those inadequacies when I was in secondary school"*. Both wanted Adi to consider teaching or at least go to university and continue her education, something Adi was diametrically opposed to doing. At that stage, it was the life of a ballerina or archaeology for her. Most of all she wanted to get out into the world and explore. Her resistance to studying created an undercurrent which never really went away. She ponders for a moment. *"I'd have thrived in transition year for sure!"* And so, when the announcement came, a career in the state airline, Aer Lingus, was met with disapproval and a lingering sense of disappointment.

Adi was close to her 3 siblings. Her two older bothers, Donal & Conchubair de Róiste, were good pals and looked after her interests in quite a protective way. She was closest, however, to her older sister, Len, who's older by four years. *"We're only 4 years apart for six months of the year!"* she says smiling. The two are incredibly close. Their bond would one day be forged forever in the late 90s…

Adi's heart soars even today when she goes to the *'trad'* sessions in Ballyferriter, West Kerry, or when she walks with her good pal, singer, Mary Black, along the beach. *"I still tell her I want to be a singer!"* Sometimes Mary will encourage Adi to sing harmonies and Mary does the melodies as the two of them meander happily, walking peacefully for miles on end.

Adi is, in fact, already in a singing group, known affectionately as *'The Bubbles'*. Where did the name come from I wonder? *"It comes from the Irish expression 'Scaoil amach an boibailín', loosely translating as 'let it hang out!'* She tells me. She came up with the name in order to play with the great singer song writer, Jimmy McCarthy. *"It was easier for him to introduce us on stage as 'The 'Bubbles'"* she smiles. The very first time she sang with Jimmy was, in fact, in the back of an arctic truck during a series of concerts he was doing during the First Gulf War, back in 1991. His concert series was themed around the messages contained in John Lennon's iconic song *'Imagine'*.

Arguably, the greatest influence in her life, her now husband, Sean, was about to enter her young life. They met at a wedding in the Cahir House Hotel, where her best friend Anne's sister, Nuala, was getting married in Newcastle church in Tipperary. She remembers going to visit her friend

Anne's grave who was buried down the right side of the cemetery when in approaches this handsome stranger from the opposite side; Sean Dunne a UCC student studying music.

She immediately enquired from her friends as to who he was. She even changed place settings at the wedding to ensure that they would be sitting beside each other. *"I felt it was Anne's way of looking out for me at the time."* Her eyes cloud a little as she thinks about her best friend, the person with whom she shared everything, from their first day at school together to their first kisses. *"We lived in each others pockets,"* she laments.

Adi proceeds to tell me about Anne's illness and that infamous day when her own life was changed forever. *"She was only 15 at the time. She fell one day in the yard and that was the beginning of the end."*

Instead of blood coming from her knee, the only substance that emerged was a light transparent liquid. She was diagnosed with Leukaemia in St Vincent's hospital, Dublin. Adi had no idea what Leukaemia was and so she opened her parent's Reader's Digest Encyclopaedia (from the set the travelling salesman would sell you), in the hope of learning more about her friend's condition. She discovered that many childhood leukaemia cases were linked with radiation. She looked up the word *radiation*. And so it had begun… So much of what drives this woman today can be linked and traced back to the tragic cause of death to her best friend, who would be dead within a year of diagnosis. Her death changed Adi forever. *"In that one moment, I learned first hand that nothing in life is more precious than life itself."* It's that simple mantra that has frequently picked her up out of the gutters of disappointment that she often falls into. Ironically, many years later, Dorrie, Anne's mum, would have another kid, whom she called Sinead. The likeness to Anne almost blew Adi away when she eventually met her many years later.

Just before Adi married Sean at the tender age of twenty, there was a remarkable ban on married women working for the state. Adi, at this point, was part of the ground staff in Aer Lingus based out of Dublin. Thankfully, just before her wedding, a challenge had been put down and the ban was eventually lifted. Of Sean, she says this: *"We're total opposites, thank God! He effectively sponsored my work in the Chernobyl Children's Project International."* She uses the word in the past tense as Sean has just retired officially from the world of teaching. No doubt he'll be sorely missed within the confines of the CBS Secondary School in Cork, a school which has, on more than one occasion, boasted the finest set of leaving cert results in the entire country. Sean Dunne's contribution to those who took English and Music will be, no doubt, regaled by those who make their way in this life. Adi describes Sean as contemplative – a deep thinker, musician and philosopher. A man happy in his own skin, who in all the 34 years of marriage has never once complained or given out about Adi's unquivering commitment to the Chernobyl Children's Project International. In fact, he shies away from the life Adi leads, happier to stay in the background lending support. He even plays in the *'The Bubbles'*, Adi's musical ensemble, arranging and being a multi instrumentalist, sometimes playing occasional pieces for the group. Sean brings the stability, contrasting Adi's free spirit.

When she's in smithereens, lost in tiny little pieces, he picks her up and nourishes her soul back to life, sometimes with just a word or a look. "*Sometimes he'd just look at me and say, 'Adi you need to take a walk'.*" More often than not, she gets her best energy when she goes for those walks.

It was on such a walk, indeed, that she put it out to the man in the sky and happily made her decision to run for President. No sooner had I asked the question "*Why did you run?*" than I regretted the utterance. "*It was a once in a lifetime privilege!*" she replies, her eyes as wide as saucers. Having been unanimously selected to stand as the People's Alliance candidate for the Irish Presidency, under the leadership of the Irish Labour Party in 1997 Adi Roche felt the time and the energy was right to make a difference. Inspired by Mary Robinson, she entered the race on behalf of the left, during that euphoric period when women were being truly empowered to make a real difference.

She was approached by Senator Pat Magner and Fergus Finlay and, for the first meeting, was accompanied by Joe Noonan, a well-known solicitor and a good friend, Helen Faughan, who was working on secondment with the Chernobyl Children's Project (now special adviser with Mary Hannifin). Fergus Finlay worked closely on the strategic planning for the campaign and for Adi "*Fergus created a very visionary role for our planned presidency,*" she reflects. They went back to the core of the Irish constitution for inspiration and guidance (in Obama like fashion). The notions of cherishing all of the children of the state and creating a greener Ireland were at the core of her value systems.

In what transpired to become one of the hardest fought campaigns ever, Adi would go from being initial favourite to second last. The final nail in the coffin was when her brother, Donal de Róiste, was described blatantly as a *'republican sympathiser'*.

Her brother, for those unfamiliar, had been dishonorably discharged from the Irish army some 30 years previously, in 1969. A young officer, he was placed under armed guard by Army Intelligence and driven to Dublin, in 1969, from his base in Athlone, where he was interrogated without being told on what basis. Interestingly, he was never court martialled, which would have required charges laid against him and which would have allowed him to defend himself. Instead, he was told he was retired by the President and given twelve hours to leave the barracks. Such was the interest that lay in the case, many, including actor Gabriel Byrne, took up his case which remains unresolved to this day. The impact of the story surfacing was underestimated by Finlay et al and would have a devastating effect, not only on Adi's campaign, but on her personally, and the health of both her brother and her father, Sean.

"I believe it simply accelerated his Alzheimer symptoms compounded by the enormous stress levels the poor man was placed under." For Adi, personally, it was extremely rough, a dark chapter that she would have to find the strength to turn over. *"I was torn apart by the dogs."* Certain quarters in the media, however, were far from done. They continued to land other sucker punches, concerning her personal wishes for the Áras itself. In certain confines she was lambasted for *'turning the Áras into a halting site'* for the travelling communities for whom she had such respect, and for her wishes to have, what some perceived, as a *'playground type environment'* created for the children of Ireland. Despite choosing to ignore the dirty tricks campaign, even though she knew who was behind it and even though there were claims that the Chernobyl Children's Project International was *'divided to its core'*, her charity, nevertheless, rode the storm and, in fact, flourished under the International microscope.

To her credit she bears no grudges and, in fact, appreciates the strength the whole entire experience gave her. She turns to me and paraphrases proudly *'Je ne regrette rien de tout'*. And though she remained more than fragile in the aftermath she picked herself up, rolled up her sleeves and went straight on a convoy mission to Belarus. Perhaps journalist, Victoria Clarke was right. Perhaps Adi was too nice to become President. Either way, this woman's convictions were not for turning.

Having been actively involved in the Chernobyl issue since the explosion in 1986, she organised and coordinated the first visit of Chernobyl children to Ireland on receipt of a plea from Belarusian doctors: The now infamous SOS message that read, *'For God's sake get the children out'*, and continues to do so under the Rest and Recuperation Programme to this day. To date, the programme has enabled over 19,000 children affected by the Chernobyl disaster to come to Ireland for vital medical treatment and recuperation, with terminally ill children attending the Paul Newman Therapeutic Recreation Centre at Barretstown in Co Kildare.

These holidays provide respite to the children during the most dangerous time of the year for them to be in Belarus, where the intense heat contributes to the spread of radioactive materials. Examinations carried out on the children following their summer break, bear testament to the beneficial effects of the children's stay in Ireland, with drops in their radiation levels of between 30-50% regularly recorded.

One of those incredible children I would get to hold in my own arms over 10 years ago in 1998, on foot of a small party that we organised for the children in the pub 'Break for the Border', in Dublin, with Adi and Ali Hewson (now a director of the project) present. That baby was called Alexei. He would soon be adopted by Len, Adi's sister, following a life-saving operation.

Doctors removed a tumour the size of a golf ball which sat in place of where his left eye should have been. It's hard to put into words what that poor child had been through, to try and describe how, with his one good eye, this little boy followed Adi's every movement as she assessed the squalor and degradation of his own pitiful surroundings, how that one good eye burrowed in to her very soul, the moment she first laid eyes on him in Belarus.

As we near the end of our extraordinary time together, I ask Adi to sum up her proudest moments and hopes for the future.

I wonder if it was the landmark adoption agreement that was signed in accordance with the Belarusian government in 1998 that helped get so many of those kids out. Perhaps it was the Oscar-winning documentary film, 'Chernobyl Heart', which brought the world's attention into focus. Or maybe she will cite her time in front of the UN assembly as her greatest and proudest moment, the time she shared her journey on the world's largest political stage. But no, despite the enormity of all of these wonderful achievements, it's something else. Another memory comes flooding to the surface. *"It was one of the most extraordinary experiences/moments that I hope will be one of the last images in my mind when I go from this earth!"* she shares profoundly.

It happened during a cardiac mission in Ukraine and it was her first time actually in the surgery when the team was about to perform the first surgery of the 'mission'. It had just followed a long and heavy debate between the team's surgeons and the local surgeons regarding the number of children to receive operations. The 20 children they had chosen were deemed locally to be 'inoperable'.

Adi politely argued back on the principle 'where there's life there's HOPE' and that they work on every child until the last breath...so they wouldn't accept that these children should be sent home to die.

In the end, they won the argument and, almost by accident, Adi ended up in the operating theatre! Nothing could have prepared her for what was to unfolded. *"I get goose bumps even just thinking about it now! ...to be given the privilege, the gift of seeing life being held in the balance. Children, previously deemed 'inoperable', seeing our surgeons living up to our motto 'heartbeat by heartbeat'...every child treated with dignity...to see the heart sitting in the large hand of the surgeon!"*

The heartbeat sound of life coming through the monitor was the only sound in that theatre for Adi and her team. The team had the power of *'life and death'!* She had a sense of time standing still...this was a defining moment...just knowing that these children put their tiny hearts and HOPES in her hands and ONE BY ONE they try and make a miracle happen! The child on the operating table was six years of age...but only weighed the size of a six-month-old baby...and he was in a much deteriorated condition...but the team saved his little life! To then see the child afterwards! He survived! *"It was one of the most awesome, humbling moments that I will treasure to my last breath."*

What next for Adi Roche?

In the summer of 2009, Adi Roche lost two good friends, one of whom was a pal and volunteer with the Chernobyl Children's Project International, Ann Carolan, died just before her 60th birthday. Adi gave the eulogy at the service in Trim. Her loss shook Adi to her very core. She was suddenly reminded that time stands still for no man or woman. Although her husband, Sean, stops asking these days, she travels less and she makes time for those she cares about.

She even stands still once in a while.

Her only hope is that the charity sustains beyond a lifetime. That the world learns its lesson, that we never make the same mistakes again.

As we dash into the car to try and catch Adi's train back to Cork, chatting about all kinds of mad and bizarre means to raise funds, she turns to me and smiles, quoting the words of Seamus Heaney, *'that one day, hope and history rhyme'.*

4

The 'Jesus' Story

Ger McDonnell

'Sin é anois a chairde. Ta an t-am ag teacht...'
'Greater love hath no man than this that a man lay down his life for his friends'

John 15:13

We had just arrived in Tarbert. Our pleasant 20 minute journey across the Shannon estuary would now link us into the heart of Co Clare. I was excited. It was the first time I'd ever been on a bike in the summertime, ever! Sure, I'd cycled to school every year and granted, we dressed up as Santa Claus every Christmas, in fact, for ten wonderful years, in the hope of raising funds for good causes. But here we now were; forty of us, all gathered together in the heart of July, 2009, enjoying the warm sunshine, committed to our 78 mile journey, committed for an exceptionally important reason....

****

Whether we climb or whether we don't, whether we understand or whether we simply cannot, whether we care or pretend not to, nevertheless, three questions fascinate us all about the world's most dangerous Mountain. Where did *K2* get its name? Why is it in fact so dangerous?

And most importantly, why oh why climb it in the first place?

In the mid-19th century, the British forces in India were mindful of a possible Russian attack into South East Asia. In order to consider possible routes the Russians might take, they began surveying peaks and passes in the Himalayas, just to be on the safe side. And so, in 1856, Lieutenant-

Colonel Thomas Montgomerie arrived in the area of the Karakoram where *K2 Mountain* lies, and he began, somewhat unimaginatively, some would say, to name all the major peaks there. '*K*' stood for Karakoram with the simple addition of a number. *K2*, therefore, was the second peak he surveyed. Interestingly, all the other 8000 metre plus peaks have since been given new names such as Broad Peak and Gasherbrum. The name *K2*, however, has eerily somehow managed to stick. The cold and impersonal name strikes genuine fear into the hearts of many of those who dare to climb her or even be associated with her. The Chinese often refer to her as the mountain 'Qogir' or Chogori (meaning '*Big Mountain*'). This '*Big Mountain*' is no ordinary mountain. The first ever successful ascent was made by two Italians, Lino Lacedelli and Achille Compagnoni, on the 31st of July 1954; one year after Everest had been summated, but not before a number of climbing disasters had already enhanced K2's frightening legend among the world's mountaineering fraternity.

An American expedition a year earlier, the fifth ever attempt, in fact, of this mountain and the first since the Second World War, resulted in one of the most dramatic rescues in climbing history, when a single climber managed to hold on to five other colleagues who had fallen, using nothing more than an ice pick. The fall was arrested by a climber called Pete Schoening. Although the seriously ill member of the party, Art Gilkey would eventually die in an ensuing avalanche fall, the heroic efforts, nonetheless, were praised throughout the world for the unfailing courage to save the life of another and for the unbreakable team spirit that the rescue fostered. Fifty four years later, such acts of heroism would be relived… Strangely enough, there wouldn't be another ascent of K2 for another 23 years, not until the second successful completion by the Japanese climber Ichiro Yoshizawa in 1977. Since then, 284 people have reached K2's summit. Compare that with the 3,681 who have made their way to the top of Everest. Of the 284 who have made it to the top of K2, 133 have also made it to the roof of the world and taken out Everest as well. The first woman to conquer K2 was Poland's Wanda Rutkiewicz in 1986. Tragically, Rutkiewicz died shortly afterwards trying to scale another of the 8000 metre peaks, Kangchenjunga, which stands perilously at 8,586m. The next five women to climb K2 either died on the way down or on their next major climb, leading some to speculate that K2 was perhaps cursed for female climbers. I should point out that a very beautiful and very talented Basque climber by the name of Edurne Pasaban made it to the summit in 2004. There was a heavy price to pay, which included the loss of two toes and a chronic 12 month bout of depression but, nevertheless, she bravely remains determined to become the first woman to summit all 14 of the 8,000 metre peaks.

If you're still not sure why it's so dangerous and why so few have made it, consider this:

"*It's enormous, very high, incredibly steep and much further north than Everest which means it attracts notoriously bad weather,*" says Britain's most celebrated mountaineer Sir Chris Bonnington, (a man who began climbing incidentally, on our very own Sugar Loaf in Co Wicklow) who lost his colleague Nick Escourt in an avalanche on K2's western side during an expedition in 1978. Just eight years later, 13 climbers would lose their lives in a 7 day period during which a vicious storm stranded numerous expeditions.

Yes, although Everest is 237m taller, K2 is a far harder climb. "*It's a very serious and very dangerous mountain,*" added Bonnington. "*No matter which route you take, it's a technically difficult climb, much harder than Everest. The weather can change incredibly quickly, and in recent years the storms have become more violent. People who have recently been there have told me that the snow conditions are also getting worse.*" Only two of the other 8000 metre plus peaks, Nanga Parbat, at the western edge of Pakistan's Karakoram, and Nepal's Annapurna, have, in fact, a higher death ratio than K2. It is estimated that 74 of K2's first 280 summiteers died, so in other words, a tragic 26 per cent of those who made it up to the summit, died on the way back down.

For, as every mountaineer including Messner, the great Italian climber, will testify, you're really only halfway there when you summit any mountain. As to why climb K2? Read on...

****

The original Killeen House in the townland of Killeen, Kilcornan, Co Limerick stands proudly erect, just over 300 years old. There's a very fine bed and breakfast, which is also known as Killeen House, just up the road but it's technically in the townland of Cowpark. Gertie grew up a mile and a half away, as the crow flies, from her family home in Killeen House in a modest "*thatched dwelling*" as she refers to it. She moved into Killeen House 45 years ago when she married Denis Mc Donnell. The property had been in his family since his great grandfather, also named Denis McDonnell, bought it in 1908, when he worked as coachman for the de Vere family of Curraghchase.

The beautiful landscaping around the family home, which today includes an intricate and ornate rockery setting as you drive into the front entrance, wasn't always there. "*Denis was a man for as many cows as possible*" she says, smiling. Her hardworking husband, who owned a mixed farm with some livestock, believed that a cow was more useful than a lawn!

Kilcornan in Co. Limerick is a very special place. There were approximately 600 houses at the time Gertie married, and scarcely 200 more have followed since. Interestingly, Kilcornan isn't a village but rather just a parish itself which begins, as you approach from the Limerick side, along the main Foynes Road, with the church on the right, followed by the local bar, the Kilcornan Inn, (formerly known as the Coach Inn) and the local community centre, where many important local gatherings take place. To describe the area as flat would be an understatement. The *'pure flat land'* surrounding Kilcornan, as Gertie describes it, is more reminiscent of the Dutch lowlands; not the kind of place you might expect then to nurture the growth of one of Ireland's greatest ever climbers. Many visitors passing through Kilcornan stop to pay a visit to Curraghchase, a family friendly parkland area and former lands of the de Vere family.

Growing up, Gertie shared close quarters with 11 other people in her house. She distinctly recalls the day electricity arrived into the family home. *"On my first night out to a dance, the electricity had just arrived. I remember looking in the mirror thinking to myself how much better I looked in candlelight!"* Her undoubted modesty and ability to make fun of herself are traits that have been passed down the family line.

JJ came first. A *'small adult'* is how Gertie describes her eldest as a child. She recalls a time when both she and Denis were out running an errand and he was left in the house looking after his granduncle. Having cycled to the shops to pick up supplies for the Sunday lunch, by the time the parents got back to the house, he had the potatoes washed, the cookery book out and the stuffing about to go into the chicken!

Martha came next, 18 months later. She was in Gertie's own words "*a very motherly type and always happy to take charge*". She was always on hand to look after the younger members of the family when they arrived on the scene. Eleven and a half months later saw the arrival of Stephanie who in her younger days would be found on her own, listening to music or watching horse racing on TV. She had plans as a young child to be a drummer and could often be found practising on the saucepans and tin cans. Four years separated her from Ger who arrived into the world on the night of January 20th 1971, ironically, in a massive storm. Conditions were so hazardous that night, in fact, that a man died in Adare when a falling tree struck his horse and cart. Denise the *'baby'* came eight years later. Daddy's little girl, she shared a love of dogs with Ger and adored the ground her older brother walked on. When she wasn't out playing with her brother and their beloved sheepdog, Princess, she would most likely be found on her Daddy's knee. Denis, whose broad white smile was compounded by his deeply tanned complexion, (an occupational hazard from being outdoors ploughing all the time), was a kind man and an excellent father. Denise was just 12 when their dad died suddenly, as a result of a rare blood disorder 'Polycythemia Vera, or PV' which resulted in him producing too many red blood cells. This was the background against which Ger developed his code of honesty and integrity by which he would come to measure himself in later life.

To say young Ger McDonnell hit the ground running was an understatement. His mum laughs as she thinks back to those early days. *"He was never in the same room as you, ever"*. One time she was making a porter cake and went to find the Guinness, only to discover a cap left in its place. Underneath the old wrought iron bed, was young Ger drinking back the remainder of the stout. He was three years old at the time.

The young boy's sense of adventure was apparent from the very start. He adored their sheepdog and if ever his mother needed to find him, they simply followed the dog's trail.

One day his mother stood motionless in relief, as she watched her son being wheeled in on the saddle of the bike by a local neighbour, *"What happened to you?"* she asked trying not to show her utter bemusement. Ger smiled at his mother and said, *"Mammy, a man said 'Christ in heaven, away, go home'."* Gertie smiled back as she realised her son of almost three had been on a mini adventure down the road to the thatched house approximately a mile away which belonged to a neighbour who began most sentences with *'Christ in heaven'*.

Two other things were very obvious with young Ger, quite apart from his big white teeth and loveable smile. His sense of humour and love of pranks were hallmark traits and Halloween appropriately became his favourite time of the year. Ger as a young boy, would organise an intricate web of fish gut to act as a transportation system for the various concoctions of scary masks and skulls that would glide past various windows in the dark of the night and scare the occupants. As he got older the pranks became more elaborate with the introduction of lights and lasers, needless to say with greater effect. In later years, Ger would religiously attend the fancy dress ball in Anchorage with disguise being the key to extending the time he could conceal himself from his friends. Ger loved disguise and this will be fondly remembered by a number of people on whom he pulled amazingly simple pranks. The simplicity made them all the sweeter.

The other constant that remained where Ger was concerned, was his love and passion for sport. He played everything growing up from hurling to draughts. The story goes that in one particular community game encounter against a female opponent, he refused late into the evening to accept defeat, moving his last remaining kings from corner to corner. He also had a flair for acting and performance. The bodhrán would become his instrument of choice, eventually forming his own band, called '*Last Night's Fun*'.

His interest in physics and maths steered him in the direction of electronic engineering and he took up his place in DCU in 1988. Ger, having moved to Dublin, kept close contact with a core group of his friends from national/secondary school, a bond that was never to be broken. It was during that period that he formed other life-long friendships with some of his closest buddies, and his friendship with his older brother JJ once again flourished as the age gap of six years melted away. Some would say that his climbing career began at college, in earnest, when he joined the rock climbing team, although his mother Gertie might dispute that. "*His first climb, in fact, was the 13 cushion climb.*" By which she was referring to the time when Ger managed to stack 13 cushions up against the kitchen wall, climb all the way up to the medicine cabinet where he chanced upon a supply of '*Panadol*', which resulted in his stomach being pumped out. Interestingly, later in life Ger was quoted as saying that all of us are, in fact, climbers and that by climbing we are simply mimicking the innate talents that we discover in our childhood. Ger graduated rapidly from the medicine cabinet to the large pine tree outside in his mother's back garden. With eight grandchildren these days to look after from time to time, Gertie is relieved that she now has a window above the sink area to monitor the next generation of budding climbers!

When he wasn't busy climbing with DCU, he could often be found in the company of his friend, John Hanley, who sparked his initial interest in ice climbing in the Cairngorms of Scotland.

His dad attributed Ger's amazing strength in his arms to '*the English*' for his time spent on UK building sites with a jackhammer in the late 80s and early 90s during summer holidays.

It was in his final year in DCU when he applied for a Morrison visa to the States.

Having applied for the lottery along with thousands of other college hopefuls back in 1992, he never expected to hear anything back. He received the positive news when he was in Cork doing a post graduate course. His initial time was spent working for a cousin, a pilot who also ran a carpet cleaning company. He stayed on the East coast, moving up to Maryland eventually to work with a software company. His time was unsettled and he envisaged himself coming back to Europe sooner rather than later. This reality looked set to unfold following a discussion with his boss, who hinted towards a move to Norway. Ger was happy to join him but requested a few months off before leaving to tour the States on his motorbike. He planned to climb his way across the States moving from forest park to forest park. His hope was to go from Maryland on the East coast to Mexico, and finish in Alaska, following a documentary he had watched on the National Geographic channel about the brown Kodiak bear. Little did he realise that his enduring love of nature would change his life forever.

On the day Ger McDonnell first saw the sunset in Anchorage, his nephew Donnacha was born. He never looked back and never left after that. As he sat most evenings in Anchorage, watching the sun go down on North America's highest peak, one hundred and fifty miles away, he likened Denali Mountain to Limerick, and the people of Dublin being able to witness that sun set on one of the world's most beautiful mountains standing at 20,000 plus feet. Having always been able to look up the classified ads and scan the many engineering jobs available, he was surprised to see how few were on offer in North America's final frontier state. But then again, a great many things surprised Ger about Alaska. He simply adored the wildness, the extremes in beauty and temperature, the tribe's people and the way in which the native tribes of Alaska, such as the Aleuts and Eskimos, came together to form working co-operatives and look after each other. In truth, the native Indian tribesmen were excellent business people. At his first serious job interview the people interviewing him joked that they would have to dock his wages on account of him being Irish, to which he responded, *"Ha, you must be Mormons"*. He laughed out loud. There was a stony silence and he was thanked for his time and escorted to the door. As he was walking out, the chief interviewer whispered in his ear "W*e are Mormons and you start Monday"*.

Much of Ger's work with the Veco oil corporation took him as a contracts engineer to the remote town of Prudhoe Bay Dead Horse (so named after early explorers who arrived in plummeting temperatures only to see their horses perish with the cold), pumping oil on the trans Alaskan oil line. For Ger it was simply perfect. Working 2 weeks on, 2 weeks off afforded him the time he needed to hone his climbing skills, photography and his music skills. It also allowed him to spend time with visiting family and friends. In Alaska, Ger found a new circle of friends drawn from a diverse multitude of backgrounds.

Ger had pleasure during a trip to Dawson City in the Yukon in bringing his mother and brother to the area's only gambling establishment, aptly named *'Diamond Tooth Gertie's'*. The location also allowed Ger to spend time enjoying the wonderful nature around him. He cared deeply about the plight of all animals but close to his heart was the plight of the Karabu who were in danger of becoming extinct due to climatic changes and increased mosquito numbers, which were forcing the herds to forage on higher grounds where food wasn't as plentiful.

It was in Alaska where Ger met Annie Starkey from upstate New York. I guess in life, each of us is looking for that someone who simply gets us... Annie got Ger for sure. She shared his love of all things outdoors, most especially his love of climbing. For Annie and Ger, the matter of a roof over their heads simply meant they could focus on doing the things that really mattered: loving life. What would start out as a friendship climbing unmanned peaks in China, would grow into a bond that lasted to the end.

Ger's first ascent of Denali, which was to raise funds for Milford Hospice, took place in 1999 where he played the small bodhrán, given to him by his sister Denise, on the summit. The ascent was made with an American buddy, Mike Mayes. It was on this trip that the world would discover exactly what Ger McDonnell was all about, as a person first and climber second. On the descent down from the summit they came across a group of five climbers who were in serious trouble, one of whom had snow blindness. Conditions had deteriorated rapidly and visibility was down to zero. The snow markers had disappeared in the resulting '*whiteout*'. Ger broke trail and led them safely to the high camp at 17,000 feet. He received the Denali bravery award for his selfless actions. Over the next four years he became intimately familiar with the various Chugach, Talkeetna and Kenai ranges. Among the many peaks he made were Mount Crosson via the north ridge, Mont Foraker, which he navigated safely, despite a severe storm on the very exposed ridgeline between Mount Crosson and the higher point at 12,472 feet, which resulted in half of his team getting frostbite.

A chance meeting with a mutual pal of his and Pat Falvey's, Leadáin Slattery, led to Ger being included by Pat on the six-strong, 50th anniversary Irish expedition team that would attempt Everest to mark the first ever ascent by Sir Edmund Hillary in 1953. The Everest bid nearly never happened for Ger, who had planned instead to climb in the Antarctic. When that expedition eventually fell through, he was more than relieved to learn that Pat had kept a place open for him. Pat was hoping to put the first Irish team on the roof of the world.

Following Dawson Stelfox's (from Belfast) triumphant first ascent in May 1993, Pat, a respected Irish adventurer who had summated Everest from the North side the previous year in 2002 and become the first person, as he put it, from the Republic of Ireland to do so, was now hoping to build on that success by putting a team of six Irish climbers there on the southern approach, the same route as Hillary had taken all those years previously. Joining Pat and Ger would be Mick Murphy, who was unlucky not to make it up the previous year, George Shorten, Hannah Shields and Claire O'

Leary, both of whom had high hopes of becoming the first Irish woman to conquer Everest.

George's summit bid ended early thanks to a bout of altitude sickness. Clare had to abandon her attempt before the high camp due to a severe stomach bug, (though she would have her revenge the following year) which had rendered her too weak to continue. Hannah who had been climbing very strongly, got to the famous *'balcony'* 300 vertical metres below the summit only to be forced regrettably into turning back due to the imminent threat of frostbite. She would, however, triumphantly return in 2007.

En route to the summit, Ger noticed that Pat, the team leader, was moving very slowly and many climbers were passing him out as they approached the famous Hillary step, the last serious obstacle pre summit, which requires the climber to scale and negotiate a 40 ft spur of snow and ice. He asked Ger to continue, saying that he'd be fine and not to worry. This was their second summit bid, with weather forcing them back down the previous night to the high camp. Undoubtedly, this extra exertion had weakened Pat.

When Ger finally arrived at the notorious Hillary Step, queues were causing severe congestion. Unphased, Ger simply free-climbed around them and made his way quickly to the summit. He only had a few moments to take it all in. His mind was otherwise occupied. Firstly there was the matter of Pat's welfare that was concerning him greatly and then there was the matter of the leaking oxygen cylinder that he had been forced to swap over reluctantly with his Sherpa. The head Sherpa or Seder, Pemba Gyalje, had insisted that Ger take the one that was working properly. As he made his way off the summit he could see that his own Sherpa, Pemba Renshe, was in serious trouble as the pronounced hissing sound became louder and louder, resulting in lost oxygen escaping from the Sherpa's tank supply. Sitting down on the hardened ice, Ger eventually somehow managed to resolve the problem and get both tanks fully operational.

When he eventually caught up with Pat he could see that the situation was very serious. Pat was being assisted by the Seder. Ger agreed with Sherpa Gyalje that at the balcony, he would shortrope Pat down to the high camp, as the exhausted Sherpa had already had a tiring 24 hours laying out the fixed lines for the oncoming climbers the previous day. En route down to high camp, they had to endure a white out and each perilous step had to be painstakingly negotiated with extreme and patient care. When they finally came into camp, Ger took care of Pat's medicine and made sure he had enough nourishment to continue down the mountain safely. They couldn't afford to spend any more time than necessary in the life-threatening death zone (areas above 8,000 metres where the body is effectively dying). By the time they eventually reached the advance base camp, Pat's spirits and health had improved dramatically and, to his credit, he was the first to rejoice in the summit success that had been achieved by Ger and Mick respectively.

Ger being Ger and despite protestations by most who knew him, was keen to clear up the matter of the world's highest 'Puc Fada'. Many had thought that he had hit a sliotar off the summit. He had agreed to do so, on behalf of the Cronin family, who were doing their *'Drive For Life'* campaign (driving from Australia to Ireland) in support of Cystic Fibrosis Ireland. Having stopped off at base camp Everest, they were hoping to auction off the aforementioned hurley at a later stage. Ger had decided to abandon his hopes of bringing the hurley to the summit after they were forced to turn back on the first summit bid. He was conscious of the weight and knew that, with such a small weather window opening up the following day, it would be foolhardy to bring it. Instead he hit the *'Puc Fada'* off the South Col below the summit. Rather than allow people think otherwise, he rang his pal in the Limerick Leader Jerome O' Connell to set the record straight. When asked why he had taken up climbing in a post publicity interview, Ger replied *"because it was less dangerous than hurling!"* Whilst most laughed, he had, in fact, taken quite a few wallops in his younger days and so there was a fair degree of truth in his words.

One year later, in 2004, Pat Falvey, in accompanying Clare O' Leary to the summit, hit a sliotar of his own off the summit of Everest, a decision that raised a few eyebrows given his association with the Kingdom, a county that was better known for gaelic and not hurling. And so, some felt that a football might have been a more appropriate gesture.

Sir Edmund signed the famous hurley that Ger had used. At an auction in 2005, which the Cronins organised, the McDonnells, spearheaded by Gertie and JJ, bought the auction item, paying a very handsome but worthwhile sum in the process for the Cystic Fibrosis charity. Perhaps it was only fitting, therefore, that the hurley, now in a glass case, with a picture of Hillary signing it, should find its way home to its rightful place. A dumbstruck Ger announced in 2008 when he learned of Hillary's sad death *"Ma, this hurley is now priceless"* . Little did he realise at the time just how priceless it would eventually become.

When he came home to Limerick as fit as a fiddle, what began for Ger as a casual bike ride to post a letter in Askeaton, resulted in a trip to Doolin in Co Clare. Parking the bike outside O Connor's pub in Doolin, he was greeted by three local elderly man enjoying a pint. *"Here for the week?"* they enquired. Ger smiled at the boys and nodded politely explaining that he had cycled from Kilcornan. They asked what brought him to Doolin and Ger replied *"a pint and a sandwich."* Having washed down the cheese sandwich with a pint of Arthur's finest, the three men were open-mouthed to see Ger get back on his bike and make the return 78 mile journey home to his beloved Kilcornan. When Ger recalled the story later, he used to say that the same three men can still be found there today with their mouths open.

China in 2004 afforded Ger the opportunity to spend some time in Annie Starkey's company. Together they climbed 3 peaks over 5,000 metres. They managed a first ascent of China's Aksai Chin West Mountain and Xinjiang Ugyur in an Autonomous Range standing at 21,693 FT.

Ger McDonnell wasn't the first Limerick man to attempt K2; that honour belongs to Mick Keys who had made his attempt in the early 90s. But, like so many who had gone before, he had to bow to inclement weather conditions. In 2006, Ger hoped to put the record straight. He teamed up again with Mick Murphy and Banjo Bannon from Newry, Co. Down. They had attempted Broad Peak earlier, another of the 8000 metre peaks often used by K2 climbers to acclimatise properly. It was on that very mountain, in fact, that Ger had gone round all the tents begging climbers to climb with him and help rescue a pair of stranded climbers who had been advised not to go up further, but who nevertheless were now helpless and in need of serious assistance. Mark Sheen, who was on that expedition, testified that not one person would go up with Ger as they were too tired, an experience which tore at the fundamental principles which Ger held dearly.

It was at camp 2 on K2 where Ger heard the mountain rumbling. Perhaps in hindsight he might have listened more intently. The following morning he was struck by a falling rock that cracked his helmet. The full extent of his injuries only became known as he began to make the tricky descent accompanied by Mick Murphy. At the next camp he turned to Joelle Brupbacher, a Swiss climbing colleague and announced, *"I think I'm hurt"* as the blood streamed down his face. She later described what she had witnessed on the snowfield as a *"whole mountain descending upon him"*. Just how lucky he was to be alive would only become fully apparent when he had the misfortune of arriving for treatment in the nearby military hospital, which was located in Skardu. Before that, his memories were hazy at best. He recalls waking up in a neighbouring Russian's tent back at base camp to the sound of the *'Dukes of Hazard'* being played on a laptop in Russian.

Tragically the Russian team that had helped him in his initial recovery were wiped out on their summit bid just days later. Ger had suffered a serious hair line fracture and had come within an inch of being killed. So primitive and disgustingly unclean were the facilities in the so-called hospital, that Ger couldn't wait to get out of there. He remembered being tied down to a slab in an operating theatre that he likened to a slaughter house. They attempted to give him a full anaesthetic with a drug that was more commonly used on animals. He demanded that they stop, fearful indeed for his very life. Unfortunately the weather prevented an airlift to Islamabad and the roads were fully blocked and impassable following heavy landslides. Despite his poor health condition, he had to hike his way to safety. It took him two full weeks to get home and to add to his complications, there were bomb threats in Heathrow to contend with. Touching down in Shannon a fortnight later, was a welcome relief. The multiple fractures at the base of his skull were going to need time to heal. The specialists in Dublin and Cork were amazed he was still alive and the scans were sent to the States. His initial fears were thankfully allayed when he got the all clear and was told he could climb again.

The following year, still keen to continue his adventures, he decided to switch focus and worked as a Team Leader along with Rolf Bae on the 'Beyond Endurance' Expedition to the Antarctic, which was Pat Falvey's project. It was also a chance to reunite with his good pals, Clare O' Leary and Pat Falvey. His love of Tom Crean made the trip extra special and he fully immersed himself in his newfound role of sweeper on the expedition. He became good pals on the trip with Rolf who was keen to climb with Ger again. They wouldn't have to wait too long....

In early 2008, Ger Mc Donnell knew he was returning to put some unfinished business to rest. The mountain had never really left him and now it was time to engage with the elements once more.

This time Ger trained even harder in the Chugach Mountain ranges back in Alaska, a place Ger considered sacred, a spiritual ground where he was most at peace. He had decided to team up with the straight-talking but trustworthy Wilco Van Roojien and so committed to be part of the Dutch Norit Team to attempt the summit. Mark Sheen with whom he had climbed before, was also along for the ride. Initially they wanted Ger to lead the expedition but he felt that Wilko had the commercial expertise to drive and support the expedition and so Wilko was the assigned team leader. Also in the crew, to Ger's delight, was his old pal from Everest, Pemba Geyalje, who this time would be there as a full climbing team member which Ger was instrumental in organizing. Another climbing pal of Wilco's, Cas van de Gevel, helped round off the team to a healthy eight. They were ready to do battle once more. Apart from climbing K2, the team was also there initially to do a major clean-up operation on the mountain akin, on a minor scale, to what had been done on Everest back in '96.

Their first window came in the middle of July but in typical familiar fashion, they were forced to abort due to weather. They had been there since May and Ger, from a personal perspective, was anxious to make a summit bid. He knew deep inside that he could make this mountain if the weather would only hold. From a climber's perspective, this was the ultimate '*climber's mountain*'. This was where you got to pit your climbing skills against the very best Mother Nature could offer you at high altitude.

On the Sunday before they would make their summit bid, Gertie received a call from Ger indicating that it was '*now or never*'. The last entry on his web page was "*Tá an t-am ag teacht*" ("The time is coming"). Spurred on with an innate belief, he approached the different climbing teams left on the mountain to seek co-operation for a mutual summit attempt. He was looking to ensure that they would work together to facilitate a successful summit bid for all concerned. He was acting as the '*Peace Broker*' so that nothing would ruin what they had all worked and strived for so valiantly, to achieve. If there was any unrest, they sent in '*Jesus*', the man with the wavy hair and long beard and a smile as wide as any crevasse, aptly named by Italian climber, Marco Confortola. Things appeared to be finally settled. Decisions were taken and roles were assigned about who would carry what, about where marker flags would be laid, and, importantly, about how much rope length would be needed.

On the 31st of July, a text arrived to say that the weather had turned again. They were at camp 3. A guy was calling out furiously, having lost his tent in a sudden horrific storm. He was seeking refuge and shelter. As no one else would give him any, Pemba and Ger obliged the young Serbian climber. His brother, JJ, while holidaying in Lanzarote, received a text an hour later to say "*happy birthday bro*". Approximately 3 hours after that, another text came in to say they were going for the summit; the weather window had suddenly appeared. JJ felt strangely uneasy. The wind had blown the snow covering away and so the perfect climbing conditions were now beckoning those who were brave enough to set forth.

The head porter who had been violently sick the night before was forced to descend. As a result of what is now believed to be a miscommunication, the ropes were laid down at the wrong place by the other porters as a consequence. When Ger and the others arrived at the famous bottleneck, more rope was needed and a six hour delay resulted.

At the bottleneck, as the climb began, the Serbian climber thought the pace was too slow and he unclipped and fell tragically to his death. A porter went out to see if he was ok and he too fell to his death. Pemba Gyalje, Ger's climbing partner, a man who had summated Everest six times, felt the omens were not good and shared as much with Ger.

A decision had to be taken. Encouraged by a brash young Italian climber, Marco Confortola, who gave an arousing speech about another Italian climber who had summitted as late as 8pm on a previous climb, a decision by the team leader, Wilko, was made - they were going to go for it.

At 7pm on the 1st of August 2008, Pemba, Cas, Wilco and Ger McDonnell all made it to the summit of K2 Mountain. Ger stood proudly with the Irish flag in hand, the ultimate reward for a lifetime of endeavour. He was the first Irish man to achieve this amazing feat... He quickly proceeded to unwrap the peace flag and was photographed on the summit with the flag extended between himself and his friend Pemba. Ger's sister, Martha, sent JJ a text confirming that Ger had made it. However, having listened to Ger so many times before recalling his various climbs, she knew that his getting back to high camp was now paramount. The text also read *"pray for his safe return"* which was a sentiment that JJ shared as he was uneasy once he had gotten the earlier text from Ger telling him that *"we have decided to make a go for it after all"*.

The family waited anxiously for more news. Nothing came for another six hours. The first communiqué indicated that Ger's friend Rolf Bae, had been killed by a falling serac (a tower of unstable glacier ice).

****

On the perilous night descent, Ger and Marco decided to rest until daylight for a few precious hours due to the fact that 3 members of the Korean team who were descending in front of them had suddenly disappeared. Having bivouacked into the snow and ice, Ger sang an Italian song to Marco to keep his spirits and self-belief intact. So much would now depend on maintaining their support for each other and the inner will to keep going... At approx 5am on the morning of the 2nd of August, as light broke, Ger began a search for the anchor of the descent rope with Wilco, in order to continue their descent. It has subsequently been confirmed that the anchor had been dislodged or broken, resulting in three members of the Korean team tragically being trapped, suspended upside down on ropes below Ger's position.. Wilco recalled he was starting to experience snow blindness and so was forced to descend. On his descent he encountered the three Korean team members suspended upside down in a distressed state. According to Wilco, he threw them a glove to place over one of the climber's feet as the Korean had lost a boot and was in danger of suffering frostbite. He then continued his descent. Marco later reported that Ger spotted the Korean team and shouted to Marco to get up quickly to help the distressed climbers. Marco and Ger spent almost 3.5 hours trying to assist the Korean climbers while in the death zone and eventually Marco was forced to descend as he felt he could do no more as the climbers were like '*puppets on a string*'.

Marco confirms that he witnessed Ger climbing back up but did not at that time understand Ger's reasoning… that reasoning soon became evident. Ger went back up to release the tension on the ropes and, eventually, some 3 to 4 hours later, the only remaining climber, Ger, remarkably managed to free the three members of the Korean team…

Marco meanwhile descended to the base of the bottleneck where he was met by two Sherpa, who were sent up the mountain by the Korean Team Leader from camp 4 to rescue his team members. They radioed Pemba confirming Marco's position and 2 hours later Pemba encountered Marco lying unconscious in the snow. Pemba received a second radio call from the Sherpa to confirm that they were descending with three members of the Korean team, and that a climber with a 'red and black down suit' was descending behind the Koreans across the traverse which had been hit by a large ice fall and had subsequently plummeted to his death…

Sadly to say, Pemba and Ger's family now know that this was the last sighting of Ger based on the suit colour, something that his mother, brother, sisters and their respective husbands, Tom, Barry and Damien, will have to deal with for the rest of their lives. However, one of the comforting things about this radio call was that Ger had been seeing descending behind the Koreans on the traverse…

This confirms that Ger, having had to bivouac above 8,000m without supplementary oxygen, and having found the Koreans, assisted them for 3 hours with Marco and, on Marco's departure, went back up for what we now know was a continued attempt to free the Koreans single-handedly, and that he managed to achieve this… Such was the act of a man whose integrity and sense of humanity were all-encompassing.

****

Later when Ger's family flew out to Pakistan, they were met by the head of the mountain rescue team in Islamabad, Brigadier Khan, and he was so touched by Ger's actions on the mountain that he was reduced to tears… He told them that Ger's respect for the Pakistani and Nepalese Porters and Cooks was incredible.

He could not believe the sadness expressed by so many fellow mountaineers, porters and cooks on learning of his tragic death. He told them that one porter was inexperienced on the mountain and Ger, recognising this fact, had shown him how to use the ropes which would assist him. The porter was amazed that a mountaineer would take the time and effort to demonstrate these skills to him. He also recalled that as the Norit team was on its way up to camp 3 from base camp, Ger made numerous phone calls to enquire about the cook who was extremely ill. He was concerned at the fact that he had to walk out and was not going to be airlifted. The family later learned that Ger gave him one of his insulated sleeping bags for his trip out, to ensure that he would at least be warm at night on the trek out. This was the true essence of the man. His concern for his fellow man transgressed all barriers.

****

As we arrived in Doolin on our bikes late that summer's afternoon, on the first anniversary cycle which Shay O' Connor and the other lads, former classmates of Ger's from DCU, had put together, I turn to Clare O' Leary and say *"He's smiling down on us isn't he?"* I ask her to describe this man's greatest quality. Many of Ger's national school friends, people from the parish, Barry, his brother-in-law, and JJ, his older brother, were all gathered together... You could sense the immense pride all around. Ger was inspiring them all even now... Claire turned to me and smiled and said "*Ger always saw the glass half full even when it was beyond half empty*".

Students studying for their Junior Cert can now learn of the kindness of this true Irish hero that has inspired a generation in their *Fonn 3* Irish textbook. As a nation, let us be truly proud. Let us never forget......

5

A New York Minute

Orla Barry

'Often attitudes are kindled in the flame of others' convictions.'

Louis E. Le Bar

It is 8.30 on a gorgeous late summer's morning in the heart of Dublin and the city is already alive. The sound of commerce fills the streets and the foyer of the Conrad Hotel is a hub of activity; airline staff checking in and out; conference organisers preparing to greet delegates; business people everywhere make the most of the technology facilities. Fortunately, my own Blackberry and phone are switched off, most unusual for me.

My focus is elsewhere. My mind is furiously playing catch up as I try to digest the pearls of wisdom being patiently passed to me from across the coffee table by an enlightened gentleman from Cork.

As Jim Barry and I take a moment to reflect on a pivotal journey that not only influenced hundreds of lives at the time but, in its own profound way, had a significant effect on his own relationship with his daughter, Orla, I stop and close my eyes.

What must Dave Buckwald have been thinking about, this very day eight years ago?

His journey would have been like that of so many on that crisp, beautiful September morning en route to a client's office in Northern New Jersey. Perhaps he was reflecting on the fact that he was just eighteen days married to his gorgeous wife, Jennifer, and remembering the honeymoon they had just enjoyed. Perhaps he was thinking about the client meetings ahead, doing what any good sales person does and visualising the potential outcomes from what might lay ahead. Suddenly, the car radio broke in on his happy thoughts – a plane had hit the World Trade Center and both

Sean Mc Sharry aged 10 training in Wicklow before his
magnificent Kili Summit in 2008

'Father and son' Tony and Kevin O'Connor on the summit of
Kilimanjaro in September 2009

Dr Austin O'Carroll pictured with his two children

Dr Austin O'Carroll taking time out from being a doctor

Adi Roche Founder of the Chernobyl Children's Project

Adi pictured with baby Anatoly one of the children on the Cardiac
Ukraine who is in desperate need of life saving surgery

Ger McDonnell pictured on 'Denali' Mountain in Alaska

Relaxing taking time out before climbing Foraker Mountain in Alaska

Alex Maguire on holiday with his wife Alison

Alex, Alison and the kids, Max is 6 next month, Toby just turned 4 in
June, Amelie is 20 months old now, 2 in Feb.

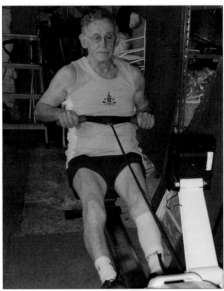

Richard Morgan training ahead of this year's world championships

Richard with his grandson Breffny, competing in the 2007 World
Indoor Rowing championships

Clare Power (right) celebrates on the summit of Kilimanjaro

Seamus Durack pictured with his daughter Caitriona aged 2

Seamus Durack on the comeback trail pictured on 'Snoopy Loopy' winning the Grade 1 Bet Fair chase in November 2008

towers were on fire. *"Surely it's a sick joke, right?"* His nerves suddenly shot to pieces as the devastating reality hit home; *"Oh My God, not the North Tower,"* he cried out in pain and panic. The North Tower, the 104th and 105th floors which housed fifty-one of his clients. The North Tower, which housed the largest brokerage firm registered on Wall Street. The North Tower that housed fifty-one of his friends... The same friends whose dreams he was party to, whose life plans had been carefully laid out and prepared, plans he personally helped to prepare.

The tears must have never stopped streaming down Dave Buckwald's face in the following days as he reflected on the shocking realities of the 9/11 catastrophe. Over the next three months Dave Buckwald and other insurance colleagues (who gave their time voluntarily) handed out cheques worth millions of dollars to forty-five families that had been utterly ripped apart. They did this because the husbands and wives of these families had taken out life assurance policies. There were seven families, however, who received no cheque whatsoever because the policies that their spouses had taken out online had lapsed. Nobody rings you, you see, when you take out an online policy to say that your policy needs to be renewed. Funny that. In this hi-tech, e-commerce driven world in which we live in today, online sometimes simply cannot replace the personal touch.

"You see Ian," Jim thankfully interrupts my thoughts, *"Our clients don't take out life policies because someone is going to die. They take them out,"* he stops to ponder for a moment, *".....so that others may live."*

The President of the Life Insurance Association of Ireland had my full attention and he knew it. Like most people when it comes to insurance I had never really thought about life cover in that way. I wondered how Jim had come to see the world from what appeared to be an entirely compassionate viewpoint and just why he'd been so successful in what I'd always viewed to be a dog-eat-dog world. I figured that in the current economic climate, businesses like Jim's would be among the first to suffer and yet his was prospering. I also still needed to figure out just exactly how his business, and the story of his American colleague Dave Buckwald, linked in with the person whom this story was really supposed to be about: his daughter Orla. So, I sat back, ordered some more green tea and did what I am often accused of never doing particularly well: I listened!

****

Growing up in the heart of Cork City, a hero to Jim Barry was someone who simply didn't take what life threw at him. He likened life to a grindstone. Just like a grindstone, depending on the angle you chose to lean on, the result can be either too sharp or too blunt. For Jim, life was about how you react to it.

His early life was certainly varied and fun. He started delivering milk at the age of seven. From there he moved on to a petrol station before graduating to become the entertainment officer of a caravan site, a position that seemed highly appropriate for this larger than life character. From the family TV business, (CT Services Ltd) he went on to do a spell with the Irish Musicians Rights Organisation. He even spent time as a drug pusher as he puts it - cigarette vending machines. The fags weren't that profitable with only a 9% mark-up to be gained, so things were tight enough, trying to provide for the growing family of three children.

One evening, out of the blue, Sean Fleming, Jim's financial adviser, called to the house. He'd bought his first policy from Sean back in 1982. Why? *"Because Sean made it about the Barry's and not about the policy,"* Jim says smiling. *"Jim, you belong in financial services,"* Sean protested. He made his case again in 1986 and again in 1988. In fact, Sean Fleming continued to protest to Jim Barry for eight years, until, finally, in 1994, Jim joined the ranks of Canada Life. He cites Sean as his greatest life mentor; the *"person who can see in us the things that we cannot,"* he reflects. To this day, they still joke about Jim being in the financial services. Jim remains unsure whether it was Sean's closing techniques or his own perceptiveness that made him join. Perhaps it was a little of both. They remain the best of pals today.

But what of the actual industry, its reputation, our perceptions of those who sell us policies? I am still curious, so I probe a little deeper.

"Ian, it's easy for any insurance guy to sell someone policies that will earn him the most commission. It becomes all about the salesperson and that simply should never be," Jim believes. And why would he? As the President of the LIA, I would expect him to say as much. He tells me about the way in which a good sales person will *'fact find'*, establishing what a person's needs actually are; imagining how those needs might change down the road; the lifestyle they require as well as desire. This discovery process seems so logical, doesn't it? And yet, when I stop to think about the way in which certain banks, for example, do business, I begin to appreciate the differences. A bank might sometimes, for example, ask the question *"How much do you want to put into the policy?"* as opposed to the question *"What do you want out of the policy?"* Terms like *'conditional lending'* come to mind. In reality, I guess a bank's *raison d'etre* is to satisfy the shareholder and therefore the customer cannot always come first. Shareholder versus stakeholder... these lines will inevitably blur from time to time.

Unquestionably, some people are starting to resent being tied in with a certain bank because their mortgage required them to take out a protection policy to copper-fasten the deal. Suddenly, it's not really that hard to see one of the reasons why Jim's business is doing so well – the banks simply don't always take the time to listen!

Jim explains that it's not about the insurance product but rather the customer's wants and needs. It makes sense when it's broken down like that. You need a car but you want a Mercedes! Do you want a mortgage? No, but you want a home. Therefore you need a mortgage. Like any good salesperson, Jim and others like him make it about the customer. How many of you reading this, for example, have ever bought or continue to buy anything because of the person or people selling it to you rather than the actual product *per se*?

But obviously we haven't all got the message. I'm told that 40% of us don't have pensions and even more worryingly, 52% don't have adequate life assurance cover.

I think back to guys like Dave Buckwald and then I contrast that image with a typically successful person in this country. He's possibly the main bread winner earning a good average income of maybe €50k. If he dies tomorrow, the state pension will provide the surviving spouse with €12,500, leaving a rather large deficit to fill.

There's one image that Jim shares with me that both scares me and reassures me. It's the notion that, when I'm dead and buried, fifty guys will be turning up to get paid but there's only one person coming with a cheque – assuming, of course, that I've thought about the bigger picture and gotten that life cover in place! I start to make mental notes to myself – (1) Get house in order!

And so, the surprisingly fascinating conversation about an industry that I really knew little or nothing about continues for a little while longer. Jim shares fondly about his role as President of the Life Insurance Association, the country's only representative body that caters for both agents and brokers alike. The LIA has 8,000 members of which over 3,000 are financial advisors. Among other things they have an educational role, through the provision of courses, and in ensuring that all financial advisors meet the minimum competency as set down by the Financial Regulator. The qualification offered is (QFA), Qualified Financial Advisor. For him, becoming President, a role he has held since December 2008, afforded him a genuine chance to give something back to both loyal members and the wider community.

Interestingly, Jim and Dave Buckwald became friends through the curiously named Million Dollar Round Table (MDRT). The MDRT is a worldwide body of professional advisers with some 35,000 members. In order to become a member of this prestigious club, you must have achieved certain levels of sales. If you are one of the lucky ones, then you're in the top 6% of sales pros in the world.

As Jim summarises the various types of policies available and products that range from income protection to inheritance tax planning, he clears his throat when it comes to the issue of critical illness cover. For those unfamiliar with the concept, it works like a life policy but it's your health that is insured not your life. So, payment (insurance company depending) is made on diagnosis of up to forty-two specified illnesses, with no restrictions on how the payout is used. The only restriction that applies, thankfully enough, is that you live for fifteen days post diagnosis!

It had certainly never dawned on Jim Barry that in February 2002, just five months after Dave Buckwald had made his visits to the poor families affected by 9/11, he would be sitting down with his fifteen-year-old daughter, Orla, to discuss the issue of her own critical cover following her diagnosis with cancer.

****

"I was spoilt rotten as a child - led a charmed existence to be fair!" Orla smiles a radiant smile in my direction, the kind that could light up the dullest and darkest winter day. Born on the 11th of January 1987, she was the youngest of four children. There was one boy in the family, Ciaran, now aged twenty-three, and two older girls; Sinead now aged twenty-six and Fiona aged twenty-nine. One thing was for certain from the get-go; Orla was Daddy's *'Little Girl'*. Leading a true tomboy existence, she became a fervent Man U supporter. She loved Beckham but adored Keane. But who else would this girl be so loyal to, coming from Ballincollig in Cork? Every August, she'd sit down with her dad to mull over the fixture listings to see which game they would go and see. She still recalls the very first game they ever went to see. Standing proudly at the Stratford end, she cheered loudly as Beckham scored and United won the game. The colourful language all around her added to the occasion. *"Dad had pinned his last hopes of finding a child who would hold any interest in football on me. The others got to be themselves. While I simply became a raging tomboy!"* she says laughing aloud.

Perhaps it's unusual to meet a young girl so close and so devoted to both of her parents. She likens her mum Anne, becoming a Barry, to a process of *'metamorphosis'* by virtue of being married to her father for longer than she'd been without him. Still incredibly happily married after thirty-two years, they met when Anne was seventeen and then married three years later. *"Dad had it sussed,"* Orla enlightens me, and *"sure he'd the house bought before he even proposed to mum!"* Orla was close to all of her family. She adored them all and they, in turn, her. Well, most of the time at least. Becoming a very close family depends, I suspect, on quality time afforded to all parties. Having a summer home in Crosshaven helped the bonding process. The Barry's never had a babysitter, at least never one from outside the family. The grandparents usually happily obliged. It spoke volumes to me about their strong family values.

"We were brought up realising just how important it is to laugh. My parents insisted almost like an unspoken rule that we poke gentle fun at each other," Orla says, recounting many fun examples. There was one particular occasion, for example, when the family were going to their parents' twenty-fifth wedding anniversary. Orla had just finished a bout of chemotherapy. Her sister had bought herself a rather elegant top that had ripped embarrassingly in the wrong places and needed running repairs. Orla simply informed everyone, dead pan, that this was understandable given that her sister had put a few pounds on and that this had inevitably caused her to burst out of the top!

Growing up, the kids really never wanted for anything despite the fact that her father Jim didn't have a great deal in the early years. *"I remember dad working so very hard for everything we had. He used to do lots of different things at first."* She recalls the cigarette vending machine days. *"For pocket money in the summer holidays, we used to tape the monies to the ciggie boxes."* She has distinct memories of pile upon pile of cigarettes filling the house – *"Fags that nobody smoked."*

One of the things that Orla particularly liked when she was younger was the fact that her parents were so tactile and loving towards each other. There was a sense of genuine fun and warmth about the house and, unsurprisingly, all the kids from the neighbourhood seemed to gravitate towards the house. *"Ours was an open house,"* she says with a sense of pride. It isn't difficult to see that she was a very contented child.

Orla's enthusiasm spilled into the classroom. She went to Scoil Mhuire, an all girls school in Ballincollig. *"A real overachiever"* is how she modestly describes herself. *"I was captain of the spellathon team in sixth class. We came second in the County Finals that year."* She did a stint on the quiz team, adored maths; so much so that she even had extra maths homework from the year ahead from 4th class onwards. *"I wanted to test myself to the full,"* she tells me. Orla considered it a genuine treat to get hard stuff to do at the weekend. So, to fill her time, she took on a secondary maths course. By the age of 10

Orla Barry was in the top 2% of the country. She was certainly capable of scoring high in a Mensa exam, unquestionably. I asked her if she had ever wanted to take the actual tests. I was amazed at the wisdom that came back. *"I guess I didn't need to belong to a club to feel intelligent."* For some it might help signify acceptance but, luckily for her, she had never felt her achievements isolated her from her friends or family. Rather they encouraged, loved and fully supported her. She was always bubbly, having fun and enjoying life with loads of friends. From the age of ten, when her father joined the financial services, Orla remembers there definitely being more money; more money for the family to do even more things together.

"It stopped the hand-me-downs for the first time – how sweet, especially being a tomboy. Ha!" We both laugh. Her dad was now able to do the house up for the first time. The kitchen was renovated and work on a two-storey extension began. *"I loved that time. We virtually lived in a caravan for almost a year, which became the social centre for all cooking to be done!"* Her dad connected a pipe over the roof to dispense water in their front garden, all on full public view, not that the neighbours minded. In fact, they often joined in the hilarious goings on. *"Just another regular day in the Barry household,"* as Orla puts it. She finally got her own bedroom, having always shared with her older sister Sinead.

Despite being whisked off to glamorous holiday locations such as Florida and on shopping trips to London with her mother, Orla still always had the best of craic with her father, particularly the time he drove the whole family to Euro Disney, Paris.

When Orla speaks about her siblings, it's with great respect. There's even a hint of protectiveness in her tones. Her brother Ciaran is a mere eleven months older than her. *"We used to be the same height,"* she muses. At fourteen he suddenly shot up and now stands proudly at 6'6". *"Ciaran's a gentle giant. A little more reserved than us Barry girls but he gets on really well with the girls. We remain very close."* One can sense an innate and unquestionable lifelong bond.

"Sinead's a total Looney tune, away with the fairies," she says and winks at me. *"It's that middle child syndrome thing."* Her sister was always smart, if a little accident-prone. She rang Orla one day to say she'd dislocated her thumb playing footie. Two weeks later, another call came in. This time it was to announce that she'd hurt her ankle falling off some steps while leaving a flat. She was a little drunk at the time! She awoke the next morning to discover it was broken. Her big sister would often baby sit and entertain Orla and Ciaran. When they still shared a room, Sinead would often run up pretending to have a weapon in her hands to fend off burglars – *"practice runs,"* Orla says smiling. She went on to study commerce and the girl who

apparently never wanted to leave college, eventually had to do so in 2009 and is now an accountant.

Of Fiona, the eldest of the children she remarks, *"The serious responsible one, a studious twenty-nine, going on forty. Ha!"* Orla laughs heartily again. She amusingly recalls the time her eldest sister crashed the car leaving a curious note that simply read *'Car has been crashed but I'm fine'*. Orla always appreciated the fact that Fiona would take her places. She was always there when she needed her. Orla's sport of choice when she was still in primary school was basketball. There were no sports facilities in the school so she couldn't play basketball there. *"It really bothered me. I hated not being able to do sports in school so I joined the local basketball team like my sisters had done before me. Ballincollig Basketball Club- we never won a thing but had lots of craic but, boy, we were shockingly awful!"*

Orla remained a tomboy in her own eyes till she was sixteen at least. Going to Colaiste Choilm, a mixed school wasn't a problem. Adjusting was easy - she just continued to hang out with the lads.

As she grew older, Orla became a bit of a trouble maker in school. *"I was a mouthpiece and had an opinion on most things. I sometimes gave those opinions when they weren't really needed or called for."* If a teacher was crap, Orla wasn't slow to let them know. The Irish teacher got a roasting on several occasions. Being virtually fluent simply allowed Orla express her opinions even more vocally, as Gaeilge!

One of the problems with being a tomboy as far as your female friends are concerned is the small matter of honesty. Sometimes Orla was simply too honest for her own good when it came to opinions about clothes and what did or didn't look good! *"I got the spade calling from Dad!"* she pleads. Some might consider it especially strange that this feisty young woman never once argued with her mother. She wasn't a typical teenager in that regard. Nor indeed, when it came to going out with lads. She preferred the idea of talking to everyone rather than not talking to some guy just because someone else had had a fling with him. So while she might have gone all girly for the odd disco here and there, young Ms Barry's passions were her mates, schoolwork and the basketball!

People who call a spade a spade tend to get straight to the point by their nature.

One October, Orla, then in third year preparing to do her Junior Cert, found a lump on the left side of her neck. It was a rather large lump that she was able to move around. It sat over the left collar bone. *"I noticed that I couldn't feel my collar bone when I moved the lump,"* she recalls. Her mum wasn't sure what the lump was, so arranged for Orla to visit the GP. Walking back up the stairs, Orla thought to herself. "*I think I have cancer but best not to worry anyone at this point.*" So she didn't say a thing. Not a word.

First speculation suggested, perhaps, that given the amount of sport that Orla played, this *'innocuous'* lump be removed. Orla was referred to a specialist for further investigation on the premise that this would be a routine operation. So, in the short term, Orla went back to normal life. She set about preparing for her mock examinations and carried on playing sport and knocking around with her pals. Christmas came and went and so did her birthday. She was fifteen when she saw the specialist in February 2002. Aside from the lump, she didn't seem to have any other symptoms apart from weight loss, something she assumed was normal given the amount of sport she was playing. In her mind she'd already prepared for the worst case scenario so whatever she was about to be told couldn't possibly be worse than that, right?

She arrived one morning at the clinic on South Terrace, Cork. Initially, seen by a plastic surgeon, he immediately called in a colleague, Dr O' Leary, a nose, ear & throat specialist. After the preliminary examination, Orla was booked in for a needle biopsy a few days later in the South Infirmary Hospital. "*And so it began. They withdrew fluid in the needle and said 'no blood' – good sign Orla, but nevertheless I was booked in for a full biopsy later that week,*" she reflects. Admitted on the Sunday, she vividly recalls the moment a student doctor asked was she in for a lymph node biopsy. She replied "*yes*" even though the word "*lymph*" had never been mentioned to her before. She knew what was coming and braced herself. She played two basketball games the day she was admitted, a final act of defiance to delay her admittance perhaps? In on the Sunday, she was out on the Wednesday, one final act of defiance followed: another basketball match on the Saturday. "*I burst my stitches going for this three pointer.*"

"*Screw it',* " she thought bravely, watching the ball make up its mind about falling into the ring. "*I'm not the cancer. It isn't who I am and it doesn't own me!*" The ball eventually fell into the ring and in her mind Orla's stand had begun.

Her mother and father broke the news to her together. The doctor had given them the choice. Her father, the man who had been her rock all of her life, was in bits. Her mum Anne was shocked but kept the show on the road. She was made of strong stuff you see. Anne instinctively had the answer. "*We've done it before so let's do it again,*" she told her husband. Just over twenty years earlier their first daughter, Niamh, was born with a lung and heart defect and died at a year and nine months old. They nursed her and took care of her for that time. They had done it before and, by God, they would do it again, whatever it took.

Orla was upset seeing her dad go off but not shocked. The diagnosis was Hodgkin's Lymphoma. Both parents seemed to blurt it out at the same time defiantly; *"Darling, you've cancer but you will be fine."* The Barry's never once discussed the risks of the illness. They just accepted that Orla was going to be fine. Jim Barry often talked about the power of visualisation. He'd often ask his clients to imagine planning if there wasn't a problem to be faced. Now he'd face his greatest test to date. And so the chemotherapy began. It was unpleasant and didn't agree with Orla, often making her violently sick. They'd hook the procedure up through the infamous Hickman line (allowing access into the chest). It entailed forty minutes of excruciating pain. Orla insisted on following the camera as it probed its way through her internal organs. She was also the first person to ask the hospital if she could she keep hers, nicknamed Lionel Bob. She was treated in the day ward. *"It was full of adults and you always knew the ones who wouldn't make it,"* she shudders. By 11.30am, after the chemotherapy, she was always in a rush to leave as the smell of the vegetable soup wafting through the wards of the hospital made her nauseous.

"Losing my hair, the only thing that distinguished me as a girl, and now that was gone too." When she chatted to her parents they decided to turn this into a genuine positive, an opportunity. Orla set about raising funds for the new Cork Cancer support group. A headshave later and before you knew it there was €7,000 on the table. *"In truth, by that stage it was bloody relief to just shave it all off!"* After her first chemo session, she had woken up her brother Ciaran one morning by rubbing her hair on his face and encouraging him to make a bird's nest with all the extra hair that had come tumbling out. The headstrong and gifted fifteen-year-old was growing up fast. The cancer was helping her to see the bigger picture in life. She was becoming more laid back, less judgemental and more accepting. She stopped taking things for granted. There was now more to life for Orla Barry than grades and sports.

Taking the Hickman Line was comparatively easy to giving a bone marrow biopsy. *"They place a very large corkscrew into your hip bone and draw out 2-3 inches of bone marrow."* Unfortunately, the local anaesthetic didn't work on her and so she felt every one of the six needles inserted into her hip bone.

In an attempt to numb the pain, she opted to have her mum feed her logical and inquisitive mind with a blow-by-blow account of what was going on at the time. Throughout the entire experience, Orla held onto an image she had burned in her mind, *"I used to imagine as I chucked up that I was chucking up the cancer cells that put your body on the line. In my mind I was cured before I started. It was the only way I could cope."* When the chemotherapy cycle concluded, it was time to switch over to receiving injections. Every second Wednesday, her mum would do the injections. For practice she used oranges! *"The texture is similar we were told."* Orla tells me they went through a great deal of fruit. Too weak to sit the mocks, she amused herself instead with house visits. One or two of the lads who she was pally with got quite upset the first time they saw her. *"The head shave combined with the weight loss, scared them a lot. They were great mates, never left me, not once,"* Orla notes.

One of the little kids that she coached in basketball, Seany, whose own head had been shaved at the age of ten, plucked up the courage to approach her one day. *"You're the coolest person I know, Orla."* It was all he could do to stop himself from blushing and running.

On the good, non-chemo weekends, her parents used to try and do something good for her, like a memorable trip to the Heineken Cup Final. *'It was my very first game! What a match too – Munster v Leicester'* and so, the Man U tomboy was being converted, in part at least, to the game of rugby.

****

As Orla and I chat a little more, she points to the gold chain around her neck. It was given to her by her mum and dad the day after the chemotherapy finally ended on the 21st of August 2002. It took her a long time to recover from the fatigue, the weight loss and gauntness that had taken temporary hold of her.

She kept playing sport throughout chemotherapy but didn't play matches on account of the Hickman Line. *"I didn't think it was fair for Lionel Bob to make any unwarranted appearances on the court that month!"* She laughs her familiar, hearty laugh. Despite everything she'd been through, despite the best protestations of the nursing staff, Orla Barry sat the Junior Cert in June, 2002. Chemotherapy couldn't stop this brave girl from Cork sitting six of the ten exams. Will it surprise you to learn that she got one A and five Bs?

It took Orla two years to fully recover, but by the time she entered fifth year in 2004, she was ready to attack her Leaving Cert. *"Those two years were like entering the twilight zone. Nobody tells you how to go on afterwards. I suddenly felt old beyond my years."* As I look across at her I can sense that this person has been on an epic journey beyond which any person of her tender years should ever endure. In 2007 she was given the all clear, the notification that tells you that they're 90% certain the cancer isn't coming back.

Her Leaving Cert yielded her a magnificent 555 points. Her first choice, physiotherapy was well within her grasp at 535.

As we finish up our chat, I look at this wonderfully inspiring and stunning young lady with long flowing hair. She's just graduated from UCD and is preparing to hit the tiles that night. With no jobs in physiotherapy in Ireland, she plans to leave these shores for New Zealand. She plans a career initially as an international sports physio before returning to Cork to train as an oncology physio specialist. She still fondly recalls the day her oncologist presented her, during her Junior Cert, with a signed training jersey from Ronan O' Gara.

As she leaves the room she turns to me to say, "*Graduating on the 24th of June 2009 was special, for sure. It was an achievement but not my proudest one – getting through cancer was.*"

Driving home that night. I make another mental note to myself: add critical illness cover.

6

An Unforgettable Fire

Dave Hughes

'Bravery has no place where it can avail nothing.'

Samuel Johnston

I believe it was Jack Handy who once remarked that the solitary difference between a man and a boy is that a boy wants to be a fireman, while a man wants to be a giant, monster fireman!

Just what is it then, about man's curious fascination with fire and those who risk their lives to put it out? I guess, as kids, some of us might have been lucky enough to be sitting around the Christmas tree wondering if it would be a Hornsby train set or a big, bright, red fire engine! And what about all those movies about firemen? The ones that defined the public's perception of what it must actually be like to be a fireman, while at the same time, perhaps fuelling our own hidden yearnings to one day become real-life heroes.

The 1970s gave us '*The Towering Inferno*', with its classic screen pairing of Paul Newman and Steve McQueen as beleaguered architect Doug Roberts and stoic fire Chief, Michael O'Hallorhan. The two men fight desperately to put out fires at the opening party of a shoddily constructed, glass tower office building that defiantly raises some 130 storeys over the New York skyline. As the fires rage out of control, the lives of everybody in the building are threatened.

Fast forward sixteen odd years later and we had the movie heralded by the tagline "*One breath of oxygen and it explodes in a deadly rage.*" '*Backdraft*', the fast-paced, testosterone-fuelled story of the McCaffrey brothers; Brian (played by Stephen Baldwin) and Stephen the '*Bull*' (played memorably by Kurt Russell in one of his finest roles) who must learn to settle their differences while fighting an obsessive arsonist intent on starting deadly fires.

The movie that most real firemen seem to agree is an accurate portrayal of the job, is *'Ladder 49'*. The film poignantly recounts attempts to save the life of Baltimore firefighter Jack Morrison. Having saved a man's life, Morrison lies trapped, with a broken leg, inside an exploding grain warehouse, recounting the events that have led him to this point. Perhaps it was the film's attempts to pay tribute to the profession itself or simply the depiction of the life that goes with being a fireman that commands a degree of universal respect among those who serve.

Personally, I couldn't but help wonder if the *'Irishness'* of the names in all three movies was purely coincidental or something more meaningful. As we approach the 150th anniversary of the Dublin Fire Brigade, it is interesting to note that the capital's first fire chief, Robert Ingram (who thankfully kept a scrapbook and news clippings of stories relating to the brigade and the service, which have been archived to safe keeping today), served in the New York Fire Brigade for more than ten years. When he returned to Ireland and established the Dublin Fire Brigade, Ingram adopted the American-style uniform and so the *'red shirt'*, based on the Federal Union Army officer's uniform from the American Civil War, became the classic image of the Dublin fireman.

The other distinct part of the uniform, the brass helmet, was worn up until 1937 and was itself invented by an Irish man, Eyre Massey Shaw (from the very same Shaw family that gave us *'Shaw's Almost Nationwide'* and the great George Bernard himself!). Originally from Cork, he himself would go on to become the Chief Fire Officer of the London Fire Brigade. He was, as they say in the profession, the epitome of Victorian London fire-fighting and literally wrote the first handbook on fire-fighting.

It may surprise you to learn that, prior to the founding of the Dublin Fire Brigade in 1862, fire protection was provided by a combination of parish fire engines and insurance companies! For example, if your home had a policy with the likes of an insurance provider such as Royal Exchange or Sun, you were given a prestigious metal fire mark on the front of your house. Highly decorative and certainly symbolic of wealth, it signified that you were insured and so were entitled to fire protection.

Things were to change radically within the fire services after the appointment of TF Purcell as the third Chief of the Dublin Fire Brigade in 1892. He remained in charge until 1917, when he was replaced by the granduncle of journalist Kevin Myers.

An engineer by profession and a volunteer fireman in Kilkenny, Purcell received a Silver Medal from the Royal Society for the Preservation of Life after saving the life of a local man. He spearheaded many important improvements and innovations that radically changed the way firemen fought fires. For example, in 1896 he designed the first extending turntable ladder. This was a hugely significant development as the arrival of the tram system to Dublin meant that the old street wheel escapes were too high to fit under the tram cables.

His legacy, however, was assured in 1909 when he motorised the fire service, a radical intervention that led to Ireland's very first motorised fire engine. It was a Leyland - the first the company had ever built, in fact. Can you just imagine convincing the Corporation of the time of the merits of replacing a horse-drawn service? Not to mention pleading the case for the possible savings that could be made in terms of bedding, vet fees and feeding, that had all been part of the fire brigade response up to that point?

However, Purcell was a persuasive man and to his credit he put his engineering background to good use and personally designed the engine, which was proudly delivered in 1909. In 1911, the neighbouring fire service of Rathmines decided they too, better get rid of the horse-drawn truck and decided wisely to get a new motorised fire engine.

However, rather than asking for the advice or support of Purcell and Leyland, they stubbornly went down the electric route! The decision had disastrous consequences as the brigade soon discovered that it took all the power the massive battery could muster, just to chug a few metres down the road. And so, the *'electric picnic'* didn't last too long and eventually the Leyland engine crossed the canal.

During Easter Week 1916, Purcell and his men fought the biggest and most destructive fires that Dublin would ever see, as the capital came to terms with the heavy price the city would pay for the Rising. The Corporation decorated each man to the last with a Chevron, an armylike stripe which also entailed an extra shilling a week in wages.

****

When I first spoke with David Hughes, he had literally just come off shift in Tara Street, where he serves as a station officer in the present Dublin Fire Brigade. I was immediately touched by his humility. *"I'm just a fireman; I'm not in their league, son."* I could sense him smiling warmly down the phone. *"Besides Ian, there are real heroes you need to look at, associated with the history of our fire service."*

Fortunately for me, Lazerian Fallon, a fire fighter attached to the Dolphin's Barn Brigade and the present day curator of the Dublin Fire

Museum (and self-described fire anorak!), had filled me in on everything I thought I needed to know about Dave Hughes and just why his inclusion in this book was so appropriate.

Laz had also filled me in on the great Ned (Edward) Doyle, one of those gentlemen who Dave had been alluding to, a genuine fireman's fireman if you will! He had come on board on February 25th, 1917. having previously been a railway porter. In 1918, both he and fireman Joseph Doyle were on ambulance duty when they received a call to go to Alexandra Basin at the North Wall end of Dublin Docks to tend to a ship called the '*SS War Cypress*'. She had arrived into the port with a cargo of grain. Six Dockers had come on board to unload her cargo only to be overcome by gas leaking from the hold. When Doyle and Lynch arrived, Lynch himself was overcome leaving Doyle faced with a choice: leave him and go for help or act immediately to try to save his life. He entered the hold and managed to revive Lynch. Between them, they tied ropes to the six trapped Dockers and eventually removed all six men from the hold. Four of the Dockers were dead but they had at least managed to save two of them.

In the Coroner's Court, Doyle was commended for his actions but the Coroner was informed that he wasn't to be given the Chevron by the Brigade, as the Waterworks Committee, who at this time ran the brigade, had decided that as firemen were in receipt of an additional wartime bonus, they simply couldn't justify the extra one shilling a week to the two firemen. Early signs that the spirit of '*An Bord Snip*' was alive and well! However, with resolute pressure coming from the Coroner, both men were eventually awarded bronze medals by the Royal Human Society and certificates by the Carnegie Heroes Trust. In addition, each man was nominated for the King's Police Medal, the equivalent of a Victoria Cross for a fireman or police officer. The Medal remained accessible to firemen until 1941 in the United Kingdom, but was quickly abandoned as a means of recognition, unsurprisingly, after 1922 in Ireland.

Lord French bestowed the award on Ned Doyle in the Royal Irish Constabulary Depot in the Phoenix Park. but Fireman Lynch declined, for political reasons, to accept the Medal.

Ned Doyle remains to this day the only recipient from the Dublin Fire Brigade.

****

When David Hughes entered the fire service back in the 1980s, things were very different. Reforms were being made in the wake of the Stardust tragedy on the 14th of February 1981, a tragedy of epic proportions in which forty-eight people lost their lives, including the son and daughter of one poor fireman's family. One of the recommendations to come out of the post Stardust tribunal was the establishment of a Fire Training Centre for Excellence. The centre was officially opened in Marino, Dublin, in 1985. Still in operation today, this centre is one of the very finest training centres for firemen in Europe. Undoubtedly, countless lives have been saved as a result of the demanding training techniques and drills its students endure.

Before joining, Dave Hughes had been a panel beater by trade. *"I felt I was in a rut at the time,"* he recalls. In 1984, before joining, he had become friendly with his future wife's next door neighbour, Stephen Brady, a senior officer in the Dublin Fire Brigade. Stephen Brady now serves as Assistant Chief Fire Officer in the Dublin Fire Brigade.

Dave was twenty-three at the time. Over a two year period, he and Stephen became quite close as Stephen enlightened Dave as to what life in the fire service was really like. Dave had a small workshop at the back of his mother-in-law's house in Walkinstown. He had grown up in the area himself, just up the road. Sometimes, he and Stephen would get chatting furiously about all matters fire-related. *"He'd talk passionately about the service."* Dave's face suddenly lights up as he recalls those days: *"There were so many great characters who he worked with in the fire service - like the larger than life great, Willie Birmingham, founder of 'Alone'. His son Willie is still in the service today."* Perhaps it isn't hard to see just why Stephen Brady would become something of a mentor figure for Dave Hughes.

This highly influential character, who spoke with such passion and never had a bad word to say about anybody, had convinced Dave that a life in the fire service was like a vocation. If you were in it, *"you were in it for life,"* in a good way, he quickly points out!

Dave had begun panel beating back in the tail end of 1976 and thoroughly enjoyed it, but somehow couldn't shake the feeling that there had to be more to life.

He had left school that same year. He had gone first to Drimnagh Castle Primary School and then on to Greenhills College, but, in truth, he hated school and so left after the Inter Cert. The mentality at the time was to go and get a job and bring in a few quid to earn your keep. His dad, Paddy, set him up after he left school with a job in Carroll and Kinsella, a place that would provide him with some of his dearest friends to this day. It's touching to hear of the respect with which Dave talks about Joe Kinsella (who now maintains the Lexus dealership in Blackrock, Co Dublin) and Mossie Carroll. He cites both men as major influences on his life, particularly Mossie, whom he recalls as:

"A driving force.......you knew you had to be working when he was around, but he looked after us all so well. You were never stuck for money or if you were in trouble on a personal matter, he'd help sort it out."

He remembers Joe as being quieter, highly capable but quieter by comparison.

Some readers may recall that at one stage, the Carroll and Kinsella empire stretched from Blackrock, South Dublin right across to Walkinstown where Dave worked initially before moving up to the Western Industrial Estate, just off the Naas road, where the body shop was located at the time. *"I did three and a half years initially and then went to Dalkey with a few of the other beaters for a brief spell and then back to the lads in C&K up until December 1985, before finally joining the fire service on the 6th of January 1986,"* - a date he will never forget.

Amusingly, when he was a kid, Dave wanted to be a Guard! *"I'd always wanted to be in the Guards but I was too small. Now, there's no height restrictions but back then you had to be 5'9" and I was 5'8","* he said with a smile. *"I was just too bloody short!"*

The irony isn't lost on his kids either. Paul is 6'2" and Darren is 5'10". It turns out that his Dad's brother had seven sons, one of whom is 6'7" and *"as wide as he is big,"* he said with a laugh. Anne, his wife is also 5'6"!

He met Anne in 1977 (he was seventeen, she was sixteen) at the Tara Ballroom in Courtown, Co Wexford. Both families used to go down to Courtown to spend the hot summers in their respective mobile homes. At the time, he was with some mates who used to make the trip down from the north just for the disco. He recalls Donna Summer and the Bee Gees being all the rage back then. The boys thought they were the bees knees, dressed to kill in their black bomber jackets. Dave remembers chasing Anne in the disco - *"We'd been asked to split up and leave the disco for some reason. I spotted this rather slim girl with a very attractive face. That was pretty much it for me really!"*

She was supposed to meet him the next day but didn't show. Eventually he found her, having tracked her down to her family's mobile home at the caravan park and so, after much persistence, she agreed for peace sake to meet him again. Those early days of the relationship were fun. Anne was doing her Leaving Cert in Leeson Street at the time and Dave recalls one day picking her up in the middle of winter on his motor bike and trying to persuade Anne to put on a set of oil skin leggings. She was wearing a short skirt at the time. Somehow, they figured it all out and have been together ever since. Dave is quick to point out, that it's coming up on thirty-three years. *"Anne's very easy-going and tolerant and puts up with a great deal from me!*

She's a very kind person, always obliging with a lift when I'd have a few, but I'd like to think I'd do the same. We have a very open and understanding relationship."

Perhaps Dave's ability to get on so well with the opposite sex stems from growing up with five sisters. *"Miriam is the eldest, then Carol, Audrey, Tricia and Fiona (the baby). I call her 'Baby",* he says with a laugh. She's now thirty-seven! *"I guess some habits die hard,"* he points out.

Two of the sisters are married. Carol and Audrey and the Hughes clan remain extremely close, to this day. The entire family all live within a five mile radius of each other. Dave's mother, Rose, had a strong influence over the entire family. *"Mum, Rose, is the matriarch,"* as Dave puts it, *".....the peacekeeper in our house, she keeps us all on our toes. Even when we were kids, we'd never outrun her. She took no 'crap'. A seamstress by trade – it appeared that she was always helping everybody out in some way, knitting curtains or just lending a friendly neighbourhood hand."*

Dave's dad, Paddy, died seven years ago. He was sixty-eight and had bowel cancer. It was Dave, in fact, who brought him to hospital in the ambulance. He was on duty that day of December 21st 2001. They had taken a call that had come in from the Tallaght Fire Station. Paddy was a proud man who never wanted his family to worry unnecessarily about anything, so nobody really realised just how ill he was. Despite his best protestations, Paddy died on 4th of January 2002.

****

Paddy had started off as a milkman but, in truth, he was really a Jack of all trades. He even drove trucks. He did whatever it took to look after his family. He was a man who would never see his kids stuck for anything, not that he didn't support Rose in running a well-policed home. Dave never forgets living at their home in Stamford Green, Walkinstown. Their estate was shaped like a horseshoe. Being a keen fisherman, he was out practising his casting, as he did meticulously most nights.

This one particular evening, he dropped the rod to reset it and can still visualise the lead weight smashing straight through the sitting room window like a bullet, and landing virtually on his father's lap!

Dave and his siblings had very happy childhoods. *"Dad drove this old VW minibus. There were nine of us, off to Courtown just like the Adams family. 'Are we there yet?' we'd all yelp out in true Shrek style!"* Those unshakably close bonds that existed between Paddy and Dave, and Anne and her father, Mick, were to prove a source of great strength in the years after Dave entered the fire service.

On January 6th, 1986, the day that Dave joined the Dublin Fire Brigade, there was a dispute. Pickets had been erected on the gates of the O'Brien Training Institute in Marino, just off the Malahide Road. Thankfully for Dave, the new recruits were exempt from the strike conditions and allowed to cross the picket line. Despite the fact that he'd been doing a panel beating job that had held little personal meaning for him, he was taking a serious pay-cut to join up. Anne, whilst supportive, thought Dave was "*off his trolley*". The training must have seemed an eternity and it would be very hard indeed to make ends meet.

Perhaps fortunately for Dave, he was cocooned away for the next three months, undergoing intense training in the Marino Institute. It was a whole new ball game for this likeable lad from Walkinstown. A real eye opener, in fact, as he learned the harsh realities of working in a highly disciplined, team-oriented environment. There followed an equally rigid six weeks of ambulance training. The lads learned to conform to living in a world where you simply had to play your part, or else you put your colleagues' lives at risk.

His first stint was six months at Tara Street, followed by a brief period in Tallaght. He eventually ended up back at Tara Street. In 1988, the Dublin Fire Brigade became embroiled in another dispute which lasted almost two months. The strike was over staffing levels. Pay was minimal and the service desperately needed more resources and support. They were tough times, especially if you had a family. But it is often in such times that families learn to rally. Both fathers did their bit, doing extra jobs and in the case of Mick, Anne's father, who was a butcher by trade, there was always an extra supply of meat put on the table to help ease the shortages.

It was in Dolphin's Barn, one of the busiest stations in Dublin, where Dave would cut his teeth and have his eyes opened to the devastating effects a fire can have on human lives. Here, he would learn the craft of being a fireman. Here, he would remain for twelve tough, but rewarding years.

"*An average night duty on the ambulance could mean anything up to 20 cases a night – we were close to James' Hospital. Not a night would go by when you weren't fighting some kind of fire, be it house or industrial. It was a great learning curve, I guess.*"

Dave's voice is calm but the tone is reflective. During his time, like so many of his colleagues, he witnessed an extreme amount of tragedy, the likes of which is hard to take in all at once. House fires resulting in kids being taken out, smoked to shreds; fires so intense that you could hear the screams of the children so clearly, but you just couldn't find a way in. Road traffic accidents were all too common (and still are); arriving on the scene to discover limbs strewn on the roadside; the stench of human tragedy would readily fill the night air at a moment's notice.

Tackling a fire back in the 1980s often resulted in what was known in the profession as the *'earrings'* effect, which resulted from blisters, which had risen on the ears, eventually bursting. It's really not that surprising when we compare the gear firemen use today with what was used then. Reflecting on those years, Dave would often allude to the differences between what we see in the movies and the reality of actually tackling a fire:

"Unlike the movies where you can see the fire unfolding before you and massive flames, in truth, it's actually smoky as hell, you can see bugger all, and you can only really hear muffled sounds, and maybe your colleagues and the cracking of breaking glass. You learn to rely on your other senses, not your sight. When the backs of the ears start to burn, you know instinctively that you are in a real fire!"

Dave's crew would have used wooden helmets, cork-based with a canvass cover. They would have worn a Melton tunic - a type of cloth which was heavy duty and double- breasted. Below the waist, the fireman wore yellow plastic leggings, plastic and rubber wellingtons. On his back, he transported his self-contained breathing apparatus, or BA set, which weighed about forty-four pounds.

Nowadays, the fireman's jacket is made of Nomex, a fire-resistant material also used in the overtrousers. He has a modern Gallet helmet, French-style, fully enclosed with a flash hood to protect the face from extreme heat and a possible flashover. A flashover is an explosion of super heated gas and smoke that occurs when a fire becomes starved of oxygen but eventually is revived. In a tragedy in Bray in 2007, two fire fighters lost their lives when a flashover occurred, while they were fighting a fire at a disused factory.

Just how does a fireman stay sane and learn to cope with the seemingly constant tragedy?

In the Dolphin's Barn Unit, there were two officers and twelve firemen on the go 24/7. A family culture had developed in which the older members would adopt a very paternal approach with the younger lads. Whilst there was no counselling service at the time, there was always the black humour to fall back on. Firemen would somehow manage to console each other with a moment of shared humour during an impossibly difficult situation. Sometimes it might be something as daft as a fireman's trousers splitting, as he went up the ladder trying to save a life. Anything at all to make it all acceptable and dilute the memories.

As Dave puts it: *"Despite everything, when we were on rostered leave, it was like a second family - you couldn't wait to get back to the lads."*

Then there were all the positives of the job too, such as the fact that women were finally allowed to join the service as fire fighters in 1994 and, of course, every fireman's delight – delivering babies! In Dave's case, several of them, in fact! His first was in Inchicore fourteen years ago, to a lovely young lady called Theresa. There's an understandable hint of male embarrassment that follows. "*It was nerve-racking! The woman does it all to be fair. You're there to use your training, to simply guide them as best you can,*" he modestly states. One can only imagine the thousands of thoughts running through a fireman's mind as the baby starts to breathe and he clamps the umbilical cord; the sheer relief mixed with wonderful pride.

As Dave puts it, "*At the end of the day, all any fireman wants to see when he brings a person to the hospital with a family member, is compassion amongst his fellow man towards their loved one.*"

One suspects that Dave Hughes's life as a fireman was very varied indeed. No two days ever the same, he could be up in a helicopter or down in the water, such as one particular Christmas Eve when he found himself in the freezing surrounds of the Grand Canal in Dublin, desperately trying to save the life of a young woman. Although this wasn't his first time being involved in a rescue operation in the water, this time the consequences of his actions would be very different indeed.

It was 1991 and Dave and Peter Murray were six hours into their Christmas shift. The lads were tired but in good spirits. A call came through about a car that had gone into the canal coming from the direction of the Lower Deck pub. It appeared, in the freezing conditions, to have lost control approaching the bad bends. For those unfamiliar with the area, the canal opens up into a horseshoe shape. When Dave and Peter arrived on the scene, the car was floating upwards pointing in the direction of the Dolphin's Barn Fire Station. The only thing that was visible was the top corner of the roof.

There were two Guards in the water trying desperately to break the car window. Despite their valiant efforts, they simply could not get into the car. Without a second thought, Dave grabbed the pinch bar (an instrument for opening window and car doors), took off his shoes and trousers and entered the water with just his shirt and underwear for company. He jumped in from the canal bank. It being a chilly Christmas Eve, it is hard to fathom just how cold it must have been in that water. With the adrenalin coursing through his veins, he swam out and eventually reached the back of the vehicle.

Unsure exactly how many passengers there were, he sensed there was at least one, possibly two, people trapped beneath the water's surface. When he got to the back of the car, he hit the back window repeatedly with the pinch bar. As soon as the window broke, the car started to sink even more rapidly, leaving only a couple of inches remaining visible above the surface.

It was now or never and Dave instinctively jumped in over the broken glass. He remembers a halogen light from a local restaurant fortuitously giving him just enough beams of light to focus on her hair. He grabbed at her freezing body and pulled her between the two head rests to the back area of the car. Once he had finally gotten her out, he began to swim back in the direction of the ambulance. *"People were yelling, saying swim this way, swim that way – a large crowd had gathered."*

Dave was programmed to get back to the ambulance, by whatever means. He swam about twenty feet, dragging the woman behind him. His stomach and his legs were lacerated from swimming in over the broken glass but the only thing that mattered as he crawled onto the canal bank was that she was alive, unconscious, but alive.

Unsurprisingly, when questioned about the incident, Dave spends more time alluding to the immense efforts the Guards made in trying to hold the car up and also the work of the first fire brigade crews that arrived after he had entered the water. They had secured the car and checked for other passengers. His colleagues that night included Dave Bell, Brendan Mc Nicholas and Peter O' Connell, to name but a few. The woman in question was revived and taken to the Meath Hospital. Between them all, she had been saved. Dave was wrapped in a blanket and taken to James' Hospital. He was dressed and back on duty as soon as possible and remained on shift until 10am on Christmas Day.

Dave Hughes became, and remains to this day, the only member of the Dublin Fire Brigade to receive the prestigious Medal for Bravery, which he was eventually awarded five years later in 1996. The Bravery Award - Comhairle Na Mire Gaile, was given, not because the fire service thought he should receive it, but because the Guards insisted that if their men were to receive Scotts' Medals, then Dave Hughes should receive the Medal for Bravery. In the Dublin Fire Brigade, they don't hand out awards. The understanding is that everything comes with being in the line of duty.

Not that that was his first time in the water, not by a long shot. On one previous occasion, also in the canal, but further up off the Parnell Road, Dave and his colleagues managed to save several lives. He has been in the Liffey several times too, but nowadays, rescues like that would be handed over to the likes of the Swift Water Rescue crews. In truth. you'd probably be arrested for even contemplating such an act!

Six years after receiving the Bravery Award, Dave's dad Paddy died, followed by Anne's father, Mick, the following year. Both men died of bowel cancer. Deirdre, Anne's sister, lost her courageous battle with cancer the same year as her father, Mick, in 2003, aged just forty. In the cruellest twist of fate imaginable, Dave's older brother Paul, the man he had looked up to all of his life, died on the 27th of November 2006.

Paul lived in Kilshanroe, just outside Enfield. In Dave's own words, the man was *"simply gifted"*. A mechanical engineer by trade, he had branched out into health and safety and ended up working on the oil platforms all over the world, often in places as far afield as Saudi Arabia.

He went on to do fire safety contract work for many big corporations at home, including companies such as Intel. *"Paul was always going on to do more studies. He was the eldest and his passion for life, his wife and all three of his children remain an inspiration."* Dave's face is sombre. Normally Paul would take his motorbike to work, but this particular morning, late in November, the weather was poor, so he decided to take his jeep to work instead. He was approaching the village of Caragh on the Naas Road when he struck the bridge and the jeep overturned into the River Liffey. The river was in full swell and Paul, despite the very best efforts of the emergency services in Naas, subsequently died. *"To be fair to those lads"*, Dave explains, *"The conditions were completely different to have to deal with – I'd been in still water, these were torrents, with strong winds and heavy rain, extremely difficult conditions to have to try and deal with. Nobody could have done more to save my brother's life."*

****

As I join Dave for a get-together in his family home, it is a crisp, bright, sunny morning. The house is proudly filled with pictures of the children and their various achievements. Niamh, the youngest, has been everywhere with her dad, even trekking and camping throughout Europe. Dave has a great many interests outside the fire service, including the Scouts, and his absolute pride and joy - two small vegetable plots, one at home and one in Offaly. An ideal way, one suspects, for one man and his dog (or two in Dave's case) to be at peace with themselves out in the open air.

Dave believes that the people of Dublin are fortunate to have such a dedicated fire service on their doorstep. I suspect as I dig a little deeper, the people of Dublin don't really know the half of it.

Perhaps next time we find ourselves in trouble, it's worth bearing in mind, that as you dial the digits 999, the service to which you are being put through, is, in fact, manned by a fire brigade service with trained personnel on hand, who are able to deal efficiently with the many thousands of public enquiries and assess the level of response required.

Dublin is the only brigade here or in the UK that provides an ambulance service as part of its work. Furthermore, all the Brigade's fire fighters are also fully qualified paramedics, something else that is unique to these islands.

The Dublin Fire Brigade is now the primary ambulance service provider for Dublin City and County. It provides fourteen Accident and Emergency dedicated ambulances, crewed by fire fighters and based in each of the brigade's fire stations, giving an excellent geographical dispersion.

And so, as we begin to wrap the interview up, Dave fondly mentions Rose, his mum, who's going on seventy-four and has just had her knee replaced.

I'm acutely aware that this man needs his sleep. These days, Dave serves over in Tara Street as a Fire Officer and he's just come off shift, making time to speak to me.

"You know Ian," he says to me going out the front door, *"if you ask my mum nicely, she might just knit you a set of curtains!"*

7

Out of Africa

Elaine Bannon

'The mind of man is capable of anything because everything is in it, all the past as well as the future.'

Joseph Conrad

Earlier this year, in August, in fact, an interesting conversation took place as I was standing in the check-in queue at Nairobi International Airport. A lady in front of me appeared to need assistance with her bags. I offered to help. She turned around and smiled at me. She could see I was holding an Irish passport. *"In my country sir, we carry the equivalent of your bags and mine on our heads every day. We carry that weight in water. We travel up to five miles on foot to get the water and 80% of our energy intake is required in ensuring that the water arrives safely back to our villages."*

There are 6 ½ billion people in this crazy world of ours, but only 1 billion people live like us, people who stand in check-in queues with their mouths open, catching flies, living in real terms, in relative comfort. The 1 billion people at the bottom of the ladder are in the *'extreme'* poverty bracket and they really need our help.

The 25,000 children who die every day of preventable diseases are in this group. They are simply too meek and weak and so die quietly. In the past ten years, diarrhoea has killed more children worldwide than all the people lost to armed conflict since World War II. Twelve million people die each year from lack of safe drinking water, including more than 3 million from waterborne diseases. Of all the renewable water available in Africa each year, only 4% is used - because most Africans lack wells, canals, pumps, reservoirs and other irrigation systems.

****

Rotary is the largest service organisation in the world, with 1.2 million members in 32,000 clubs, in over 200 countries. As you might imagine, such an organisation when fully mobilised on the world stage, can be a formidable proposition, as well as being very effective in local communities. Rotary International has chosen the irradiation of Polio as its main challenge. It is one of the few organisations, therefore, that can mobilise over 100,000 people in one weekend to innoculate an entire region, in conjunction with the World Health Organisation, in order to stop the spread of Polio. Rotary, via its members from around the world, has donated over 600 million USD to this cause.

Recently, Bill Gates asked Rotary to match his donation of 100 million USD each year for the next three years, in a final attempt to irradiate this terrible and preventable disease. Rotary has again stepped up to the plate and met this challenge.

However, for all their wonderful high profile global projects, Rotarians mainly work quietly in their local communities and on small bespoke international projects. One such international project was brought to the attention of the local Dublin club, the Rotary Club of Dublin Central.

Matt Porter is a member of the Rotary Club of Dublin Central. It would be fair to say that having worked hard for it, life's been kind to Matt. After concluding several successful business deals, Porter was in that privileged position to give something back. There was an old work colleague and friend who Matt knew who was now giving her life to making a difference to those who needed it most in the heart of Kenya.

He and his colleagues in Dublin Rotary, like the current President, Grainne Bagnall, were touched deeply by the difference one person could make with so little funding or resources. Matt flew down to meet this remarkable woman to witness her work first hand. He was moved by the need and encouraged by the vast difference she was making to these local communities. He and his Rotary colleagues set about raising awareness and funding. He made important connections with the Ambassador of Kenya in Ireland and eventually helped to register the charity over here. Solid connections were made with other helpful organisations like Electric Aid, Belgrove Senior Boys School, VSO and Rotary International. He has travelled the length and breadth of this country raising awareness and funds to help make a difference to the children of Rombo in Kenya. With thirty plus members, between the ages of 30 and 50 years, the Dublin Rotary Club was asked to support one remarkable Irish woman, with her outstanding work with Maasai children in Kenya.

****

It's one of life's many clichés I know, but for some, the notion that life begins at forty is so much more than just a cliché. According to a report that appeared in *'Science Daily'* last year - growing old is a happier experience than many of us imagine - that's according to the findings of a study conducted at Queen's University, Belfast, on behalf of the Changing Ageing Partnership (CAP). The study, which was conducted by Dr John Garry from Queen's University, looked at young people's attitudes to happiness in old age and how these attitudes affect their current health-related behaviour. What made the report interesting when it drilled below the surface was what it actually revealed about our attitudes to life in general.

According to Dr Garry *"We have all heard the saying 'life begins at forty'. But it seems that many people, particularly young people, actually associate growing old with being miserable, meaning they don't see any benefit in preserving their health for old age".*

He goes on to point out that *"Young people like to enjoy themselves, but this can mean behaving in ways that can damage their future health. The harmful effects of alcohol, smoking and poor diet and fitness are well known, but many young people still binge-drink, smoke, avoid eating fruit and vegetables and fail to do regular exercise. This study aimed to find out whether this risky behaviour is associated with young people's estimates of happiness in old age".* And so the survey raises an interesting question. Do people in their early twenties actually *'live it up'* while they remain what they perceive to be still young, because they are convinced that as they grow older they will become more and more miserable? Surely not!

Undoubtedly the media plays its part too. We've been hearing this *'40-is-the-new-30'* chatter for a little while. Ever since stars like Sheryl Crow, Courteney Cox (Arquette), Sarah Jessica Parker and other fashion-forward female stars turned the big four-o, the fashion industry, marketers and, yes, the media are rethinking the way they look at those over 40. Perhaps they are right? One woman, who certainly believes that her life is only truly beginning and only began to do so in any kind of meaningful way, when she turned forty, is Elaine Bannon.

****

We agree to meet near the airport close to Elaine's family home in Beaumont. As we sip a beer and chat, it's plain for anyone to see that this woman is truly content. It's hard not to envy her. She used to work as the General Manager for ASTROTEK Ireland Ltd in Dublin's Ballymount, a company that specialised in commercial and industrial light fittings, tailored around the needs of the construction industry – kitting out offices, factories, hospitals and the like.

"*They were interesting days,*" she reflects. "*No two days were ever the same - laying out the lighting plans from the engineer's report for a whole variety of customers.*" Often contractors would try to undersell her trying to buy the various fittings cheaper. It was an ongoing battle, all '*part and parcel*' as she describes it, of the world of '*Sales Purchasing*'. She got her first '*big*' order as part of the first phase of the Wyeth's Pharmaceutical Plant development in Clondalkin. The margins were good. Her boss Martin Stapleton was her employer. They would go back to the suppliers and look to increase the profit margins – "*it was a never-ending circle of profit hunting*". Ireland was booming in that golden period - the late 90s, early 2001/02. For Elaine, everything at the time appeared to be about the money, about status and keeping up with the Joneses ... not that Elaine wasn't enjoying life herself at the time.

She'd bought her own home back in 1992, which she cites as her "*greatest achievement at the time*", a two-bed bungalow in Lucan. She enjoyed her two holidays a year; "*One big one and one small one,*" as she put it. She would go to far-away places like Cuba and Egypt, always interested in how other people lived. Her favourite holiday was in Cuba. "*I loved the fun-loving Salsa ways of the barman,*" she said laughing. The country was in a paradox, "*capitalism underneath the communism*" but she admired the fact that everything from education to dental care was free. They had one of the greatest orthopaedic experts in the world; they just lacked the equipment to work their skills. "*I guess all pigs are equal. Some are more equal than others.*" She applies this metaphor to what she perceived as Cuban Utopia. "*All we can hope is that people have enough,*" says Elaine. "*That's free Utopia.*" It's obvious that this woman had seen a great deal to inform her opinions.

She cites her mum as her real hero. Maureen is 68, a carer who looks after her father Dan, a charming gentleman who was diagnosed last year with Vascular Dementia. "*Mum is very positive – always has been, despite all the setbacks and she takes fantastic care of dad. Just maybe doesn't take enough care of herself. It's hard for her to get breaks.*" Elaine's grateful, however, that her parents made the most of their lives, even if they only started to travel late on. They took their first long trip together to Thailand to mark their 25th wedding anniversary. Ironically, they would even make it to Kenya long before Elaine. The tragedy with dementia, of course, is that her father has no recollection of making those trips. They remain a very close couple, and have never needed any other company except themselves. Her dad's sense of humour and ability to always see the glass half full was inspiring. He thought Maureen always reminded him of David Frost, because when she'd meet someone for the first time, she'd have their story before the day was out!

Her father had lived an active and rich life. He was proudly on every committee, from the local residents to the football team. "*We used to have a gala week in Beaumont where we lived, in Elm Mount, our estate. We did it all really from egg and spoon races to cheering on the girls' local soccer team.*" The festivities always ended up with the traditional barn dance. She doesn't remember it ever raining (a problem many of us who grew up in the 80s have!). Her vivid memories of going to the beach as a family to eat their crisp or banana sandwiches filled with loads of sand, stand out for Elaine. "*One time we were walking for miles along the sand dunes along Portmarnock beach, when we suddenly saw this dog covered in oil and as black as soot.*" It took them several minutes to recognise Rex, their own Labrador who seemed to revel in the journey home, dripping all over the family.

As we sit and chat, Elaine notices that I'm eating fish and chips; "*most expensive bag I ever had, came from Burdock's,*" she remarks. The famous fish and chip establishment located just off Christchurch is something of a landmark in Dublin.

Dan, her father, was a butcher and for a treat used to bring them all home a bag of fish and chips salted and dripping in vinegar, of course! One wet night he was in the queue, when he noticed this drunk wearing a hoodie, drop his money in front of him. Dan bent down to pick it up for him only to realise that when he got to the counter, his entire week's wages, were heading south down Castle Street!

The caring nature of her mother, Maureen, was best exemplified when it came to others. She used to make hampers for those in the community who were in trouble. Perhaps they had lost their jobs. Regardless, she would do a tour of the generous neighbours and make up food parcels.

When Rex was put down (her parents told her he'd been sent to the country. He didn't care much for people in uniforms and that included police men, nuns and priests!), they replaced him with a stunning Rhodesian cross, a mix of Labrador and Ridgeback called 'Chloe' which had originally belonged to her brother, Eamonn. Three years ago, Dan who used to take the dog for a walk arrived home one morning to announce that the dog had brought him home. Maureen replied "*I'm getting rid of that dog!*" It was the first time Dan had begun to display the onset symptoms of Vascular Dementia.

When Elaine was just 7, her cousin Terry, aged 13, moved in with the family after both her parents died. Maureen, who was only 27 at the time, and Dan, 30, welcomed her in as if she was one of their own. This new '*big sister*' rapidly became part of the Bannon household. She recalls Terry always doing her make-up and one time arriving home at Christmas with a puppy dog that she hid away in her bed in sheer excitement. There really could be no denying the Bannon's positive attitude to life. Her last grandmother with whom Elaine was especially close, Maureen's mum, Kathleen, smoked 3 packets of cigarettes a day and took a daily glass of Guinness *'to help her appetite'*. Before she died, she was doing a full highland fling in the living room. *"Mum and dad made me who I am today!"* she acknowledges proudly. I guess like so many of us, we are by-products of who we are from our upbringing.

Having attended Whitehall House Secondary, like so many women at the time, Elaine went on to do a post secretarial course. Luckily, given the economic climate back in 1980, Elaine managed to get her first real job as a receptionist working for a lighting company. She was eventually promoted in the Hanratty family business to go off to London to buy light fittings. Back then, as a young woman in her twenties, she worked to live and not the other way around. She was struck by how tough it was working in a male-dominated environment. *"As I discovered how few of us there were, I got tougher and eventually more streetwise."* Fellas, Elaine felt, only interfered with her social life and despite the fact that all of her friends had pretty much settled down by the tender age of 25, she had no intentions of settling for anything less than what her own parents shared together. The guy who would eventually rock her world, Elijah Kilempu, would come much later.

Elaine's twenties mirrored those young women who grew up in the 80s … trips to Tomango's where the *'gang goes'* as the old slogan went. Many great nights were spent in Dublin's *'McGonnagle's'* pub and *'The Baggot Inn'*, watching great bands perform. As anyone who grew up during this period will testify, there was a wealth of great Irish bands back then to choose from; among her favourites, great acts *'Bagatelle'* and the *'Look a Likes'*. She witnessed the late genius of Michael Jackson performing 3 times, twice in Cork and once in Dublin. His *'Off the Wall'* album remains one of her favourites even today. Like so many Dubs she can remember seeing U2 perform for fifty pence in the Dandelion market back in 1980. *"They were ok but the 'Look a Likes' were better!'* she reckons.

Her next company assignment took her to a company called EWL where she spent two years. She was offered the chance to go to Cork to open a new branch, her first time away from home and had an absolute ball. She kept two jobs, the second of which was working in a little restaurant, Jacque's (owned by the daughters of the Barry's Tea people). It was there that she got a call from Falk's Lighting and the chance to rep on the road. Despite not being able to drive, three weeks later she passed her test, the same day she got the company car. Freedom at last! She drove to Cork that very day determined to prove a woman could cut it in this competitive business. Elaine painted the picture back then. *"There were female architects arriving on the scene back then, but no whisper of a female consultant engineer."*

She got a call 18 months later from Martin Stapleton, a former colleague in EWL, who was setting up on his own. Elaine had been let go from her previous job suffering with serious back problems. *"I'll pay you to stay on the dole if you wait three months for me to open up,"* he told her. The deal was done and for the next eleven years, Elaine and Martin slowly, painstakingly built up 'ASTROTEK', the light fitting business. In 1991, she got her first car from Martin, a Nissan Micra van, which may as well have been a Mercedes. Her annual review with Martin would consist of *"you're not doin' the job right!"* to which she would reply *"replace me so"*. A silence would follow and a red-faced Martin would reply, *"no, because nobody else would do the job!"* Their relationship glided along over the next decade with the smoothness of plate tectonics in the Pacific Ocean. Being a smoker, one time he offered her 500 old Irish pounds if she would quit (she's been smoking since she was 14). She used to follow people around who did smoke, just to get the whiff. It almost broke his heart having to pay up a year later. Of course, as soon as she'd won the bet, she was back on them straight away and normal service resumed.

Like so many, when they turn forty, Elaine had promised herself something special. To make the event special on the 23rd of April 2002, she split proceedings in half. A week in Cyprus pre-birthday was followed by a murder mystery weekend with the family in Cobh, Co Cork. The *'craic'* for the eighteen who made the train journey down, was simply mighty. Dan, her father, who had brought his own costume, right in the middle of the murder mystery decided to dress up as a priest to give the murder victim the last rites! The players were completely confused and had no idea who this lunatic was!

The second part of the celebrations was a trip to Kenya. Elaine had heard stories as a kid about the Maasai tribes and the Serengeti plains and the migration of the wildebeest. Accompanied by her pal Marguerite, they set off for the trip of a lifetime. They did it in style with 5 star hotels and a trip to the Amboseli National which gave her her first glimpse of Kilimanjaro Mountain. They visited Maasai tribes and then flew north of the equator to Samburu for 2 more days on safari. Their Maasai guide was informing them about their beautiful surroundings when he asked them if they knew what to do if a massive stampeding elephant approached them out on safari. The girls were expecting the Maasai warrior to offer them words of wisdom, when instead he smiled his wide smile, white teeth gleaming at them both, *"Run like fuck ladies is what you do!"* It was all they could do not to wet themselves in hysterics of laughter. Elaine finally got to see her wildebeest first hand, when they flew on again to the incredible Maasai Mara plains, north of the Kenya-Tanzanian border, famous for the migration of this magnificent animal. The trip was capped off with a relaxing week in the sun in Mombassa in the luxurious 5 star White Sands Hotel. Their rep was talking to them in the hotel about a friend of hers, Carol, who ran a school which provided free education and also housed some orphans in the hope that the two girls might wish to leave some stuff. The conversation coincided with a weekly visit of the Maasai. They would arrive in the large resort hotels to perform their traditional dances and sell local produce. Elaine enjoyed their company and was fascinated by their attitude to life. Before setting off, they stocked their suitcases with bits and pieces - happy mementos of their trip to Kenya.

That September, when Elaine got home, she recalled getting a massive order for ASTROTEK, and at exactly the same time, getting this incredible sick feeling in her stomach. *"I felt sick and empty inside."* The client in question had just bought his third house. *"The boss was complaining about profit margins. Contractors were looking for more discounts and I'd just come from a place where clean drinking water for the masses wasn't an option!"* In that very instant, Elaine had her epiphany. She decided to give two fingers to the materialistic world in which she was living.

She was tired of trying to keep up with the Joneses and the Smiths and all the other people who cared more about what they had than who they were as people. She sent an email to the rep in Africa asking if her pal Carol would like a volunteer for a year. Martin was given six months' notice appreciating that he didn't think anyone else would do the job. Her mum and dad told her to go with their blessing. Her pal, Mags, said she wasn't in the least surprised. Of course, there were the usual begrudgers who asked *"who does she bleedin' think she is, Christina Noble?"* I couldn't help but laugh at the irony; another woman who discovered there was so much more to life in her 40s.

She decided to go out in January to visit the project which was called St Joseph's House. When she came back she raised 15,000 euro from various clients and sponsors. She finished up work on the 30th of March and just before departing went to the bank in Walkinstown to do her final bits and pieces. She was held up by a guy wielding a shotgun, who took her wallet, her cards and even her make-up. Badly shaken up, she put the trip back two weeks to the 16th of April.

One week later, the local Maasai who had visited the hotel on her birthday, the previous year, returned. This was where she first met Elijah who hadn't been in the original group which she had met the year previously. He was one of the dance leaders. They became friends at first and it blossomed from there. *"We all have expectations from our respective cultures."* She pauses for a moment... *"In Maasai there is no word for 'please', they will say 'yes' or 'I don't want"*. At first, it was hard for Elijah to come to terms with her saying *'please'*. It was even harder for him to accept her smoking, for in their culture, a Maasai woman could never smoke! The Maasai believe that all the cows in the world belong to them. When Elijah came to visit Ireland recently, he couldn't understand why we have so much grass and so few cows. They have the opposite problem! Another time, he asked Elaine what women did in Ireland. *"But you have machines to do everything,"* he said. *"Machines to do washing, to do drying and even hoover your carpets!"*

At first, Elaine taught some classes and lived in a compound just north of Mombassa in a place called Kikambla. She taught all classes except Swahili including Maths and English.

Their official language was English, so getting them to practise was extremely important. *"There were 42 tribes all speaking their own dialects!"* When the makeshift school fell down, the funds Elaine had raised in Ireland helped to fund a new one and went towards a stand alone room which would be used as a clinic. The simple accommodation consisted of two small rooms. Her living quarters were behind the makeshift school which had a thatched roof or *'makuti'* which was the local term used to denote *'thatch'*. Close by, there was another small dwelling which housed five boys, some of whom were orphans. They lived, slept and worked there. Elaine also learned to run a small clinic, treating wounds and cuts that stenched when the wrapping was taken off, having festered for so long. Here she also administered antibiotics. Carol's sister-in-law was married to a man who helped out in the clinic and that same man remains Elaine's best friend today.

She shares a story of being in the clinic one day and everyone was being given a card to record their relevant history. An old woman whose name was *'Kache Kiti'* from the local area, came in complaining of a very bad chest. *"What age are you?,"* Elaine asked the old woman. She thought about it for a moment and replied *"I must be old 'cause I have a son and he has son and he has a son... so I must be 21."* It was the highest number she knew to count up to.

Elaine's days were her own after 4pm. One afternoon, the local Maasai decided to give her a Maasai name. There was a local ceremony held in her honour - a very big deal indeed. All the Maasai living in the Mombassa region gathered together. There were great celebrations and goats were slaughtered in her honour. The warriors selected her name. Henceforth, Elaine would be known as *'Narikuinkerra'* or *'Nariku'* for short. In Maasai, they don't call you by your name. She was invited to Rombo to witness the real Maasai local culture ... Elaine was amazed at what she witnessed. Life was so much harder here and yet people always smiled. *"They somehow managed to maintain this romantic view of life."* For *'Nariku',* there was simply no going back. This was where she truly belonged, body and soul. And so in September 2004, she moved permanently to Rombo. *"I worked initially under the local Catholic Mission doing administration support having secured a three year visa."* Her partner, Elijah, and the other two Maasai shared their vision with Elaine of what they wanted to do for the local area in Rombo and so the *'Light of Maasai'* charity was founded by a group of four: three Maasai and one *'musungu'* (Irish NGO worker, Elaine Bannon). The three Maasai men were Joseph Nkanoni Lempira, Elijah Kilempu Joseph and Jonathon Kipanu Ole Nampa.

Their shared vision was mapped out: *"Our greatest wish is to see a day when no woman will have to walk 20 or 30km for water every day, and where girls can start school at the age of 4 or 5 years, happy in the knowledge that they will not be removed from school at the age of 13 or 14 years to be circumcised and married. We wish that children won't have to walk more than 3 or 4km to school and will be educated to a level that will allow them to achieve employment later in life."*

What Elaine witnessed the first time she visited Rombo was an area that hadn't seen rains for 24 months. Animals were dying all around her. There was a serious shortage of food and the immense starvation was driving the wild animals to leave their plains in search of grass.

As we chat, Elaine tells me there's a serious famine looming in Kenya. *"The Government doesn't seem to have enough maize in storage. Remember our famine?"* she asks me. *"Well instead of potatoes, these people need maize!"* Even simple foods like the porridge they eat are maize-based. Their staple diet consists of *'sima'* which is like a solid porridge. It provides, as Elaine points out, *'cement for the stomach.'* The Maasai live by their animals, sleep on cow skins and barter using animals, selling milk to get maize flour. In simple terms, their bank account is denoted by the cows they own.

Elaine tells me that the World Food Programme will not be giving food to schools in 2009. *"How can you expect kids to go to school to learn without any nourishment to sustain them?"* she asks. Last year was a difficult year for all of them post Presidential elections, where hundreds were killed and thousands displaced in violent eruptions following claims of election-rigging. Much of the violence was directed towards Kikuyu communities, the tribe of the former President Kibaki who was re-elected. A ban on live media throughout the crisis meant that bloggers became one of the few valuable information sources available. Elaine and her team try to break down tribal hatred and differences by giving out foodstuffs.

Over the past five years, Elaine has raised a staggering 600,000 euro and for that, they now have clean water, lots and lots of it; 15 shallow ground wells and 2 pipelines. *"We've also built 9 classrooms with 2 under construction – supplied 3,000 desks to schools – 300 kids have been sponsored into primary, secondary and the university".*

Back home, a family friend, Sr Kathleen, sets about raising funds to help. When she's asked at church gate collections how much goes on administration, she replies *"I'm the administration".* Those who help out are sent regular reports with pictures and updates of what's happening.

Elaine's team has helped HIV sufferers by renting a small farm so that they can plant seeds and grow crops in order to sell half and eat half. *"Give a man food and he will survive. Teach a man to fish and he'll eat forever,"* she says smiling.

Perhaps not unlike Captain Jean Luc Picard of the *'Starship Enterprise'* who was bound by the *'First Directive'* forbidding him to interfere in other cultures, so too does Elaine have to be very careful about how far she tries to push the boundaries. In Maasai culture, a woman is not perceived to be a woman until she has been circumcised and had her clitoris removed. It's hard for Elaine to accept the widespread female genital mutilation taking place all around her, so she attempts to educate the females as subtly as she can.

It's hard for most of us perhaps to contemplate waking up worrying that a herd of buffalo might prevent our kids from getting to school, or elephants might destroy our crops, that a black Mamba or scorpion might be lurking in the garden. Every time Elaine comes home (every nine months or so) her plane trips are filled with thoughts about the technology we have and the differences it could make to the people of Rombo.

As we walk out of the hotel, Elaine lights up a cigarette. *"We're building a volunteer house – it will be ready by next February. You should come and visit. Oh and by the way, next time you're putting money on a horse, place it on 'Trafford's Lad'."*

The owner, Jim Butler, had agreed to donate the profits every time the horse won a race.

After I left this remarkable woman, I dropped into Paddy Power's to see when he was next racing.

8

Give Me Ten

Matt Craughwell

'People come out to see you perform and you've got to give them the best you have within you. The lives of most men are patchwork quilts. Or at best, one matching outfit with a closet and laundry bag full of incongruous accumulations. A lifetime of training for just 10 seconds.'

Jesse Owens

Reflecting back on the sad spectacle that was, for all of us Jackeens in Croke Park, that fateful Bank Holiday Monday... as we sat, waiting patiently for the heavy pillars of history to finally come crashing down on a Kerry team that oozed utter self-belief above all else, I believe that Mick O'Dwyer was right - the problem with the Dubs wasn't in their feet but their heads.

Funny thing that, how some things can be over before they've even begun! One thing is for sure my friends; whether you're standing in the middle of the pitch, in the cauldron that can be Croke Park, waiting for the referee to throw in that first ball, whether you're preparing to finally ask the girl of your dreams to marry you and you can feel your heart beating through your ear drums, or perhaps you're simply about to tempt the great temptress herself, fate, in some mysterious way, and make a little history by becoming the first crew in the world to row an ocean in under 30 days - just be sure in all cases that you visualise how you're going to achieve the end result in your own minds first.

The reasons why a person would want to risk crossing an ocean in the first place are as varied and multiple, I suspect, as the reasons relationships break down - why men choose to behave like they really are from Mars and why women choose to forgive us when they're wrong! Why indeed do any of us do anything for that matter? For me, it was a purely functional thing.

This was a chance to learn about team dynamics and to see how a team functions or fails under real pressure. We could, in truth, have been crossing space, it wouldn't have mattered. I knew as much about ocean rowing as I knew about being a spaceman, nothing. This was a chance to see if the skills I'd acquired climbing the seven summits could hold up in any environment, a chance to see just how much of a determinant attitude and optimism could be in terms of performance and outcome.

For Matt Craughwell, it was a far nobler thing. It was about showing the world just what he could be, and finally being proud of the person he really was. After all, in the bigger scheme of things, over 700 astronauts had ventured into space, several thousand mountaineers had climbed Everest, but only some 300 odd had ever rowed an ocean. Who wouldn't want to become a Spartan of the sea, right?

We first met on Operation Hop Scotch. Or, was it Operation Pink Salmon? Forgive me if my memory seems a little hazy at this point. What I can tell you with certainty is that we'd both just completed the first five kilometres of a proposed gruelling forty kilometres hike in the highlands surrounding Lough Tae in Central Scotland, Perthshire – by Aberfeldy, to be precise. It was the tailend of a bloody cold October and the windchill was making the going '*testing*' as the Scottish locals might have put it. Still I had to smile. Further south in the Lake District, they'd been forced to cancel the celebrated annual marathon that same weekend due to flooding and '*hazardous weather conditions*' as the locals down there, I believe, phrased it. Personally, I was glad to be finally up in the mountains. We'd just completed the first phase of our Tabata training (so named after a Japanese team instructor who trained the national ice-skating team through a series of intense interval-based cardio exercises where the ratio of maximum output to recovery is 2:1).

There followed kayaking down to Ardeonaig, and then, in true triathlon style, it was straight out of the Malibu's (single moulded kayaks) and into a brisk run in the wetsuits up to the High Ropes Course at the Abernethy Trust Outdoor Centre, with a little British Military Fitness thrown in for good measure.

We learned somehow to negotiate the tricky '*Jacob's Ladder*', a series of massive poles that rise about 60 feet, linked by a chain suspended in the middle, with the distance between each pole becoming tantalisingly further and further apart. We then climbed up the logs of the infamous totem pole known quaintly as the '*Pizza Box*', a seventy foot pole with a small square platform at the top – edging out to allow four people to eventually stand on top, trusting each other not to fall off. All of this took place under the watchful supervision of the team of Mr David Fox Pitt (ex SAS British

Forces), and his talented team - all former soldiers, all highly trained, and all as fit as the proverbial butcher's dog.

'Teams need to think about all aspects of speed. You do not win a race, necessarily, by going fast – you have to be fast in the right direction with proper co-ordination.'

I believe these were the majestic words of our Scottish skipper, Leven Brown, uttered in response to someone's foolish enquiry as to why a bunch of highly trained SAS guys would ultimately (in part at least) decide the fate of who was going to be selected for the two crossings being proposed; the South Atlantic in January and then '*Big Brother*', the North Atlantic in June 2009. He should know, having skippered the crew that held the existing world record, and also having a host of other enviable achievements to his name - including being the first man to row solo through the Bay of Cadiz. He was one of the world's foremost experts on ocean rowing, and was as tough as they came, physically and mentally.

Overlooking fundamentals is a path to defeat, he believed. Preparation, familiarisation and execution of any act can never be hasty unless it has been practised in an unfamiliar environment. "*Spending time thinking about your move(s) is not time wasted,*" he would often reflect over a dram of the finest Balantine whisky. Just how right Skip would turn out to be, seemed a million miles from the thoughts of the other rowers who had turned up for their shot at fame, and a chance to be considered part of the '*Mondiale*' boat crew which would take on these massive challenges. Assisting Leven in the week-long military-styled operations were his two able lieutenants, both of whom were part of the crew which held the world record for the fastest ever crossing of the South Atlantic in a commendable time of thirty-three days. From Glasgow, there was Don '*The Machine*' Lennox who ran ultra marathons of 100 plus miles for fun, with the same appetite I suspect that Arnie might have eaten Green Berets for breakfast in his breakthrough film, '*Commando*'. Juxtaposing this mild-mannered and rather amiable Scottish beast was Galway's answer to the terminator, Ray Carroll - about 6'5" and weighing in at just under 200lbs. In this good-cop/bad-cop relationship, Ray was the latter and he played it rather well. To this day, Matt Craughwell would refer to Ray as '*driven* and *single-minded*' in nature.

Ray had a plan, and part of that plan included breaking Matt. He'd made his mind up from the off. Just when the off had begun, I'm not entirely sure. Perhaps it went back to the first training camp, in which we'd all assembled at Port Patrick the previous month. As far as he was concerned, Matt didn't belong. Perhaps he didn't look the part? He was 5'10" in height, the same as me, '*shorties*' by rowing standards, it must be acknowledged. Perhaps he was concerned about the reach he'd have on the boat. Let's face it; the only thing I was bringing to the party, apart from my fitness, was an indestructible will. I was no rower and as far as the man from Salthill was concerned, neither was Matt. Either way, Ray had decided in his own mind that Matt just wasn't made of the right stuff and so had purposely decided to make his life a living hell, and it was only day three.

I first met Ray at a Junior Chamber function five months previously. Towering *over* me at the bar, with a bottle of beer in hand, he had a presence about him. He didn't waste any time with bullshit, but chose instead to cut straight to the chase, like a man on a mission. "*You don't really think it's over, mate, do you?*" By over he was referring to the Seven Summits and the notion of hanging up the adventure boots to focus on working to help other people to achieve their goals. "*You need a real challenge, Mc Keever!*" he suggested, looking me straight in the eyes. "*Oh, what might that be then, Ray?*" I replied smugly. "*Rowing the North Atlantic in fifty-five days or under, the last great record on offer and the oldest one at sea too,*" he replied rather matter-of-factly. Before I'd time to digest the notion, he bent down, as if turning to whisper in my ear, his eyes focusing on the red head that'd just left my side for the ladies toilet. "*By the way, she won't last either*". As we approached the next RV point, I cursed the '*son of a bitch*' for being right on both counts. I did need another challenge and the relationship sadly disintegrated as predicted. Things were going from bad to worse and I seriously wondered for a moment whether he was right about Matt too.

The poor guy was burning big time, trying to get himself over the next ridge. In his mind he thought, for the team's sake, it would be better if he perhaps called it quits. The pace was killing him and it would take its toll on several others too before nightfall. Ray's job ultimately on this exercise was to feed back to Leven, and Don was doing the same with the other South Atlantic crew who'd started from a different grid reference point. I waited, curious to see Ray's strategy unfold. "*Are you sure you want to quit Matt. If you ring that bell, you don't want to have any regrets. None.*" Matt's calves were on fire and like the blood draining from his reddened face, he could feel his chances of rowing an ocean evaporating. "*Hey Matt, I could sure use some company to get over that ridge mate. If you want to quit, then I'll ring the bell for you. How 'bout it?*"

These were the first words I'd spoken to him. Thankfully for the next three hours, Matt did most of the talking. They were three of the most memorable hours of my life. He opened up about a great many things, including Helen, the woman who had saved his life, he told me. "*Every day mate.*" He stopped to catch his breath as we meandered stubbornly up another lousy hill and looked at me like a man whose soul had been touched by an angel. "*Every single bloody day, I wake up and look across at that woman and think to myself, I've won the Lotto.*" There were tears in this guy's eyes. She had changed everything. She made the boy who grew up on a council estate in West London, and whose father had done a runner when he was just a kid, feel like he was worth something to himself a.id to the world.

I knew in that moment that Ray was very wrong this time. This guy had more passion coursing through his veins than Ray and I combined. He just needed the chance to channel it. And so we shot the breeze for a few more hours. I guess it helped a little to take Matt's mind off the obvious pain and discomfort he was in. We chatted about our school days, about his hilarious tales from Walford High and my contrasting life in the Christian Brothers; about his stepfather Steve, who he met when he was thirteen; his mum, Anne, who he adored and his little 'bro', Danny, who was eighteen months younger and 6'4", and who had waited patiently most of his teenage life until he was tall enough to exact retribution on his older brother for the number of times he'd kicked the almighty crap out of him.

Talking will, of cours,e only get you so far in life. By the time we reached the massive peat bogs, which stood some eight feet tall, standing defiantly against the 60mph winds, it was freezing cold, and Matt's brave adventure was all but over. Two hours later, having literally crawled on his hands and knees down to the next RV, which was on a roadside beside a massive dam reservoir, it was time to say enough is enough. Matt was seriously worried he'd blown his knees. Working as a gas engineer, (repairing and installing domestic appliances), he needed those knees. Helen, his wife, had gone back to college and was undertaking her legal practitioner training course, having just completed her law degree. They depended at that point on Matt's salary. As he bade farewell, you could see in his eyes a huge sense of perceived failure.

Looking back on that weeklong experience in Lough Tae, which included four more days of Scottish hell on earth, three things stand out. There was David Fox Pitt's memorable speech, post-trekking in the mountains, in which he had commented on the state of the dishevelled tents, and in particular his reference to one of the lads' gear bags - which in fairness looked more like something Coco Channel might have designed. *"If you think this kind of fucking preparation will be accepted aboard a 40 foot boat with communal living quarters for fourteen grown men, then think again, as Leven tosses your gear overboard and a whale swims by three days later with your jocks hanging from his snout, just to really piss you off!"*

There was the embarrassing moment when I had to get into my wetsuit, which had completely frozen, as we recovered from two hours sleep in the forest on the aptly named Operation Fat Trout. We faced a daunting ten mile kayak back to base camp and it eventually had to be thawed out several hours later in the tent with a blow heater.

And then there were the classic arm-wrestling encounters - over many a bottle of whisky - between Skip and Livar, a paradoxical artist and whale hunter from the Faeroe Islands, one of the many bidding for a spot on the rows ahead. This man had arms like Popeye and I swear he was made out of granite. They wrestled all bloody night.

And so, as we filled out the last of our psychometric assessments, said our farewells, and awaited the 'letter' from Leven to say whether we'd qualified for thirty days of ocean rowing, luxury or not, my mind drifted to the West End boy, our *top banana* from London. What of Matt's fate? We all know what it's like to have those nagging feelings at the back of our minds, the ones that just won't let you be at peace. Despite having enough painkillers for his troubling knee, enough to sedate a horse, in fact, Matt just couldn't settle back home. He remained anxious as he sat under those black clouds. At the back of his mind there was that constant, unsettling feeling of failure. Sure, he'd done the best he could on a bad knee, (a knee that still troubles him today) but he chastised and berated himself for not having been better prepared. *"Craughwell, you're a twat son. That was a bloody pointless exercise, a bridge too far."* Say these things enough times to yourself and you will become those thoughts. In his powerful book, 'The Inner Game of Tennis', Tim Gallwey proposes that performance, be it in life, on a tennis court, a Gaelic pitch or an ocean, equals perception minus interference.

"Dear Matt, There is a place on the South Atlantic crew this December, should you wish to accept it." It's hard to imagine the mixed emotions, never mind the genuine shock, that must have greeted Matt several weeks later when he checked his inbox. Skip must have drunk too much whisky that last night, surely? Delighted naturally to be getting his chance to fulfil an ambition that had been with him for many years, all Matt could really think about at the back of his mind was how the lads would take him or not take him - the possible weak link in the chain. He could feel those teenage insecurities rising to the surface once more. As he packed his bags for sea survival training in Lowestoft, Helen helped assure him that everything would be alright.

"When we are creating a team, it is important that the team ethos and unit is present at all times... Rowing an ocean is as much about looking after your crewmates as it is about looking after yourself. Their interests are your interests!" Matt took it all in, listening carefully to Skip as he laid it out to the team about what would lie ahead for all of us. *"If we fail to look after them, we fail to look after ourselves as a whole, thus weakening the unit".*

Matt was impressed by the team selection: Our motley crew comprised five Irish, five English, two Scots, a Lithuanian and a deranged Faroese arm wrestler with a heart of gold. This was a chance for the team to finally do some bonding. People no longer had any reason to be fearful of each other. They were no longer competing with each other. Very quickly the characters in the group emerged. Among them, *'The Jackal'* Yaacov, our Lithuanian friend, who was fifty-three years young. Many suspected that he was actually ex-KGB. The fact that he held four different passports, was licensed to carry firearms in several different countries and held a post doctorate degree in quantum physics, did little to quell the rumours.

From an early age, this man had made his decision where marriage was concerned. "*Men have a choice in life,*" he would often say. "*We can be right or we can be happy,*" and so he chose to be happy. Among the English selected there was George, a quietly spoken soul who, despite being selected, had passed up a career in the Royal Marines to have a future with his girlfriend who he had met in Harvard, where he'd also prestigiously rowed first eight. There was Gareth, a beast of a man, a former rugby player, and talented rower. James, who had done all kinds of interesting things, including swimming the channel and Danny from Christ College, Cambridge University, for whom he had rowed. He was the baby in the crew at twenty-three, and he planned to do some postgraduate studies while on board the boat, looking at man's evolution from a seafaring perspective.

Training to row across an ocean is a curious thing. In my case, the call to be included in the South Atlantic crossing had followed surprisingly, in the wake of the Loch Tae training. One of the Irish lads, Breffny, a former Harvard rower felt that it would be good preparation for what lay ahead on the North Atlantic.

Skip and the rest of the crew were in agreement, and so I set about learning how to row on an erg machine. I had eight weeks to get up to standard. Eight weeks to be able to comfortably row thirty kilometres in two hours. On board the '*Mondiale*', our amazing rowing vessel which was made out of carbon fibre and weighed four tonnes, we would row in shifts of eight and six, two hours on and two hours off, twenty-four hours a day. We would consume 7,000 calories daily while burning up to almost twice that amount. And so the lads set about getting fat in the process.

Matt trained in his local gym, The Hearton in Hertford, about fifteen miles North West of Greater London. He would build up to rowing for two hours, going home for two hours, and then going back again. People in the gym thought he was a raving loony. "*I had my gloves, a memory foam pillow under my arse, my blue slam jacket and my trusty iPod. I was happy out, mate*". Matt would sometimes row up to fifty kilometres in one day. In his own words, this man "*trained his ass off!*" I often wondered if there was a picture of Ray Carroll at the end of the erg machine spurring him on.

As it happened, putting on the weight for Matt was easy. He simply ate twice as much pizza as normal, along with stacks of protein shakes, and so made up the required 4,000 calories a day that allowed him to put on the extra sixteen pounds in required padding. I was gob-smacked the next time I saw Matt - he'd turned into a virtual tub. He'd come up to me, put his hand on my shoulder and say *"listen mate, some bodies can take it,"* and then he'd smile looking look down at me and say, *"and some bodies can't!"*

We took the '*Mondiale*' into the water in late November, again off Lowestoft. The boat needed three to four hours work. A sliding rail system was required to be in place for the seats and Matt knew that his practical skills would now start to come in very handy indeed. Matt quickly realised that he had skills to offer in abundance that the rest of us simply lacked. The simple and honest truth is that without Matt's help, our departure date would have been pushed further out. This knowledge of how everything worked, and where it all belonged, offered Matt a lifeline, a sense of security and confidence on board the boat. While the boat was technically ready to be rowed, all of the life support systems had been delayed because of an unforgiving set of suppliers who had messed Skip around. And so, all the technical installation that should have been carried out in Lowestoft had now to be put back to pre-departure in Port Mogán on the Canary Islands. The next time I saw Matt on St Stephen's Day, he was like a kid in a sweet shop.

It was fascinating for all of us to witness him set about his business. First up, he sorted the fuel cells which supply the boat's power – these use methanol as a fuel source to create an electrical reaction, leaving a by-product of only water. "*It's like super green electricity!*" he'd remark excitedly. This military grade technology was overseen by Leven, with Matt positioning everything just so on the boat as the rest of us looked on in amazement and tried to make ourselves useful. Next up came what Matt liked to describe as the '*bad boys*' on board, the water makers! A water maker operates as a desalinator, taking salt water and filtering it through a five micron filter. This goes through a first stage pump, and then goes through a secondary pumping system, which eventually squeezes the water through a very thin membrane, trapping the salt, and leaving us with fresh drinking water. There were two systems (one back-up), capable of making fifty litres an hour.

The rowing deck on the boat was out of line, it was off-kilter. All the hard work done in Lowestoft had to be redone in the Canaries as Matt and the boys set about re-drilling the seating positions. This was followed by the varnishing of the boat with anti-foul to prevent the growth of algae. As Matt, Skip and Don did the hard work, Cork man Peter Williams, a superb technical rower who had rowed underage for Ireland, set about getting the rest of us organised with task lists in hand. Those tasks included regular visits to the local chandler's store run by the amiable *'Sunshine Mike'* and his lovely wife. Among the things we learned to do was to knit nets for the two small cabin areas where we would sleep on board at opposite ends of the boat. To let off steam, most nights ended with the crew on the proverbial lash. We all hit it hard that New Year's Eve to be honest. Because the weather systems were changing, our departure had been put back another three days and we were all running out of cash. To make ends meet, George, the eternal student, lived on the ration packs that were supposed to keep us alive on board. These were made up of re-hydrated mountain food that had to be stored below the boat's decks from bow to stern to keep the boat properly balanced.

One day, rather memorably, George walked the streets of Mogán in nothing more than a bin liner, with a sign over his shoulder saying *'Free hugs'*. I believe he made €30, not bad considering! Ryan Corcoran and Robbie Byrne, tough-as-nails former National Skiff champions (coastal rowing, which is a brutally tough endurance form of rowing), formed the backbone of the Irish quintet on board. Ryan, who trained the senior cup rugby team in CBC Monkstown, made sure that the walls of the second cabin (the one which Matt and I would be sharing along with six others) were lined with a curious mixture of FHM pin-ups and quotes to get us through the tough times that lay ahead. *"Pain is just weakness leaving the body"* and *"Everything must pass"* were just two of the more memorable ones.

When the tasks were finally completed on the 3rd of January 2009, the new Cleaver oars sanded and installed, and the boat sea-tested, the entire crew jumped off the marina in celebration. Having completed the weigh-ins, with me being the lightest with just eighty-three kilos in body weight (you were allowed no more than sixty additional kilos in bag weight), we were finally ready to depart. The moment had come.

Departure was signalled by the sound of a klaxon going off, and a large crowd had gathered at the marina to see us off. The adrenalin was pumping and you could feel the excitement tingling down to the back of the spine. The first two-hour shift seemed to fly by in an instant as, leaving the harbour lights behind us, we set out upon the first of the 3,000 miles that remained till we touched down in Barbados.

The water was extremely calm at first. The second cabin, in which Matt and I were sleeping, was a rather tight affair. The actual space afforded us was no more than seven feet in length and five foot in width, tapering at one point to no more than two. The other cabin was even less delightful, a place where the air temperature was never below 30°C on account of the fuel cells being kept there. If you were lucky, you got maybe twenty minutes sleep. Matt and I had been paired together in the classic buddy-buddy system. At first, after our shift would finish we tried to politely negotiate our way past the monster, Gareth, very politely asking him to move his enormous arms so that we could crawl underneath him in the hope of getting some sleep. By the time our second shift came around, however, the notion of sleep was about to go out the window. That first night was hell. Skip had warned us about the changing weather patterns and so it came - the massive weather front that heralded force seven conditions, rampaging waters and a boat which happily tossed its cabin occupants into the air like rag dolls.

Seven-foot waves frequently came crashing over the bow side for fun, and so I was christened with my new nickname, '*McCleaver*', as I caught several crabs (wrong side of the wave), eventually breaking my oar in half and with it what felt like my lower back. Half of the crew were violently seasick and the two worst affected, Danny (who was on stroke, setting the rowing rhythm) and Ryan, were sick for five days straight, unable to keep any food down. It was cruel to watch such big lads becoming dilapidated and losing ferocious amounts of weight in the process. They never once moaned or complained, and to Ryan's eternal credit, he never once missed a shift. Through it all, Skip drove us on with one eye on the speedometer which required us to keep a constant speed of four knots (or close to 4.2 miles an hour) regardless of the weather conditions. For the first seventy-two hours, I just couldn't sleep. It took me two full days to get the rowing stroke right – there was much relief among the rest of the crew when I eventually did! Matt was loving the day shifts and hating the nights, as was I.

Over the course of the first four days, the normal teething patterns that you would associate with any crazy adventure began to emerge. Cleaning yourself with baby wipes was done to the rear of the boat. You were roped in as you made your way out to sit on *'God's throne'*, a makeshift toilet seat which sat above the ocean water below. Toilet breaks, however, did become an issue because when you rowed you were invariably sitting downwind of the toilet throne, and some of the smells that greeted you were simply nauseating. Sometimes you might have to duck as tissue paper would come flying back across, landing often on poor James' arm (he had the worst seat to endure, front left opposite Danny and George who stroked on alternate occasions). More often than not, in choppy waters and heavy winds he got urinated on. The fact that Pete *'went'* to the toilet as often as a racehorse before and after every shift, probably didn't help matters. Most of us were developing serious sores on our backsides and so Skip devised a special combination of antibacterial ointment mixed with '*Sudocrem*' to alleviate the excruciating pain that followed.

Our hands blistered badly too, even when wearing gloves, as they toughened up under the strain of rowing twelve hours a day. By nightfall, all these little problems seemed to melt away like lemon drops. Matt and I had mastered the art of sleeping between the 11pm and 4am shifts. We were eating properly and the '*esprit de corps*' among the crew was really starting to take form. We'd cracked our first hundred miles in one day, keeping us nicely on course for the world record, which was all the sweeter for Matt and I because our six-man shift had two hours to complete the final six miles that would take us over the 100-mile mark. Matt was sensational. His good-natured humour, attitude and willingness to get stuck in whenever any task was required, were outstanding. He drove our six-man team over the line that evening. On one particular shift, looking out to sea, he spotted a lone yellow buoy, bobbing its head above the water. "*Come back Wilson, come back,*" he cried out in Tom Hank's fashion, which had us all in convulsions and offered a welcome respite from the task in hand. On another occasion after his hamstrings had tightened up very badly, he ran down the decks kicking his leg in the air, shouting, "*I'm the Kung Fu Panda!*"

By the fifth night, the seas were calmer and the stars became brighter, guiding us like giant beacons in the sky. We'd never seen stars burn so brightly, or so high up in the sky for that matter. When you looked overboard as your oar glided into the water, fluorescent algae appeared to light the way. It was breathtaking and we knew we were on the adventure of a lifetime.

"*Give me ten!*" Breffny Morgan would burst out with the same line every morning, and so the crew would offer up ten strokes for literally anything, from the Brian O'Leary dealership in Co Cork to the Marguerites Club (Danny's club in Christ College in Cambridge), whatever it took to keep the crew in good spirits and keep them focused on the prize. A little humour always helped, of course. Matt was now beginning to realise that he'd been born to row an ocean.

He was now in an environment where he knew exactly what was supposed to happen, but, in truth, had no idea what was actually going to happen, which just added to the excitement. As the days became hotter, Ryan and Robbie stepped up to the plate. "*Give me honesty boys, good honest strokes,*" they would say, propelling the entire crew on as we went in search of the unthinkable - a sub-thirty day crossing. At night, the boys led us in song as we rowed as a unit, "*together lads, together,*" and our pace was increasing steadily every day - 104 miles, 109 miles, 112 miles. George and Danny continued to do Trojan work on the stroke, mixing the stroke lengths as and when the waters required them to do so - longer if we had no wind, shorter when we did. Everyone was now in sync with the sound of the ocean. To the rear, our two powerhouses, Livar and Leven, provided the boat's engine room, rowing as a virtual pair of Siamese twins, while the likes of James, Pete and Bref made sure there was some artistry in what we were doing - each and every one technically sublime in their respective deliveries. Every night before my final shift, when Yaacov, who sat in front of me (to be replaced by Robbie), would depart for his well-earned rest, I would take inspiration. This man was fifty-three years old and rowing as well as anyone.

By day seven, we knew in our hearts that this world record was on, and the belief that we could possibly smash it was firmly entrenched in each of us. With each stroke we breathed in confidence and breathed out any lingering doubts. We were starting to pick up the blessed trade winds from the African plains, which created a *'rip wave'* effect. The sweet sound of us moving through the water filled the air as we thrived on the extra two to three knots an hour difference which the winds created. Our daily patterns seemed more palatable. Before noon every day, we'd bilge the boat of any water which had managed to seep anonymously into the lower decks through the gunner rails. The ration packs were then issued to everybody.

Matt still hated the flap jacks (they tasted like powdered flour he reckoned!), I loved the chilli con carne, and Danny loved the muesli, while James hated chocolate. People had found their niches, settled comfortably on their strengths, and the team was functioning in a way that Skip could be proud of. Even the things that couldn't be cured, such as the excruciatingly sore asses, were now made more bearable in the knowledge that we were committed to a common goal, a world record. Matt warned people to use body glide – do you think we listened to him? He would also cleverly alternate his seat cover, while Don and I persisted with sheepskin. I'd also managed to put a small hole in the back of my left foot with the pressure I'd put on my ankles, but after each shift, Don or Matt would help ensure that the dressings were changed to avoid infection.

It was 2pm on day ten when it happened. The sun was high in the sky and we'd decided to have a go at the record for the most distance rowed in a single day (measured between 6am and 6pm) which stood at an impressive 117 miles, set by Ray and his merry band of men a year previously. We were on course for a possible 120, when suddenly, as we came over a massive wave, we could feel our oars being suspended in the air. The speedometer shot to zero in a millisecond! Within thirty seconds, the boat had drifted beam-on into a twenty-foot wave. We'd gone a full 360. There was genuine confusion at first. What was happening? Matt thought the auto helm had been turned off and so went to check. Meanwhile, Skip was suddenly up out of his rowing seat and had sped down to the stern to check on the rudder. A moment later, he announced that the rudder had gone, vanished! The gravitas of the situation was immediately apparent. We knew in that moment that our record, like the bloody rudder, had plunged to the bottom of the sea.

The first thing to do was to set out the sea anchor, which was designed to keep the boat's bow pointing into the wave as opposed to the beam onto the wave. We were suddenly in a very dangerous situation.

Meanwhile, Leven asked Matt to come up with an idea; a way to produce a rudder out of a piece of daggerboard using whatever power tools had remained on board with us. Matt got busy drilling enough holes into the daggerboard to create a tiller rudder system. Because the rudder had been connected to the auto helm, we were now deprived of our automated steering, which would mean manual steering - a job Leven and Livar took on in difficult waters - twenty foot waves in twenty knot winds. It was becoming mission impossible. The dream was turning rapidly into a painful nightmare.

I don't know exactly how many miles we managed to make – maybe forty before nightfall. Now we were blinded. No auto helm and no moon to guide us. How could the lads possibly steer when they couldn't even see the waves coming? The boat breached time and time again as we went beam-on several times. At one point, I'd come off the erratic shift, sat in the cabin, and heard the screams coming from the lads. Skip had gone into the water, trying to set down the sea anchor in horrendous conditions. The gravity of the situation was becoming too much for many of the lads. They finally got Skip out and dried him in the cabin below. The lads, understandably, had been visibly shaken. Although, to his credit, he remained extremely calm in difficult circumstances, Skip was aware of the heightened state of alertness that was apparent in the crew. We could smell the fear. Matt and I spoke with Don and offered to support Skip in whatever decisions he felt were best to make. I was aware that many of the crew wanted to call it quits, but it had to be Skip's final decision. He was the captain and we had to respect him. He knew best.

That night, we set a two-hour shift pattern to watch the conditions on board. Rowing ceased. It had become impossible to sleep as the sea anchor continually pounded and crashed against the waves. The next morning (to everyone's immense credit) we tried to row again. The last of our spare ropes was now required to maintain the tiller system.

By lunchtime, a mutual decision by skipper and crew, acknowledging our current situation whereby we'd run out of rope before we'd run out of the will to carry on, forced us to give up the ghost. A pan-pan call (a call that requests assistance at sea, but without immediate threat to life) was made to the Falmouth coastguard services and we were duly informed that two shipping vessels were in the vicinity - one bound for Brazil, the other destined for Ravenna in Italy.

Getting on board the *'Island Ranger'* twelve hours later that night, is an experience that will live deep in the memory of all of us. Picture if you will a 40,000 tonne vessel (ninety feet from sea level to deck in height) approaching the 4 tonne streamlined *'Mondiale'* on the portside, then drifting onto our bow to shield us from the twenty-five foot waves, which were swelling in force seven conditions. To ensure a safe and efficient exit, we had all been given numbers. The plan was for the Ukrainian crew to throw the rope ladders down and we'd each grab on and jump across to begin our ninety foot ascent up the ship's side. As the first ladder fell, we could feel the *'Mondiale'* being tossed by the crashing waves into the hull of the *'Island Ranger'*. We were being breached. The situation had become highly dangerous and we had to act fast. And so, on the peak of a wave, each crewmember made their jump across. One slip and you were a goner, resulting in a fall to certain death between the two vessels.

Matt was the third off. I went tenth. By the time the last of us had crawled to the top, there was just Skip to come aboard. We watched from above, horrified to see the *'Mondiale'* being destroyed, praying that Skip would make it safely on board. He did finally. It was a miracle that nobody had been killed that night. Later, as we sat in the ship's kitchen, we thought only of two things, the fact that despite being nearly 270 miles ahead of the current world record, none of that would now count for anything and the cruel tears that Skip shed as they cut the *'Mondiale'* loose.

Nobody died but we'd lost our fifteenth crew member and with it the chance to make history on both the South Atlantic and the North later that summer.

****

When Matt returned home, he received a call from one of the crew who held the existing record, which had remained intact despite all of our best efforts. They were having a reunion and invited him to come along to share memories and toast the *'Mondiale'*. On his way home on board the London tube that night, drifting somewhere along the central line, Matt had an epiphany. A surreal moment occurred. He suddenly realised that at that exact moment in a parallel world, he'd be just coming off shift on board the

'*Mondiale*'. It was day twenty-two! He smiled to himself and thought of his pal Dominic who had died some years earlier, losing his brave fight to cancer. "*Who decides when anything is over?*" he thought out loud. In that moment, Matt decided he would buy a boat himself. *"Screw the economy!"* he said laughing, '*I'll borrow the damn £40k myself to get it up and running. I'll do my yacht master courses. I'll skipper the boat. Some of the crew will come with me. I know they will.*' He had now burst into a veritable chuckle. The few remaining passengers on board were staring intently at him. He thought about Peter Williams from Douglas in Cork and how determined, for example, he remained to become the first Cork man to complete an ocean crossing, Matt would start there.

The West End boy from a London council estate, with the English passport and the Irish genes handed down from two sets of grandparents, will depart Port Mogán this Christmas, bound I believe for Barbados in his very own rowing boat.

9

Conquering Clare

Clare Power

'There would be nothing to frighten you if you refused to be afraid.'

Gandhi

By any measure, Clare Power is a remarkable woman. Although her achievements alone would make interesting reading, as I was about to discover, it is her inspiring attitude to life itself and the manner in which she treats the obstacles that attempt to block her path, that make her inclusion in this book both a pleasure and a privilege.

To fully appreciate Clare, we must first pay tribute to a woman who greatly inspired Clare.

Maria Montessori is a woman to whom the world's children owe an enormous debt of gratitude. Born in the town of Chiaravalle, Italy on August 31, 1870, many of the books written about her, describe Maria from a young age as self-confident, optimistic and greatly interested in change. Like the dilemma facing so many modern day parents, Maria's had difficulty agreeing on what might be best in the long run for their *"talented, headstrong daughter"*. Her empathy for people was demonstrated clearly from an early age, for example, the manner in which she treated her neighbour, a disabled little girl whom she befriended and brought out for walks on a regular basis. Clearly a child that knew her own mind, it was not uncommon for her to interfere in arguments her parents would have. At that time, elementary education was a very local affair and the schools were usually dirty and crowded. However, Maria learned very easily and did exceptionally well in exams.

Graduating from technical school in 1886, Maria attended Regio Instituto Tecnico Leonardo da Vinci from 1886 to 1890, where she studied modern languages and natural sciences. By the time she was ready to graduate, she had decided she wanted to go into the biological sciences. At that time in Italy, it was considered futile, indeed impossible, for a female to consider medicine as a career. Unsurprisingly, her father was shocked and disapproved greatly. In order to give herself a chance to find a route into the medical arena and fulfill her ambitions, she decided instead to enroll at the University of Rome to study physics, mathematics and natural sciences. While other students were reading or writing novels, dreaming of romance or considering an 'ideal husband', Ms Montessori kept her head in the books.

True to form, in 1892, she passed her exams with distinction and received a Diploma di Licenza which made her eligible to study medicine. But one problem still remained: how to overcome the gender factor? When running short of divine inspiration, why not accept the next best thing, papal intervention? Allegedly, Pope Leo XIII stepped in and helped her get into the school of medicine in the University of Rome. She would eventually become Italy's first ever female doctor. To put such an achievement into perspective, in these times in which we live, is difficult. Or is it?

If somebody had told you thirty years ago that Ireland would be led by a female President, what might you have said? Perhaps the simple truth that Ireland's best ticket to a gold medal in the next Olympics may lie in the hands of a brilliant young female boxer from Bray, is a good example that the gender gaps are finally closing.

How incredibly shocking it must have been to Maria Montessori's male colleagues, some 115 years ago, that a woman had been accepted into the decidedly male inner sanctum of medicine. A woman standing side by side with her male counterparts treating patients and studying the human anatomy, imagine! The story goes that in 1896 she had to present her thesis to a board of ten men. Highly impressed with her work, they granted her a degree, making her a doctor of medicine. Not only did she graduate, but she did so with an exemplary record. At this time, anything over a 100 was considered brilliant. Maria scored a 105.

Shortly afterwards, in 1897, having joined the staff of the University of Rome as a voluntary assistant, she made a discovery that would lead her inadvertently to that with which we now associate her. One of her responsibilities was to visit asylums. It was here she came across so-called *'feeble-minded'* children, unable to function in schools or families. They had no outlet. She saw that they were starved of experience and started to think about what she could do to help them. In 1904 she was offered a job as a

Professor of Anthropology at the University of Rome. Two years later, she quit to work with sixty young children of working-class families. And so, the Montessori methods of teaching were born. These methods of teaching were so successful that even children with serious learning disabilities began to pass examinations for so-called normal children.

Maria began to notice how the children absorbed knowledge from their surroundings, almost effortlessly, like sponges. She felt the children were teaching themselves. They inspired her lifelong pursuit of educational reform. It was this highly empathetic approach, that touched a chord with Clare Power.

On a cold winter's day in 1984, she made a conscious decision, in setting up her own modest crèche facility in her family home on Sidmonton Road, Bray, to adopt a different approach where children were concerned. *"What Maria Montessori gave us was a system which teaches children to progress step by step. Each step overlaps. Best of all,"* she smiles, *"children are never set up for failure. They learn self-discipline – instinctively the children know when they have something wrong and they learn to positively support each other in the process."*

Clare's facility caters for children from as young as two and a half up to pre-school age. As she kindly offers to show me around the family home, I can't help but think about the notion that children who venture into this Narnia-like playground are never set up for failure. How positive is that? I wondered.

Clare patiently explains the role of the materials and various equipment that the teacher uses in the teaching process. Following the Montessori model quite faithfully, the learning experience is broken into five sections: *language,* (the materials used help develop the child's listening and oral skills using a phonetic approach to language) *maths,* which introduces the children to numbers, where the child learns through 'actual doing' and is seen as a continuation of the third of the experiences, *sensorial,* whereby children are given the chance to arrange things by shape, colour, touch and sound - an experience all children love. Here they learn that making errors are essential to the learning process. Next, we have what Clare refers to as '*practical life*'. Here the child gets to do what they really want to do. For the girls, that includes copying many of mum's daily routines; from setting the table to arranging shoes. In this section of development, the children are encouraged to develop control and coordination of movement, orderly thought patterns and a better overall awareness of their environment. The section that Clare's school specialises in, and the one that to my mind brings this magical world to life most vividly, is *cultural studies.* In one simple but ingenious exercise which Clare shows me, children are brought on a virtual geographical journey, beginning with the solar system, where a compelling jigsaw represents the stars, showing how the world began. They then explore the globe, discovering Europe and finally they find out where Britain and Ireland fall into the equation and the journey then comes full circle as we end up back in Bray.

Her splendid home, which dates back over 120 years, is now transformed into a children's paradise, the kind of place that CS Lewis would have drawn certain inspiration from. The tour begins with the beautifully decorated Baby Room for children one or under. The toddler's room caters for those up to two years old, while there are separate lodgings for the Junior and Senior Montessori kids.

The fact that several of the staff, including June and Yvonne, have been with Clare for over twenty years, through thick and thin, speaks volumes about the positive environment the school has created, not to mention the resilience that Clare has shown.

In 1984, things were even worse than they are today economically (just!). Across the water, the *'Thatcher Years'*, were dominated by the plight of the miners fighting pit closures across the UK, a struggle which was memorably captured in Billy Bragg's classic anthem *'Between the Wars'*.

Back in Ireland, the retail sector took a massive hit. Power and Moore, which began as a small chain of retail clothing shops, (the city's first stockists, in fact, of the classic *'Teddy Boy'* clothing) and was run by her husband Eric, had all but evaporated by the end of 1983.

Money was tight and despite the understandable dent to Eric's pride, Clare needed to think on her feet and find a way to support their four children. *"Necessity was the mother of invention back then. I had to earn money plain and simple."* Clare set about thinking about the various things she could do to bring in cash. She could cook, certainly, and sew. For years she had made all kinds of clothes, including nearly everything worn by her own children. But the thing she felt most comfortable with was looking after kids. Having thought carefully about her various options, she bravely decided to open a crèche.

Their home dated back to 1896, a beautiful house that would need serious attention if it was to be converted. Each of the kids, to their credit, mucked in to help their mother prepare. Of the six bedrooms, two were going to be used for the new crèche. And so, Niamh, Cormac, Ciaran and Brian (the boys would now share their room) set about stripping the bedrooms and painting the walls. *"We even had giant insignias of Jumbo on the walls!"* Clare laughs as she recalls the efforts they went to. *"The kids will love this if I can convince them to come!"* she thought to herself. Clare informed Eric that her intention was to have ten kids and charge £40 per week. In simple terms, she would bring in £400 every month. He loved his wife but it was all he could do to stop himself from laughing. Had she lost the plot completely?

There were two stairs in use in the house at the time and so they decided to use the backstairs to avoid disruption to the household, particularly to Eric who was having a hard time coming to terms with not working himself. Originally the crèche was to be called Bosco, a name that Clare thought the kids and parents would identify with. It was neighbour, Al Butler, whose wife June had been so helpful to Clare in the initial phases, who pointed out that were she to call it the Clare Elizabeth Crèche, using Clare's first and second names, then people would naturally assume that there were two people involved in the running of the operation, which might help engender a better sense of trust and comfort to the perspective parents.

Ironically, Clare had never even stepped inside a crèche before she decided to start her own. Her first priority was to undertake a child minding course, which she completed through the Preschool Playgroup Association. Over the first year or so, a small group of about six like-minded crèche owners would meet in the Pembroke Hotel in Dublin. They would swap ideas and share concerns. Clare's involvement at the time, helped ensure that the seeds were sewn for the establishment of the National Children's Nursery Association. Twenty-three years on, it is a highly respected organisation, often approached by the Government when child-related policies are being considered. Although it took over four years before Clare saw any kind of return, she felt certain she had made the right decision. Despite the difficulties in putting food on the table for her kids, throughout the entire period her family stood by her giving support as and when it was required.

One of the first employees to work for Clare was a Montessori teacher named Susan. Clare was fascinated by Susan's teaching methods and the manner in which the kids would respond to them. It was at that point that Clare decided to go to the St Nicholas Montessori Training College to start a teaching diploma. She immersed herself in the teaching methods, making the crèche a complete learning experience for children. The link with Maria Montessori had been well and truly forged. Given the fact that Maria herself had only opened her first London centre some forty years earlier, Clare had a distinct feeling that her teaching methods would now play a crucial role here in Ireland.

Over many years, Clare was aware of children in her care, some of whom she suspected would have difficulties academically in 'big school'. She was not satisfied with the children being given 'labels' – dyslexia, dyspraxia, ADD, ADHD etc – she wanted to find the cause of their difficulties and help them to overcome them. So, with fellow student, Bernie Dwyer, she embarked on a post-graduate course at The Institute for Neuro-Developmental Psychology, (INPP). The course was the result of many years of research and practice by Peter Blyth and later his wife Sally Goodard, and was the answer to Clare's prayers. The results of the specially researched and designed exercises with the children performed each day were amazing. It was a joy to see a child begin to achieve their full personal and academic potential and such a relief to the parents, and in a huge way, to Clare herself.

****

In many ways, the relationship Clare had with her own mother and father while growing up, mirrored that of Maria Montessori and her parents. There were seven of them growing up in the very pleasant surrounds of Dalkey, Co Dublin. Clare describes her upbringing as the *'only child'* in a big family, a feeling familiar to any of us who have ever found ourselves being the middle child. Clare came third - a free spirit! Anselm and Patricia came first and second, followed by Jimmy and Maureen and then Jackie and Roddie. It felt to Clare that everyone else had been neatly paired off, which just seemed to fuel her inquisitiveness and urge to explore the quaint surrounds of Colimore Harbour. They lived on top of a hill, known locally as the 'Green Hill', which peered out over the harbour. The house, called 'Island', afforded splendid views of the Dalkey Islands and the surrounding hinterland. Her childhood consisted of swimming in the harbour, exploring the many hills, roaming in the local parks and climbing the biggest trees she could find with a pal of hers. They even had a *'call'* that they would use to tell the other person that they were there.

Her father Jim, who had grown up in Cork, was *'Edwardian'* in character. A strong disciplinarian, he would summon the children to the bedroom when he wanted to scold or admonish them for some misdemeanour or other. They always knew they were in trouble when the housekeeper would announce rather sheepishly *"Your father wants to see you!"* Despite being particularly strict, their father was a very good provider and good to the family. He ran a successful steel and engineering business. He was also an inventor of sorts, though Clare reckons his inventions might have seen ever greater fortunes had the man been a better delegator, something which Clare observed from a young age, astutely aware of the need to share tasks.

The remarkable get up and go spirit that Clare possesses comes straight from her mother Aine, (born Anny in 1912) who was sent to school at the tender age of three, as she had no kids to play with growing up in the local village of Noville, just outside Kinsale, Co Cork. Her mum had lived her entire life by the Chinese motto *'The journey of a thousand steps begins with the first'*. Indeed, her mum only took up walking in the true sense at the jolly young age of seventy-six, when her first trip abroad with her daughter Clare brought them to Cordoba in Spain. Clare recalls an incident which occurred on a famous bridge as they were crossing a local river bank on their second day in Spain. She said *"Mum, it's not a good area. Maybe we should turn back."* No sooner were her words out than a young guy ran past them both, grabbing Aine's bag and dragging her behind him as he tried to escape. It was her mum's first time abroad. He'd taken everything: their passports, all their money, even her mum's cigarettes. When she finally caught up with her mum, she discovered Aine was shaking. Not with tears but rather with laughter, she turned to her daughter and laughing, said *"Oh well Clare, seventy-five years it's taken me to get a passport but only one day to lose it!"* They ended up having to go to the British Consulate in Malaga. Her mum best described the whole experience: *"Look at the new places we are getting to see in the back of a police car to boot!"* After that, the annual trip to Europe became a much anticipated event on the family calendar.

Some ten years later, aged eighty-six, Aine started taking writing classes at Killian's School in Bray. She wrote a story about her school headmaster, who had been shot by the IRA when she was just three years of age. It was subsequently published in a book called *'No Shoes in Summer'*.

For some of us, certain dates and numbers have more significance than others. We try not to be superstitious, of course, but sometimes certain patterns just continue to emerge. In Clare's case, the number '17' would come to have huge significance. She should have been born herself on the 17th (would have been too, for but for a late carry over). Her eldest Niamh was born on the 17[th.] She had been 17 years a house wife when she went into the crèche business. She got engaged to Eric on the 17[th.] And after thirty-three years of marriage, her husband was diagnosed with cancer on the 17th of March. They met at a rugby dance through her brother Anselm. It was ladies' choice and, as Clare put it, she chose well. Six months later, Eric announced it might be a while before they could get married, to which Clare replied *"I'm in no rush, Eric."* They married six years later.

She describes her worst quality as being too hard on herself, particularly where her dyslexia is concerned. She recalls being on her honeymoon and asking Eric en route to Limerick, as they passed Paddy Power's, what a betting office was.

For forty-four years, Clare and Eric enjoyed a wonderful marriage - *"lots of arguments but lots of laughs,"* as Clare puts it. In 2006, Eric went in for an operation on an aneurysm. Doctors discovered when they opened him up that he had pancreatic cancer. He died a week later. *"He may have died at sixty-three but he had lived a hundred years, Ian."* Clare's eyes water a little as she recalls the tremendous influence Eric had had on her life and the way in which he helped to build her character.

Clare reflects on a certain trip to Gambia where they visited a local kindergarten school. It took two hours to cross the sand roads, impossible to figure out which side of the road people drove on as the track was so dirty. When they arrived they found the kids were taking shelter under the bushes. They had literally nothing. *"What can we possibly do to help, Eric?"* she asked. Pencils were simply no good as they didn't even have the paper to write on. They couldn't even get the kids to make playdough, as the flour that would have been needed to make the plasticine substance, would have been eaten. And so began a seven year commitment to build these children a school. Eric and Clare threw themselves passionately into making it happen. They raised considerable funds and the parents of the children in her crèche got right behind it. Clare's neighbour, Al Butler, chipped in through his trade union which had surplus funds to offer. Four years later, with real mahogany school tables to boot, the Gunjur Pre School was founded. Soon afterwards, they managed to finance the college education of a young boy called Yusphar. That same young man now lives in England with a family of his own, thanks to the generosity of one Irish couple who believed that everyone deserved a fair chance in life.

The seeds of Clare's love affair with the great outdoors were undoubtedly sewn over a twenty year period, thanks to weekends spent renting a cottage in the very beautiful Glenmalure in Co. Wicklow. *"Eric loved to shoot and the kids loved it too, despite there being no running water and no electricity."* She remembers coming over the last mountain on the final approach into Glenmalure many times. She likens the whole experience to a giant curtain being drawn and moving into a different universe. Fittingly, Eric is buried in the cemetery at the bottom of the mountain.

After Eric's death, to help fill the gaps, Clare joined a local walking group quaintly known as the *'Knockadosan'*, named after the townland in Rathdrum, Wicklow. She joined in 2006, six months after he had died.

Clare Power never set out to become the oldest Irish person to climb Kilimanjaro any more than she had planned on having to beat cancer four times. She was first diagnosed with cervical cancer in 1990. *"That was fine, Ian,"* she says smiling at me through her blue eyes. *"They just surgically removed it."*

Nine years later she overcame skin cancer on the back of one of her legs. The only thing that remotely bothered her at the time was that she might not be able to hillwalk any longer!

Nine years later again, the idea of climbing Kilimanjaro was mooted. As with many of these bright ideas, the original complement of eight climbers quickly dwindled down to just one. But Clare was not to be defeated. Deciding on the famous Shira route, she would allow herself a total of eight days to conquer the largest free standing mountain in the world. At first she was worried about travelling on her own as a woman, but then she was quickly assured that the eclectic group that awaited her, featured an array of interesting and varied characters.

Having never spent a night in a tent nor climbed higher than Ireland's highest peak, Carrountohill, Kilimanjaro was going to be a serious challenge for this gutsy sixty-five year old lady. Before leaving, she joined a group and spent three nights in a tent on the Wicklow Mountains, which consisted of "....*one very wet, cold, stormy night and two more pleasant ones. It gave me an idea of what to expect, enough to jump at the chance of hiring a mattress when it was offered on arrival in Tanzania's Arusha,*" she recalls. On arrival in Africa, she met her team which consisted of her and eight strangers – four Icelandic females, four others from the UK and Clare. Remarkably, all would reach the summit. Keith, the fittest in the group, struggled badly with vomiting and bouts of diarrhoea. He had tried five years previously and failed, but sheer determination got him there this time.

"*You can do anything so long as it's one step at a time.*" This became Clare's brave mantra as she set out her stall to climb Africa's highest peak. On her journey up the mountain, she met a boy called Edward from the Maasai Tribe. He was working as a cameraman for Thomson's Travel Company. Clare asked him about his tribal markings. He told her that at the age of three years, the branding wire was put in the fire and his face was marked. "*I am proud of my markings,*" he told her. "*Everyone knows that I am from the Maasai Tribe.*" He studied in Kenya for three years to become a cameraman. The greeting *'Jambo'*, meaning *'Hello'*, became very familiar to them all as they walked. *'A Coona Ma Ta Ta'* (*'There is no problem'*), a phrase used by the guides, was a regular source of comfort; the perfect answer, Clare felt, to all their little anxieties.

She recalls her long, drawn-out summit night suffering with the effects of the altitude, as she tried desperately to reach Stella Point, knowing that if she could get that far, she could crawl the rest of the way onto the summit which was just one more lateral hour of walking away from that point.

"*My main memories of our nine hour trip to the summit included my water freezing because it was in the front pocket of my backpack. I was without water until I reached Stella Point, not a good situation, slowly taking a few steps for each of my Mum's ninety-five years. I thought about all the stories of her childhood and youth.*"

In the end, Clare prayed to the angels to tie sticks to her legs to give her strength to complete her epic journey; *"I actually felt them tying them on."* She recounts those last few steps with such clarity. *"It's as if we're right back there on the mountain."*

Although Clare doesn't cite summiting as the most amazing moment in her life, she remains extremely proud, if not a little modest, of her outstanding achievement. When she finally came down from *'Kili'* in September 2008, Clare felt extremely lethargic. She sensed her iron levels were low. By November she was constantly surrounded by that *'drank too much wine'* feeling. So finally, she conceded and visited her local GP, Rita Doyle. Her iron levels were down to a frightening 2! Her doctor was naturally concerned. *"Clare,"* she said *"I think you're bleeding on account of the iron loss and I'm sending you for a colonoscopy."* The bright pictures made stark reading. Not only were her iron levels low but she had bowel cancer and it was travelling to her liver.

As I join Clare in her living room, she's just taken a chemotherapy tablet. She takes Xeloda, in the form of pink tablets, six times a day - three in the morning and three in the evening. She chooses the tablets over the weekly intravenous treatment instead. *"I think of it as pregnancy,"* she says smiling at me again with those piercing blue eyes. *"...you just get sore feet, a little tiredness but thankfully, in my case, no nausea. At least not yet. I haven't lost any weight either,"* she says with a wink. As we chat a little more, I discover that she's just over half way through the fifth of eight cycles. Her symptoms, she feels, are improving. *"I'm back swimming,"* she tells the nurse. *"Just doing little hills I promise, not climbing the big mountains."*

Perhaps it's just as well the nurse can't hear the plans for her next adventure - off to the French side of the Pyrenees. She gets the map out to show me. *"There's so much to do still, Ian."* Her eyes light up.

"I'll be walking the St James' walk, going from the St Jean Pied de Port to Santiago de Compostela. I'm planning to do the whole lot. What do you think?"

As I walk out the door, smiling inwardly, feeling as if my own silly little woes have all but evaporated, I can't help but wonder if St James himself might be smiling from up above.

10

The Walking Miracle

Seamus Durack

'How long should you try? Until...'

Jim Rohn

The equestrian sport of horse racing is almost as old as time herself....
From the *'Ben Hur'* like chariot races of old Roman times or the contest
of steeds of the God Odin in Norse mythology, the sport had existed, in
many forms, for a very long time indeed. For just how long exactly,
perhaps nobody really knows for sure. What we do know today, is that
the common sobriquet we use for thoroughbred horse racing - the
'Sport of Kings' holds its race-going public spellbound, be they *'prince or
pauper'* alike. Horse racing as a sport, has led to one of the greatest ever
love affairs that this country has ever witnessed and has managed to
hold many of us captive for decades.

Just when that love affair actually began, is a wholly subjective thing.
Growing up as a child, my father who wasn't particularly sporty himself
(though he encouraged me to play all sports), was passionate about his
horse racing. Although I could never claim to know a great deal about
'form' and such like, as a child, nevertheless, I was mesmerized simply
standing in places like Leopardstown Race Course, wholly enthralled,
watching these magnificent athletic specimens go by in the ring: these
fascinating creatures, which each had its own special relationship with
the rider on its back, as it paraded politely for an appreciative public.
Sometimes you could almost *'sense'* who was going to win the ensuing
race just by paying careful attention to which horse seemed most
comfortable with both its surroundings and the person on its back.

Ireland's rich history of horse racing is well documented; from the
very popular Point-to-Point which has its origins here – (a form of

amateur horse racing over fences for hunting horses), to the National Hunt scene, to flat racing. As to which form of racing we prefer, jumps or flats, is perhaps a matter of divided opinion. But there can be no question that our love of jumps is best exemplified by the sheer numbers who travel every year to the highlight of the National Hunt Calendar across the water – the *'Olympics'* of jump racing, *'The Cheltenham Festival'*. More often than not, Irish owned or bred horses have dominated the event in recent times.

As we all know, this country enjoys a thriving thoroughbred breeding industry, stimulated in fairness by favourable tax treatment. The world's largest thoroughbred stud, Coolmore, was established in Fethard, Co Tipperary in 1975. It was first inherited by a retired *'Battle of Britain'* pilot, Tim Vigors, in 1968, who went initially into partnership with the leading trainer, the late great Vincent O' Brien and Robert Sangster, the 'Vernons Pools' magnate. Eventually, he later sold his shares to Vincent O' Brien and his son-in-law John Magnier who would, of course, eventually take over the ownership outright.

Among our many great current crop of trainers stands John Oxx from Kildare, who trained the magnificent colt, *'Sea the Stars'* to victory in October of this year in the *'Prix de l'Arc de Triomphe,'* in Paris. Aidan O' Brien, who enjoyed similar success with the horse *'Dylan Thomas'* in 2007, was named Champion Trainer in Britain last year, 2008, for the second time in a row. In the same year, he equalled former Ballydoyle resident Vincent O' Brien's magnificent record of six winners in Royal Ascot.

If horses themselves could possibly be nominated as *'heroes'* in this book, then surely the horse *'Vintage Crop'* would take its rightful place among the greatest of the greatest. Dermot Weld, our third wonder trainer, did something in 1993 that had never been done before, never thought even possible before; he beat the Aussies in their own back yard by winning the *'Melbourne Cup'*, the greatest horse race in the Southern Hemisphere bar none. He did it with *'Vintage Crop'* (foaled in Ireland in 1987). Though he would repeat this success again 9 years later with the horse *'Media Puzzle'*, it was overcoming the impossible odds with this thoroughbred that will earn both the horse and the trainer a special place in racing folklore. Not only did the horse have to travel in excess of 90,000 miles just to race for a distance of 2 miles, not only did Weld have to get the quarantine laws changed in Australia to allow the horse suitable access, but the horse itself had to overcome incredible odds of its own to win, including stomach ulcers. He simply had an indomitable spirit to win. If you travel to the Curragh Racecourse, you will see the statue in his honour and if you're very lucky, you might just catch a glimpse of this legend in the National Stud where he is now happily retired.

As to the greatest ever Irish horse? Now, there's a question that could divide the Irish public as quickly as a discussion about the greatest ever Lions team or closer to home perhaps, the greatest ever hurling team. For me, as a child growing up, the greatest of them all had to be *'Dawn Run'*, the great mare. She won twenty-three races and is the only horse to have ever won the *'Champion Hurdle'* and the *'Gold Cup'* at Cheltenham, where she is commemorated, along with the brilliant *'Arkle'*, with a bronze statue. Trained by the great Paddy Mullins, she famously won the Irish, English and French Champion Hurdles, but sadly was killed racing in France.

What of our great jockeys? There are so many to choose from: Mick Kinane, who at 50, showed his true colours once again in Paris on *'Sea the Stars'*, John Joe O' Neill who we fondly associate with *'Dawn Run'*, Ruby Walsh, Tony McCoy, Johnny Murtagh, Kieran Fallon, the list goes on and on. Jamie Spencer, a top Irish jockey who shared the British Jockey title with Seb Sanders in 2007, was asked recently about the person/jockey who he most admired and would want to be like. Interestingly, the person he chose wasn't on that list of greats above. Instead, he chose a fellow Irish jockey, a father too, like Jamie, a man who has overcome incredible odds to still be in the game; a man often referred to as *'freak'* in the weigh-in rooms by his fellow jockeys and a man the *'Racing Post'* recently dubbed the *'Walking Miracle'*.

****

In England, the jewel in the crown of Haydock's National Hunt season is the *'Bet Fair'* sponsored Chase that takes place every November. It's a prestigious Grade 1 race and last November (2008), the focus was firmly on the brilliant 8-year-old horse *'Kauto Star'* who had previously won the *'Gold Cup'* at Cheltenham and was now bidding for a hat-trick (the *'King George Stakes'* among those three) in the fourth renewal of the *'Bet Fair'* Chase. In fact, there were several brilliant horses racing - among them *'Exotic Dancer'*, the top class chaser who was beaten into second by *'Kauto Star'* in the previous year's *'Gold cup'*. There was also *'Cloudy Lane'*, an excellent jumper who had made stunning progress in the 2007/08 season.

Nobody really expected that Seamus Durack, the *'Doctor's son'* from Clogheen, Co Tipperary, could really win this race. Not that they doubted his talent. No, nobody could question that. Since bursting onto the scene eleven years previously, this likeable Irish jockey had had his moments, his highs and his terrible lows. Most thought his career should, would have been finished in May 2005, after racing at Towcester, when in a horrendous accident he dislocated his hip and broke his right femur. Another jockey, Ollie McPhail, who had fallen independently, but safely at the same hurdle, the third last, picked himself up, dusted himself down and turned to see what had happened to Durack. What he saw made him vomit his guts up. Durack had broken his thigh and pulled the leg clean out of its socket. It was now dragging up behind his back. At first, Durack felt something lying beside him; he thought it must have been the horse and so he tried to move to get up in case it trod on him, only to discover it was, in fact, his leg.

It was Durack's third leg break in four seasons and he was placed on a '*morphine drip*'. He had to undergo further surgery yet again three months later. When he broke his femur he didn't realise how bad it was. Some would say he probably came back eighteen months too early, but he'd been off for fourteen months already, so it was understandable that this young man had thought if he didn't make some sort of effort, he might not come back at all. But it's not just the breaks he had to contend with. He had to somehow find a way to get his body back into sync, get the massive muscle, tendon and nerve damage sorted out. Watching this young man in the paddocks in the intervening years before now, must have been soul-destroying for all concerned, for all who loved and cared about him, his gait more resembling that of an arthritic pensioner than an athlete of immense promise.

In the end, he had six operations on the last injury alone. He had all the excuses in the world to quit but he didn't. He had to cope with the type of pain that most people would have found unbearable to simply walk, let alone, to consider riding top class horses. After his second break, he somehow managed to persuade the doctor that it wasn't broken at all. He drove home that particular evening to Lambourn from Doncaster in the UK, taking the motorway which was longer, but meant he wouldn't have to contend with any roundabouts and so put his foot on the brake, which nearly caused him to pass out with the excruciating pain. No, nobody really thought he could win this race in 2008, except the intensely focused Seamus Durack who had a tendency to switch off rather than worry about things too much, and, of course, '*Snoopy Loopy*', his ever-willing ride.

Seamus' gutsy ride which saw him pull away in the final home straight, gave him a coveted Grade 1 race win, and placed '*Snoopy Loopy*' to the fore in the '*Order of Merit*' series; a gratifying reward for the young man who may have been a long way from Tipperary but refused point

Orla Barry on the road to recovery, pictured with Mick Galway

Pictured on her graduation day 2009, graduating with her
mum and dad

Ma Sheahan Making a presentation to former Taoiseach Jack Lynch
on the occasion of his visit to Mallow to launch the Red Cross
50 year book

Ma Sheahan with the late Fr Mossy Brien C.C. in the grounds of
St Mary's church after the planting of a tree to mark 50 years since the
founding of the Red Cross in Ireland

Emma Farrell pictured with her dad learning to play the accordion

Emma proudly approaching the finishing line of the Dublin City Marathon

Dave and Anne pictured at 'icy point' in Alska beginning a well
earned break together

Daves 3 kids Darren, Paul and Niamh relaxing togther in Portugal on
holiday over the summer 2009

Matt Craughwell

Matt's new boat arrvies proudly onshore the boat that will take him
back across the south atlantic ocean this Christmas

Elaine Bannon pictured with Matt Porter getting their project work underway in the village of Rombo

Elaine Bannon pictured with an elder of the Maasai tribe in Rombo

Dave Campbell salutes the crowd after winning the 1,500 metres Cork City event in 2007

Dave Campbell at home relaxing with his brother Philip and sister Jane

Gary Keegan pictured inside the Olympic stadium before the
Olympics commence

Gary Keegan's two daughters Kellie and Kate

blank to quit on horses or on life. After the race, he stood proudly in the parade ring with trainer, Peter Bowen, the pair having just pulled off one of the biggest upsets in recent Grade 1 history. It's worth remembering that '*Snoopy Loopy*' was 33-1 and 10 years of age. Moreover, as the crowds watched Durack in the paddock, the change was obvious. His movement was now fluid… There was a restored confidence back in his face. How did this tenacious fighter do it? Just how did the dance techniques learned from the programme '*Strictly Come Dancing*', help restore this young man back to prime health and give him back fitness levels that he hadn't enjoyed for almost 10 years.

****

The '*150th Grand National*' in 1997 was famously postponed and the racecourse evacuated, after an IRA bomb threat, just minutes before the race was due to start. The threat led to the evacuation of Aintree and an estimated 20,000 people were stranded in Liverpool, as their cars and coaches were left inside the cordoned-off racecourse. 60,000 people were moved out of the course including the world's media. I believe that BBC Radio Merseyside's Mike Hughes, using a radio microphone, was the only reporter able to still broadcast live from the course, as racegoers were being driven away from the main areas, many of them scrambling over fences. While undoubtedly, most will reflect on the event as one of racing's darker moments, for the intrepid young Seamus Durack, aged 22, it represented a glowing opportunity to light the fuse on what he believed in his heart was the start of a promising career as a jockey.

While everyone else, including his fellow jockeys, were being rushed out of the weighing room, as police began the evacuation, Seamus was busy trying to use the hour or two of uncertainty to seek out the country's top jump jockey's agent, Dave Roberts. Having found him, he begged Roberts to give him a shot promising him he could win the Amateur Championships that year and become the first Irish man in fifteen years to do so. Roberts, whose books were filled with leading lights like Tony McCoy and Norman Williamson, as well as the two previous British Amateur Championship winners Richard Johnston and Robert Thornton, admired the Irish man's guts and tenacity and courage in sticking around Aintree, knowing that he could get into serious trouble if caught. In Robert's eyes, The '*Tipperary Boy*' had earned his shot.

****

Seamus Durack was, in fact, born in Australia. His parents, Tish and Bernard, had returned to Ireland when he was just four years of age, together with his little brother Conor, who was one year younger. His mum and dad had been working (as a doctor and nurse team) firstly in Perth and then in the famous *'outback'* in extremely testing conditions, where they were nestled on the *'Tropic of Capricorn'*, working for a mining company called BHP. Getting home to Ireland was something of an ordeal, to say the least. They left Port Mantle in Australia in a Russian container ship. The waters were so unstable at times, that Tish had to place the two children in a set of Chester drawers to prevent them from becoming constantly seasick.

Tish was from Ballinagare in Co Roscommon and Bernard had grown up in London. When they returned first, they lived in Ballina in Co Mayo, before Bernard took up a GP post in Clogheen, (6 miles outside Cahir), Co Tipperary. As part of his post he would also cover the hinterland of Ballyporeen as a dispensary doctor (there are only two left in the country, in fact). Tish, as nurse, would order and he, as GP, dispensed. They lived initially on Lower Main Street, before building on a site in neighbouring Cooldevane eighteen months later. Back in those days, pre mobile phones, the patients used to come to the house and the husband and wife team found themselves working on a literal 24 hour callout basis.

In May 1995, due to an unfortunate accident, caused by a grinder catching fire to slates on the roof, the house was burned to the ground. When the home was finally reconstructed, Tish decided it should be appropriately called *'Sin Scéal Eile'* (*'That's Another Story'*). The reasons behind the name were explained rather humorously to the President herself, Mary Robinson, who was down to open a local day care centre, which Bernard had been involved in setting up. It was a memorable day for the Durack family, as Niamh, their youngest daughter, gave the President flowers which her grand aunt Cath, had prepared.

Of her eldest, growing up, Tish smiles and considers her response carefully. *"Seamus was stone raving mad!"* By that, I suspect she was referring to his explorative nature, always pushing the bounds of possibility. *"One time when he was about seven, he made his sister Alana, who was about four at the time, drive his police jeep over a sand pit out the back of the house, that had been covered in plastic, just to see if it was possible!"* But Seamus was, in fact, a sensitive, caring soul and always watched out for others. His love of animals and his optimistic nature were apparent from the start. Before their house was rebuilt in Coldevane, and they were renting on the main street from a local, Mitch Collins, Seamus, along with his sisters and brother Conor, were minded by May Burke (she would go on to baby sit these kids on and off for the next twenty-five years). One day, Seamus aged 5, arrived at the house with a chicken's egg and a piece of hay. He placed them both carefully in a bowl. As May recalls, *"the next morning he awoke as if it was Christmas morning, devastated to discover that the egg hadn't, in fact, hatched into a chicken!"* They were good days for the family and May's own two sons, 'Pabby' and Johnny, and Seamus all palled around together.

When he was about seven years of age, something inside Seamus changed. He arrived home one day in floods of tears – a group of lads had bullied him, slagging him off saying he lived in a mansion, that he was the doctor's son, who did he think he was? He told his mum that he didn't want to be different, that he just wanted to be like every other kid. His mother Tish told him that he was, in fact, no different to anyone else and to never *'judge a book by the cover'* where people were concerned. Her words of wisdom stuck and although, by his own admission, he became a little more introverted, *"the cheeky, mischievous side, independent with a bit of a rebellious streak"* developed with time.

Seamus went to the local primary school in Clogheen. At seven, he was Mensa tested and his results indicated clearly that he was extremely bright and alert. He continued to explore ways of doing things differently. *"It was as if he didn't fear any danger. Anything in his mind was possible"*, Tish recalls. One of his most endearing qualities growing up was his humility. *"Seamus came to see everyone as equal. Strangely enough, by the time he was nine, he didn't want to grow anymore!"* Tish reflects; admittance, in fact, that coincided with his own realisation that he wanted to be a jockey. A discovery that was made, having spent summers in the company of his mother's brother, Patrick Bruen, a successful show jumper and horse trainer back home in Roscommon. His uncle encouraged Seamus bit by bit to try some small jumps. His uncle recalls a defining moment when he was about 14. *"He had been riding a pony called 'Shorty', when one day he asked could he ride this particular horse called 'Ledato'. The horse, a gelding, was particularly tall."* His uncle advised him to do push ups and try and build up his muscle. To practise, he would saddle a bale of hay at home. If one of these wasn't available, there was always his sister Alana who was a willing assistant. On her back he'd shout enthusiastically, *"Is my back straight, is it Alana?"*

Back home Seamus applied the rudiments of his trade, at a small training and breaking yard, near his family home in Cooldevane, near Clogheen. His mentor was John Fennehessy, a man with a reputation for having looked after the Gold Cup winner, *'The Thinker'*, when he used to work for trainer, Arthur Stephenson. It would be fair to say that Fennehessy's methods were somewhat unorthodox. Every time, for example, Seamus fell off one of his bucking yearling horses, he would get thrown into the nearby river. Seamus recalls it vividly. "*I was chucked in twice and then for a bit of variation if I did things wrong, my clothes were taken and I'd get chased around the yard without a stitch – tough loving you might say!*"

Although he lived to ride, he thrived academically in school. He attended the famous Rockwell College in Tipperary and played football for the local Fr Sheehy's Club where he won an Under 14 county title. "*One of my proudest moments when I was younger,*" he tells me proudly. In addition, he picked up plenty of tips along the way from other local trainers including '*Mouse Morris*' and Michael Burns in nearby Coolpucca, between Cahir and Clonmel. He would get up faithfully on every possible morning at 3am and his mum, Tish, would kindly drive him to get in his rides before going to school. One of the great highlights of his young life was to meet John Joe O' Neill and Lester Piggott at a race meeting in Limerick Junction. A picture of his autograph signing ended up in the local '*Tipperary Star*' Newspaper. His mother asked John Joe what she could do to stop him riding, to which he replied "*The fact that you're driving him to practise on the horse in the first place, means you're simply driving him further down the line*"… Tish knew as much in her heart – her son was destined to be a jockey.

Seamus got 600 points in the Leaving Certificate. He could have done most anything he wanted. "*Most of all I wanted to keep mum happy, so I went to the University of Limerick to take a degree in Equine Science.*" His tireless routine of early morning rises continued throughout the year before starting college. Despite coming top of his year, Seamus Durack couldn't put off doing what, in his heart, he felt was the right thing to do – become a jockey.

His first competitive rides would come in the Point-to-Point meetings in Roscommon. His first ever winner was on a horse called '*Killer Lady*', which he rode for a local Tipperary trainer originally from the UK, now living in Fethard, Co Tipperary, Cliff Wilkinson. Other trainers who helped Seamus, in those early days, included Tom Hannon and Michael Byrne. On one rather forgettable afternoon, one of his rides, the aptly named '*Risky Galore*', decided to whip its bony head back in the direction of its unsuspecting rider's face, resulting in the loss of all of Seamus' front teeth. Three weeks later, the same horse unsaddled him leaving him with a broken collar bone. Despite just having three winners to his credit, he knew in his heart the time had come already to try his luck in the UK. "*I felt there were more opportunities for me to get a break and besides which, the minimum weight in Ireland, taking into account the 7lb claim, was 9 stone. In the UK, at least, it was 9 stone 7lbs.*" And so it was, despite the initial heartbreak it caused his mother, this shy, but fiercely determined 9 stone 6lbs, '*jockey in waiting*', with the sky blue eyes, stuffed his battered suitcase and carried his two pockets filled with dreams across the Irish Sea in pursuit of the elusive, holy racing grail.

Before he could even ride a horse, he had to first pick up his mucking shovel, get stuck in and earn his keep which he duly did at trainer Philip Hobb's Somerset yard. Like everything else this young man did, it was no fluke that he arrived as a stable hand in Hobb's back yard. He had been studying trainers and their statistics before leaving home. The Somerset trainer had figured highly in the Clogheen man's calculations. Two years later, he got his break and grabbed it with both hands, riding his first winner on British soil at Newtown Abbott on a particularly determined horse called '*Orswell Lad*'. As one of his early mentors, Dai Williams said of him, "*Seamus can go all the way because he has an eye for a fence and horses jump well for him*". And so it had begun. Seamus Durack was on his way. Over the next season, he would go on to dominate the amateur scene. In 1998, he won the British amateur championships outright with a total of 41 winners, (just 2 more than his closest rival) including the memorable highlight of winning at Cheltenham, in the '*Kim Muir Chase*' aboard the brilliant '*In Truth*'. He was the first Irish winner in fifteen years. In June of that year, he turned professional and began his entry in dreamlike fashion, just missing out in that 1998/99 season by the narrowest of margins, to another jockey Joe Tizzard, in his bid to win the Conditional Jockey title. Seamus' star was rising and it was looking so promising... He was due to take over as Sir Robert Ogden's retained jockey, when Richard Dunwoody was preferred at the last minute. It wasn't in Durack's personality to moan or complain. Besides, Dunwoody was his racing idol.

He simply moved to ride for another trainer, Sue Smith, and was well on his way to the summit when in September at a race meet in Worcester, he broke his right leg. "*Everything just seemed to stop. I had a plate fitted,*" he said smiling at me. I sensed there was more bad news coming. "*It never healed properly if the truth be told, and remained weak.*" Worse was to follow for Seamus. In March 2002, he broke it again and then in 2005 he suffered the horrendous dislocation at Towcester in a comeback season which had seen him bag 55 winners at the time, his second ever best tally. '*With all the injuries,*" he reflects, "*you start to compensate. You end up being lame as a duck because you are not using yourself properly. I couldn't get on a horse without hurting and I was always getting my tendons snagging on parts of my bone. It used to be horrendous and very, very sore. Sciatica used to go down my legs."*

Perhaps it was the considerable knowledge he had picked up at University or perhaps it was his insatiable appetite for answers that led him to buy dozens of books on human anatomy and physiology, or maybe, just maybe, it was seeing BBC broadcaster John Sergeant's success on *'Strictly Come Dancing'* that finally lit the spark. Whatever it was, something made this young man go back to the drawing board, pick up the pieces and hone his will to put himself back together physically and mentally. Perhaps Seamus is just one of those guys who gets hit so hard and just comes back stronger and stronger, perhaps.

****

Ironically, when we meet in October of this year, he's recovering from yet another fall. It's the pelvis this time. *"I'll be back next week, just badly bruised,"* he tells me nonchantly - the voice of a man who's seen more brutal pain than Rambo. He's a dad now. *"What a feeling,"* he tells me, his blue eyes lighting up at the very mention of his beautiful daughter Caitriona. *"She's changed me inside. They've both changed me!"* he says laughing, careful not to forget his partner Sam. ''Will you quit, Seamus?" I ask him. He looks at me across the small table of the Arrivals lounge in Heathrow. *"Will you?"* he asks. I'd been stumped. There I was, about to turn 40 soon, with lofty and rather grandiose plans to try and break Eamonn Coughlan's world record for the over 40s in the 4 minute mile… Who the hell was I to ask this man such questions?

The word *'quitting'* simply isn't in this man's vocabulary and I knew as much. Smiling back at him I ask him instead, *"So what victory or what race, if any, might help make you feel like you've done enough to turn your hand to something else in the horse world then?"* He stops to ponder the question. *"I'm thinking perhaps Gold Cup? The Grand National would be nice."* If he stays healthy, which he is, (pelvis notwithstanding) this man will one day win the National, mark my words. Before we go, I ask him to show me his rather agile right thumb (the legacy of another dislocation). Seamus stands up to politely excuse himself. He's got a physio appointment in London.

There's no time left to ask him about the horses he buys and then rides, on behalf of certain players on the Welsh Rugby team. I believe he had a winner earlier this year at 33-1. Amazing. As he leaves, I simply raise my hand to salute this wonderful gentleman, the one they dub the *'Walking Miracle'.*

11

From the Heart

Alex Maguire

'When we argue for our limitations, we get to keep them in the end.'

Peter Mc Williams

We underestimate the power of language. We always have. As respected US social psychologist Michelle Toomey puts it: *"Words can inform our mind, caress and comfort our feelings, excite and thrill our spirit, or warm and kindle the flame of our hearts."*

But the converse is equally true, right? How often have you felt slapped in the face; punched hard in the stomach; had your nerves rattled to the core or felt your self- confidence evaporate slowly because of the power of words? Granted, the analogies that Toomey and others in the field offer, are purely metaphorical. Nonetheless, the metaphors still convey the strong and intense physical reactions we can have to words and, more importantly, the manner in which we say things. In short, they capture the true power of language.

Unquestionably, words can move and affect us as powerfully as any physical actions. Anyone who has ever been bullied in a relationship, more often than not, will have been bullied first through the power of words. Throughout history, man has been inspired and brought to action by those with the gift to orate profoundly. Sometimes those gifts are used for good, as in the case of the great motivational leaders of our time, from JFK to Martin Luther King. On other occasions, words can have devastating consequences. For example, just how did a being as physically unthreatening as Hitler become so alarmingly powerful by merely opening his mouth? Fast forward almost seventy years and along comes an African-American who shakes many of us to the core with his choice of words.

Granted, these words may have been offered by a speech writer barely out of nappies.

But the manner in which Obama used those words during the run up to the US Presidential election, created an effect which rippled throughout the US and, indeed, the entire globe. Even here in Ireland, we got in on the act, adopting certain slogans and phrases in the worlds of advertising and marketing.

Experts such as Toomey argue that we still fail to recognise and legitimise the great power of words. We must personally interpret language as best we can with the tools we have adopted and learned. Words and terms that we don't understand often frighten us and can create powerful images in our minds. For example, a word such as *'cancer'* conjures up stark images. We may not fully understand the term *'cancer'* but we have a very definite image in our minds of what we think the term means; an all-pervasive and powerful entity eating away at our very core, for example.

Other words, because they become *'colloquialised'* and assimilated into everyday usage, can sometimes lose their impact. An example would be a word such as *'depression'*. Because we are so used to hearing the word in a casual, everyday setting, we may fail to understand its impact and levity in a clinical setting. Of course, certain terms, through perhaps sheer ignorance or a simple lack of understanding, can cause some of us offence and a certain sense of unease…

Take the term *'life coaching'*. It is probably one of the most misunderstood terms you could encounter in Ireland today. For many, the very idea that their life needs coaching is wholly offensive. The very mention of the words *'life coaching'* generate an automatic disinterest, even disdain. For others, it's seen as yet another *'Americanization'* of Irish life to endure. For some, it's neatly filed away under that perplexing term *'Self Help'*; a section of the book shop that makes one shudder as you scurry past, frantically trying to find something that might encourage young Johnny to put down his Xbox and read this Christmas.

Perhaps unsurprisingly, when corporate leaders are informed about a process that can help workers unlock their potential beyond the 30% they are most likely operating at now; a process which can empower their staff professionally and powerfully; a process which can help to accelerate their own personal goals and Key Performance Indicators; a process which enhances their abilities to relate to customers and each other; the penny suddenly drops and the MD thinks:

"Okay, I don't really care if it originated in the States. Just give me a strategy that

works!" And so the journey begins. The Life and Executive Coach gets busy doing what he or she does best: empowering people!

****

Alison hated being late. Perhaps it was a throwback to corporate life. Five years operating as a sales trainer had instilled in her a sense of discipline and respect for people. Perhaps it was even more basic than that. Growing up and having to compete in a busy comprehensive school just outside of London, had given her an early appreciation for timeliness and making the most of the time we have. As she parked her car and began the five minute walk to the training room, she smiled, allowing herself a generous smile as she thought about her impending motherhood: her third child.

"Be still, little one," she told the baby rolling inside her. *"We need to stay on our feet for this one."*

Tonight Alison had to present a talk to her class in the Business Coaching Diploma, on Deepak Chopra's book, *'The Seven Spiritual Laws of Success'*. No mean task. Even for a mother and career woman like Alison.

The problem as she saw it would be trying to give everyday meaning to said laws. *"Got to try and make this stuff relevant,"* she thought. Alison had been coaching people long before she had decided to take on a formal qualification and go on to teach a diploma course herself. She liked the idea that, as a coach, she too grew in the relationship process. She also liked the notion of becoming a better listener, something which all coaches are forced to do, to actively listen. In Alison's case, having a pretty low threshold for boredom in the first instance, she found that the process of teaching others to be more in touch with their own listening skills on the Diploma course was helping her to become a more tolerant and less judgmental person. Apart from the parking and easy access that the small hotel just outside of Wexford afforded her, she also liked the people on the course; a small diverse group that had come together for a plethora of different reasons. She knew that the course had already touched their hearts, and today – if she could find the courage to deliver this the way she hoped – she could show them a new way to understand life's trials.

Some of the spiritual laws made obvious sense. The *'Law of Least Effort'*, for example, teaches us not to swim upstream, to accept others as we find them and to take responsibility for our own actions. It teaches us that we don't always have to cling desperately and to defend our own point of view. *"Right I can start there,"* she mused. Perhaps what was really troubling Alison was the idea that in order to make these laws come to life, in order for her to put everyday perspective into their application, she'd have to share a little of her own life, of her own experiences. That would mean having to open up and share the story of the greatest hero in her life past or present, her husband Alex. She couldn't begin thinking about Alex without going back to the start, replaying the moment that they first shook hands as trainer and trainee all those years ago in the company where Alex had just started work. She sensed immediately that he was different and going to be special to her, and apparently so did he: the flirting began that day and has never quite ended…

One of the vows they made to one another in those heady first few weeks after Alex came bottom of her class, (well, he may have been cute, but no preferential treatment was in order!) was that together they would rewrite the rules, and it still stood. Even after their first child was born, less than a year later, and they were married and, to all intent and purposes, settling down, they never gave up dreaming. They strove to open their business together, buy the house they had dreamed of, and have another baby, and still they talked of the life in France they wanted and pursuits they would take on when they had more time. Alison realised as she walked through the door of the training room that all along it had been Alex's attitude which had kept them going. He saw his goal and he went for it, and through the sheer force of his will, he made things happen. This was what she'd always hoped for in a mate: someone who could keep the vision in amongst the 'nitty gritty' of everyday life; someone who could inspire action even when life seemed to rain on your parade. After all, as Chopra might have put it himself, the 'Law of Karma' teaches us that every action generates a force of energy that returns to us in like kind…

****

Alison cleared her throat. Looking around the classroom, she took a deep breath and began…

"Imagine, for a moment, that in about fifteen minutes, your entire life is turned upside down, and you discover that you've lost everything you had worked so hard for. Imagine, then, amid the chaos of that moment, that you realise that life for you changes irrevocably from this second; your way of life, your home and everything in it gone. Now imagine a voice, like a mantra, or a prayer, playing over and over in your mind: we're so lucky, we're so lucky. Does that seem possible?

So now imagine that at that precise moment, you know for sure that everything is lost, you turn to find the most powerful person you know, a person you love and cherish above all else in the world, standing shoulder to shoulder with you, alongside the children you have made together. Now how possible does it seem to find yourself thanking your lucky stars? I've been inside that moment, and I recall it with the perfection of a newly developed photograph. Yes, the sense of devastation and loss shook me to the core, but I also recall thinking: "My God, we are so lucky. That was so close."

It was Halloween night, 2007, and we'd been to Wexford to see the fireworks, four-year-old Max dressed as an impressive Spiderman, two-year-old Toby resplendent in green tights and a furry dragon outfit. We'd taken along a flask of hot chocolate, toffee apples and sweets to keep the children going – oh, and me as well, as I was six months pregnant with our third child. Alex had always complained about Halloween and this evening was no different, grumbling all the way there that the whole thing put him on edge and brought out the worst in people. We chided him into submission between us though, and in the end I think even he enjoyed the fireworks.

I guess we'd come home about nine or ten in the evening, and without even undressing the sleepy boys properly, we plopped them straight into bed. Downstairs, I realised I was too tired to really do much else. Our dog, Poppy, was bugging me. Her nerves were on edge, from the fireworks I thought, and she was doing what she always did when she felt unsure: sitting on me. With a six month baby bump, this was just plain uncomfortable, so I shoved her off and went to bed, leaving Alex downstairs for a while in front of the TV.

What I didn't know, as I was sleeping soundly upstairs, was that Alex had switched off everything downstairs, as was his routine, put Poppy to her bed in the utility room and had then gone back to the living room to sleep there. This was rare, but he'd developed a tickly cough over the evening and didn't want to disturb me, so had decided to sleep on the couch. I had no idea.

The next thing I knew, some time in the middle of the night, I was dragged abruptly into wakefulness by the sound of Alex storming up the stairs screaming: 'Get out of the house! Get out of the house!' I'll never forget the sound of terror in his voice. I was awake in a moment and leapt from the bed, instinctively grabbing my phone from the bedside table, my initial thought being that there was an intruder in the house. My thoughts of nothing else, I raced across the landing to the children's rooms. Alex had Toby in his arms and was already running down the stairs, yelling at us to hurry. I grabbed a panic-stricken Max from the top stair, oblivious to the strength it takes to lift a lanky four-year-old child with a huge bump in front of me and I followed soon after, trying in my sleep-fuddled mind to grasp the reality of the situation.

So what the hell was going on? Here's what Alex had woken up to, alone in the downstairs of our house.

Some time around half past two that morning, the blackest part of an early winter's night, he had been woken by a sound that had him on his feet in a split second. There was a strange stomping noise coming from somewhere in the house, like someone walking around with boots on upstairs. As he opened the door from the living room, *he heard Poppy from the utility room, half barking half whimpering: it didn't sound like her and it was unusual for her to be up in the night, and he didn't like it one bit. He went half way up the stairs, the stomping sound still seeming to be around him, over him and under him all at once. Backing down the stairs once more, he looked in the hot press in the hall, and behind the utility room. There it was: a buckling, metallic sound, and now a smell as well, chemical, choking… Half realising what this was, half hoping he was possibly wrong; he sped to the kitchen, looking quickly at the door closed onto the utility room. He couldn't hear Poppy any more, only that grinding, banging. He opened the door, for one instant only, seeing with horror a blast and huge billow of black smoke: the heat was incredible.*

Poppy was nowhere to be seen. Going in was impossible. Slamming the door was the only thing he could do, his thoughts turning instantly to getting his sleeping family out of there as quickly as he could. Shutting the kitchen door between him and the fire, he raced up the stairs, yelling to get his family on their feet.

There we were, in the hallway by the front door, a child each, Alex telling me there was a fire in the utility room, and we had to get into the living room to be safe. He quickly explained that there were no keys to be found; they were probably thrown carelessly on the side in the kitchen, so at our safe, friendly front door, right by us, there was now an enemy, firmly blocking our escape. "We'd be able to get out of the patio doors," Alex said. My mind fought against the reality that was closing in around me, and suddenly three things happened all at once: the smoke alarm in the downstairs hallway finally triggered, it's high-pitched wail stoking the panic up a notch. Alex grabbed me by the shoulder and pulled me into the living room, and just before I moved under his pull, I turned and saw what I can only describe as the most evil thing I've ever seen. A billow of ugly black smoke curled around the corner of the hallway towards where I stood, clutching Max. The same instant I saw it, I felt it catch in the back of my throat, stealing my breath in a stinging retch. Alex thrust me into the room and slammed the door. The electrics blew, thrusting us further into darkness and panic. We were trapped. Earlier that night, when one of us had let Poppy into the garden for her last run out, we'd locked the patio doors, taken out the key and put it in the kitchen somewhere. The larger windows out of the room were also locked.

In a thought process that far outstripped my own in that panic, Alex grabbed the likeliest thing he could find: a piece of old bog oak that a friend had bought us for a wedding present – could I ever thank her enough? In one shot of superhuman strength he put the piece of wood straight through the toughened glass of the door, shattering it into a million tiny pieces.

Ask Max what he remembers of the fire, even now, and he'll tell you: "Daddy smashed a window, and smashing windows is bold, but sometimes when you have a fire you're allowed to, so that you can get out of the house."

Alex spread the quilt he'd had over him as he slept on the sofa, over the worst of the glass, and we ran over the rest of it in our bear feet, carrying the children to safety.

And then, there we were. I'd had the emergency services on the phone, and the fire brigade was on its way. Carnew has a voluntary service, and those guys were amazing. While we waited, we stood on the back lawn of our garden, shivering from cold and fright, fully expecting to see our house burn to the ground completely. We felt for the entire world like the luckiest people alive. There was Max, in his vest and pants, Toby slightly better dressed in green tights, the baby inside me not even turning in her sleep; and Alex and I, bare feet cut by the glass and otherwise unscathed entirely, all of us, except Poppy. She was our only loss, and we felt it keenly from the first, each having to stop the other from going back in to find her. We were lucky to be alive, lucky to have got out of there, lucky that none of us had any smoke inhalation at all. It felt like a miracle.

This feeling became like Alex's motto over the next few days and weeks. "We are the luckiest people in unlucky circumstances," he used to say. Even three days later when Toby, our smallest son, was attacked by the dog belonging to the neighbours, who had taken us in after the fire, Alex's sense of finding the positive in amongst all the ruin was unshakeable. Poor Toby didn't have to have any stitches, thank goodness, and he suffered no infection as a result. Alex kept us firmly focused on the good, while all I felt like doing was cracking up.

This was what made Alex our hero, and no doubt about it. Over the days that followed, we talked about what had happened together. We cried and we even joked about it.

I would ask Alex for some small favour – a cup of tea, or a sandwich – and he would say: "I just saved your life, isn't that enough?" My reply would be: "Well, that was last week!" Somehow we found it funny at times.

Yes, Alex had pulled us out of a fire, completely unscathed, but it was the heroism of his attitude that really pulled us through the worst of it. We didn't realise the hardest times were yet to come. We were a family displaced, which is a strange sensation. We called several places 'home' over that time, without even a hint of irony either – it was simply whichever place we laid our heads as a family at the end of the day. Alex kept us real, kept us laughing, kept the routine going, and above all kept reminding us how lucky we were to be there, altogether. Over the coming weeks, Alex worked tirelessly to rebuild our lives, single-handedly keeping the business we had run from home going, as much as he could, project managing the rebuild of the house, and replacing everything from clothes and bedding to toys and books for the children. Even after we moved back into the house and our third baby was born, Alex went back to work fulltime to support us, kissing goodbye to the life we'd made for ourselves. And he never complained.

To this day, it's the strangeness of the experiences we had in those days after the fire which strikes me: going shopping for shoes with no shoes on; giving the children the run of the toyshop to replace some of what they'd lost, and seeing the utter exhilaration on their faces; burying Poppy, who was as blond and unsmudged as the last time I ever saw her; finding routine in the oddest places. It makes you think.

So what has all this to do with Seven Spiritual Laws? Well, I don't know. Like anyone else, I guess I'm still trying to unravel the depth of the implications that try to offer us a way to regard this life of chaos, meaninglessness and meaning, loss, love, relationships and connections.

Between Alex and me, we have a theory that the moment in life where you go: 'Oh, I get it!' well, that's the moment when you're plucked off to go on to the next life, whatever that may be. Or this life just throws you another curve-ball to make sense of.

What I do know is this: sometimes all we can do is look back and apply these laws in retrospect. Even from the first day after the fire, looking over the garden wall at the charred remains of our kitchen laid out on the lawn, we knew the only way to stay sane was to find a purpose; a lesson in all this mess. In my thoughts, there are two sides to this. The one side encapsulates the first five laws; the second one is really described by the final two. Here's how it goes:

The 'Law of Pure Potentiality.' What is 'Pure Potentiality' but a blank canvas? What better example of a blank canvas than losing it all and starting again? Even amid all the confusion and grief we felt during that time, Alex kept on trying to get us all to see the excitement of recreating and rebuilding our lives from scratch, and raising a home for us again from the ashes. Alex, quite simply, had a vision. A vision of us returning to our home, before the new baby was born, and being content once more. This vision kept us all going: it was pure potentiality until it was realised.

'The Law of Giving and Receiving.' This law is really about giving and receiving, because one can't exist without the other. Humanity - and friendship, being the greatest expression of our humanity - hinges on this one law. You know it yourself. How many times have you heard that a relationship is give and take? That you have to take the rough with the smooth? Well, that's giving and receiving, and allowing yourself to receive is part of this law. We remain amazed and humbled by the response of the people around us during that time. Friends, family and neighbours all gave us their time, their support, and whatever was to hand in the way of clothing, bed linen, and whatever else we needed to keep us going day to day. The staff at the Amber Springs hotel, their compassion and generosity, keeps us going back there even to this day. As people, our natural disposition is to give. By receiving, we were also obeying this law, building ourselves back to be able to give once more, to someone else. Round and around.

'The Law of Karma or Cause and Effect.' This one is simple for me. It's about accepting responsibility without verging toward blame. It would have been so easy for us to berate ourselves for not having more smoke alarms (just one, in the utility room,

would have saved Poppy and the worst of the damage) or not keeping the keys somewhere a bit handier. But we didn't dwell on this too much. Chopra asks us to ask ourselves: "What can I learn from this experience?" Then, it becomes simple: we learned to appreciate one another in a way that's changed us forever. And to put in more smoke alarms!

'The Law of Least Effort.' Well, this hardly describes the time we had after the fire, and Alex will laugh when he reads this. The work he put in during that time was hardly what you'd call 'least effort!' But looking at it another way that comes with distance and time and another perspective, it becomes a little clearer. Chopra says that "All problems contain the seeds of opportunity" and this is so true. Just off the top of my head, some things I am grateful for which could only have happened as a result of that night: friendships and people we met; a new determination to live out our dreams to the full; seeing the birth of our third baby as the miracle it truly was; writing this now, here, for you; having a really nice kitchen! Just seeing it all differently, makes the effort fade and the opportunity becomes the purpose.

'The Law of Intention and Desire.' I talked already about Alex's vision for us to return to our home and resume our life together. That, to me, is what this law is all about. I only have to look around the room I sit in now, the same sitting room we smashed our way out of that night, to see once more how one person's intention and desire, once realised, is a reality just waiting to happen.

I said that there were two elements to what I felt was the purpose or the lesson in this experience. The first one is what we take away as a family, Alex and I; what we felt, what we learnt. This next part, this is for us also, but for anyone else who wants to take it away too. This is for you.

'The Law of Detachment.' You'd have to read this yourself to get the real meaning, but underneath lies a sense that in holding onto security in our lives with all we have, we distract ourselves from really living. I'm as much in this as the next person, with kids, a mortgage and all the trappings and trimmings, so I'm not about to say to hell with it, give it all away to charity and go and live up a hill for the rest of my life. Really, this is just about knowing that if it came to it, if you lost it all, you'd still have enough strength and sense of yourself to get up and keep going. And you do; we all do. Just know it.

'The Law of Dharma, or Purpose in Life.' This emerged quite soon after the fire. We knew that if we spread the word of what had happened to us, eventually it would ripple out, and someone somewhere would make a choice because of a story they heard about a fire somewhere in south County Wicklow, which might just save them from going through the same thing. If the purpose of us going through that was to stop even one death from a fire, that's enough. So, this law is about looking at what's in your life, and making it bigger than you; making it about all people, everywhere, and making life better overall.

So, buy a lot more smoke alarms than you already have, and always know where your keys are!

I'll end my friends, with a beginning: Deepak Chopra prefaces his book with a quote from The Brihadaranyaka Upanishad, by Swami Krishnananda, which reads:

'You are what your deep driving desire is;

As your deep driving desire is, so is your will;

As your will is so is your deed;

As your deed is so is your destiny.'

To this day, Alex's belief in us, our life, what we do, and above all, me, is an inspiration to me every day. It was a quiet act of heroism I suppose. He didn't change the course of history for a country, or set free a race of people, but what he did do, and what he's done ever since, is give me a shining light to follow. In the darkest hours, when you think you've lost everything, having someone there to make you feel like you can go on, and even make you laugh, is truly to be in the presence of a hero.

Trust me, I know."

****

Alison looked around the hush of the room, looking for signs that her story had been understood. Someone cleared their throat, and another shuffled in their seat. *"Oh God,"* she thought. *"They have no idea why I've just told them all of this."* Then she saw it: someone wiped a tear away, almost imperceptibly, and another blew out a breath. Slowly the spell lifted and each of the people in the room looked at one another. Small smiles and looks were exchanged and eventually they all turned their gazes back towards Alison. Some nodded, others offered a smile, and Alison smiled back. Then she grinned. She knew she'd got there. She'd made it real.

12

Walking Back to Happiness

Emma Farrell

'You gain strength, courage, and confidence by every experience by which you really stop to look fear in the face. You are able to say to yourself, 'I lived through this horror'. I can take the next thing that comes along.'

Eleanor Roosevelt

The sun had finally come to pay its first visit. It was the second Saturday in May, and summer had arrived with aplomb. The welcome heat from the warm rays re-energised our tired bodies as we entered the Upper Car Park in Glendalough. It was a familiar routine by now; Tabata training on the waterfall steps followed by several intense jaunts up and down Camaderry Hill. The team was starting to bond in earnest. Some sixty odd people of varying fitness levels each with their own very personal motivations, had signed up to climb Kilimanjaro in support of the Irish Red Cross. '*A tough but doable challenge'* was the general consensus and they were enjoying the weekly training sessions in the heart of Wicklow. Through careful planning which went way beyond simply cardio training and took other extrinsic factors into account such as diet and bloods, I was hopeful that we could achieve at least a 90% success rate.

They say Ireland's a different place when the sun shines and as we gathered to do some warm down exercises; I was amazed, as I was every time the weather changed, at just how quickly the car park had begun to fill up. It was barely 10am and already there was a lengthy queue for spaces. As we prepared to huddle in a circle and begin to stretch out, I was greeted by a warm and familiar smile. It was President McAleese. Accompanied by plain clothes members of the special branch who were also enjoying the surroundings, she was out with her husband Martin for a walk. They were regular visitors to Glendalough and came down as often as they could when their busy diaries permitted. *"How's that godson of yours? Climbing any more mountains?"* she kindly enquired. The President had taken a keen interest in Sean climbing Kilimanjaro the previous year at the tender age of ten. She was so good that way, remembering people and their interests. I could feel a huge sense of guilt filling up inside me waiting to burst out. *"He's great, thanks for asking. Enjoying being a regular kid again, I reckon!"* The truth was I hadn't spent any quality time with Sean for some time. I had gotten too caught up in my own little world. Not for the first time I'd skewed my priorities. But as we chatted, I was nevertheless grateful for the fact that Sean had been given the opportunity to be a kid again and do regular stuff like play with his mates and support his favourite soccer team, Arsenal (a team choice I could never sadly influence).

The last time I had seen the President was about six weeks previously at the Gaisce Gold Award ceremony.

As always, President McAleese had thoroughly enjoyed presiding over the achievements of the young people of Ireland. She was a wonderful Ambassador for the Awards because she genuinely cared about the welfare of the youth of Ireland.

Conscious of her time, I asked her finally if she had enjoyed the ceremony. *"As always Ian; what a privilege it is to share in such wonderful achievements,"* she replied modestly. I asked her about one of the participants, in particular, a young lady from Wexford. The President took a moment to reflect. Turning towards the car, she looked straight at me and said *"That, was powerful!"* Like the President, I too was simply blown away by what had ensued in Dublin Castle that Tuesday afternoon.

****

Certain school text books we remember, others we forget. A lot depends I suspect, on the English teacher you are fortunate enough to have to inspire you. Jim Byrne was mine and he inspired me a great deal.

In the wonderful *'Lord Jim'*, Joseph Conrad tells us that it is necessary for a youth to experience events which *'reveal the inner worth of the man; the edge of his temper; the fibre of his stuff; the quality of his resistance; the secret truth of his pretences, not only to himself but others'.*

In my humble opinion, the youth of Ireland, indeed the world, owe an enormous debt of gratitude to one man whose shared vision would empower young people in a way that had never been possible previously nor indeed since. One man whose vision was thankfully adopted in this country in the summer of 1985 and brilliantly championed by two men;

John Murphy and John T Murphy. A vision which thrives today under the very excellent stewardship of Barney Callaghan and a wonderful team of development officers who continue to grow the vision from strength to strength in the form of Gaisce (an old Gaelic word meaning deed of valour or proud moment), The President's Awards. But what of the man whose vision inspired the award's origins? Just how did this person come to make it all possible in the first place and why do the awards matter so much? More importantly still, just how did these awards give one young lady back her faith in herself as a person?

It all began with The Duke of Edinburgh's Award which was founded in 1956 by His Royal Highness, Prince Philip, and The Duke of Edinburgh, to help young people develop a sense of responsibility to themselves and to the wider communities in which they lived. The principle of the Award is one of individual challenge.

But its secret and beauty lies in the simple fact that it offers young people a balanced, non-competitive programme of voluntary activities which encourages personal discovery, growth, self-reliance, perseverance and responsibility. So regardless of background, social standing, relative standing to others, the young person sets the objectives, chooses the goal posts and decides the level of difficulty and input entirely for themselves. They become in real terms, the *'Masters and Commanders'* of their own destinies. The Award currently runs in over 130 countries worldwide, and to date, almost 6 million young people have challenged, changed and empowered themselves by participating in this incredible Award. In Ireland, that includes over 10,000 young people of which 400 have undertaken Gold. But just where exactly did the Prince get his vision from and how did he make it a reality?

The actual Award programme is, in fact, based on the philosophy of Kurt Matthias Robert Martin Hahn, often referred to as an *'eccentric, charismatic educator'*, who was himself born into a cultured Jewish industrialist family in Germany in 1886. Today he is recognised as an inspirational founder and significant contributor to many well-recognised, innovative, experiential social developments, and outdoor education schools and programmes.

Hahn developed many of his ideas, in fact, from the study of Plato. Among other things, he was the founder and headmaster of Gordonstoun School in Scotland, where Prince Philip was a student. At Gordonstoun, Hahn instituted a novel badge system which included Athletics, Swimming and Expeditions on land and at sea. This was later extended to include any boy in the county. Plans to extend this system nationwide were shelved by the outset of the Second World War. However, it was during this period that Hahn set up the first Outward Bound School in Wales. In the UK in the early 1950s, there was growing concern about the problems of youth which were aggravated by the gap between leaving school at 15 and entering National Service at 18. It was against this background that The Duke of Edinburgh's Award was set up in 1956, by HRH Prince Philip, Kurt Hahn and Lord Hunt (leader, in fact, of the first successful ascent of Everest, three years previously). Up to this time, worldwide development had depended almost entirely on resources derived from within the UK.

These arrangements inevitably imposed constraints on the ever expanding UK Programme and whilst consultation with other National Award Authorities took place, the UK remained in a lead role in determining policy and practice. But the time had come, the Prince felt, to share more universally the responsibility for both the promotion of the Award worldwide and the provision of resources to meet that commitment.

Thus in the early 1980s, the first steps were taken towards international partnership which led to the formation of The International Award Association (IAA) in 1988 and the World Fellowship in 1987, to provide a proper financial base. The first International Forum was held in 1982 in Edinburgh, to provide all Award associations with the opportunity to sit together to discuss the Award, its relevance and its future. And so in 1985, Ireland followed suit.

Indeed throughout the 1980s, the Award spread to more and more countries, noticeably outside the Commonwealth and by 1989, nearly 50 countries were now operating the Award on a national basis and there was growing considerable global interest in the Programme, particularly amongst French-speaking countries. *'Mais oui'*, the Duke had left the world with a legacy he could truly be proud of....

****

Emma Farrell felt confident, jittery, almost giddy inside. It was show time. "*Ok, deep breath, just breathe and smile,*" she kept telling herself the line over and over again in her head. The question was, what exactly was it she was about to do?

What was her role exactly? - To tell the audience about the awards? Share a little about herself? Make a simple speech? She chastised herself for overcomplicating it. "*Analysis paralysis*" she said, smiling to herself. As she entered the great hall in Dublin Castle, she felt like she was stepping back in history itself. The magnificent surroundings provided the perfect backdrop for this very prestigious day. She certainly felt excited to be finally receiving her Gold Award and humbled in the extreme to be making one of the keynote recipient speeches. As the select award invitees began to take their places in the audience, her mind began to wander down the path which had led her here today. She just wasn't good at sitting still. Her hands were starting to fidget, probably why she didn't watch too many movies. *'Mindless chewing gum'* was how she would have described so many of the films she had tried to sit and watch. *"What if they don't get my humour?"* She could hear that inner voice being given a little too much volume. Mind you, by her own admission, her humour was certainly quirky. The one film which she had thoroughly enjoyed, *'The Bucket List'*, captured her humour to a tee. In it, the character played by Morgan Freeman Carter who is dying with cancer, is somewhat hesitant about getting a tattoo and Edward, played rather stylishly by Jack Nicholson, who is in the same predicament as Freeman's character, says to him; *"What, are you afraid of not being able to be buried in a Jewish Cemetery?"*

As far as Emma was concerned, without humour we are soulless. Without humour, how could she possibly have come through her own darkest hours?

****

We agree to meet in Waterford close to where she lives, just out beyond the Regional Hospital. Emma Farrell grew up with the loving support of her parents and family, something she is always proud to reflect on. She grew up six miles outside Enniscorthy on one of the highest points outside of the Blackstairs Mountains – Curraghgraigue (debates still rage over the 'h' being included). *"You're always either going up a hill or down a hill."* Her dad's cousin was one of the main strawberry growers in the country and to earn extra pocket money during her summers, she and her buddy Yvonne would put in long and gruelling 12 hour days. *"I hated picking to be honest,"* she freely admits. Back in those days the strawberry picking season ran from May to the end of July. They would pick for up to 12 hours a day with the aim of going home with £5 in their pockets.

When the two girls picked together, they used to share a headphone each, glued to Today FM. Emma was a massive Ray D'Arcy fan and enjoyed the chat and banter throughout his morning show.

Being the youngest of three can have its advantages… Her brother was five years older and still treats her like the baby of the family to this day. He's just gotten involved in the family business, in fact, which specialises in custom furniture, covering everything from hotel desks to customised kitchens.

She recalls her older sister beginning college when Emma was just eight years of age. Her older sister attended college in Cork where she studied European Studies. *"She's very bright. We share the same sense of weird humour and have similar personality types."* These days her sister works in Brussels as a diplomat. She grins at me and says *"Trying to take over the world in a grey suit!"*

"Just working on a coup in Moratemia! I'll be with you soon sis!" The patterns are familiar to Emma each time she goes to visit. *"She's a great sister and a great friend."* Emma even concedes happily that she spoils her on her European trips.

Her father is an avid hurling fan and never misses a match. He came originally from the other side of Enniscorthy – a small townland, in fact, called Finchogue. With both of Emma's parents working, growing up, she spent lots of time with her Gran, who's still incredibly fit at the young age of 88. *"I practically lived there! She's as sharp as ever! It was Gran who insisted I be called Emma."*

She was brought up with a strong work ethic. Her own father left home to go to work in Dublin at the age of 15 and he instilled a sense of valuing things and people in all of his children from an early age. Perhaps that's why she fidgets so much – she can't sit still not even for a moment...

In talking about her parents, she diligently takes her time to describe them both.

"When I decided to walk the Great Wall of China as the final part of my Gaisce award, I asked Dad to come along. I wanted him to be part of what was to be a most incredible experience for me. I was delighted to have him there. Of course, only my dad would look as comfortable leaning against the Great Wall chatting to people as if he was leaning against the wall at home chatting to the neighbours! He's very relaxed, easy going and endearing." Happy to be tagged as Daddy's *'little girl'*, she blossomed under his support. When Emma decided she wanted to take up horse riding, her Dad knew her well enough to know that she was serious. It wasn't long before she was a member of the Irish Pony Club Games team. Their weekends were spent largely together driving endlessly from event to event. They were happy days indeed...

Her mum is a teacher. These days she's a Home School Liaison Co-Ordinator in a large primary school. She's from Screen outside Curracloe (famous to many of us, of course, for its very long, golden, sandy beaches). *"You always know a teacher when you meet one,"* she says laughing out loud. Emma's mum is highly organised and efficient. *"Believes in getting things done!"* Emma recalls when her mum used to teach inside the classroom. *"When mum speaks, she's a gifted communicator and the pupils just get it."* While on her first day in 6th class, she called her *mammy* instead of *teacher*. She describes her parents, in terms of being a couple, as being *"devoted to each other, never pretentious and never too emotional"*.

Undoubtedly many of those childhood memories are best encapsulated spent on warm days, helping out on the farm, occasionally even climbing into leftover plastic manure bags and spinning endlessly around the fields, tied carefully to the back of the trailer - good fun days indeed.

****

In her first year at secondary school, Emma's world was slowly turned upside down. In that first year she got nine Certificates for high achievement. However, the academic success hid the misery she waded through each day. She was bullied continuously. Out of a class of just eight girls, none of whom she knew, she was singled out for having a pony and for not being into GAA. She felt isolated and awkward.

She knew nobody in the school, with the notable exception of her brother, who was in fifth year at the time, but couldn't be seen talking to his kid sister and so he often passed her in the corridors with his eyes pointing down to the ground. In a desperate bid to fit in, she tried to be bold and cheeky to gain some attention. *"I wasn't even good at that,"* she reflects sadly.

When Emma was just eight years of age she was badly hit by a car and the impact of her back hitting the windscreen with such force caused the screen to shatter. *"I remember lying on the ground on the other side of the road listening to someone screaming. It was a while before I realised I was the one screaming."* As her days in school became longer and darker, she stopped remembering. She was becoming dissociated.

Emma escaped as best she could through her horses. To her eternal credit, she won the European Club Championships. *"There were no English competing,"* she points out modestly. The Foot and Mouth had kept them away. She continued with the pony games up until the age of 16.

Her father used to play the accordion and so she began to play the abandoned instrument at the age of 11. Traditional music was always played in the house. She remembers the tapes always being on. *"We'd have the Chieftains or De Dannan on or The Bothy Band."* At 14 (largely inspired by Lisa Simpson) she took up the sax. *"It was a choice between the clarinet and the sax!"* She played with the school band and despite the absence of a strings section, they even got to record a live album from the National Concert Hall and got to tour the States into the bargain. She became pally with one of the girls, Laura, who happened to come from the same local village, through their shared loved of music. But despite her achievements, her sense of self-worth and esteem continued to plummet. Her music and horses couldn't prevent her from despairingly trudging through each day. The dreaded 50 minute bus ride to school, surrounded by some of the girls who were making her life sheer hell and torment, was made all the more unbearable because the old bus driver insisted on staying at his self-imposed driving speed limit of 15 miles an hour. Each and every school morning, for Emma Farrell, time became suspended, teasing and taunting her as the knots in her stomach turned tighter and tighter...

"It's ironic you know. These days" she says, *"people associate me with being this sporty person. Back then I couldn't get picked for one school team!"* In Emma's eyes she was now *'crap'* at school. She began to believe that she was *'crap.'* She began to believe all the other crap that other people were telling her every single day. *"When someone tells you something enough times, you believe it and you become whatever they say you are. Teachers have such a capacity to empower their students, with just a few positive affirmations, no matter how small. Guess that never happened."* The non sporty, friendless, hopeless, helpless girl was the one who stared cruelly at Emma Farrell in the mirror every single morning. She had begun to internalise external reinforcers – she was a loser. By the time she reached 6th year, just before Christmas, the so-called *'Enniscorthy Epidemic'* had tragically begun. The authorities had begun to patrol the Slaney River 24 hours a day, fearful of what they might find. Two of the deaths which had occurred were of kids who Emma had been in school with. *"One guy drowned himself and one shot himself."* It's naturally hard for Emma to describe those memories of sitting on that same school bus looking over at two of the empty spaces across from her, where a girlfriend of one of the lads used to sit beside him. He had taken his own life just the night before.

****

Emma bravely sat her Leaving Cert in hospital. It was 2003 and everything had simply become too much. It wasn't that she was feeling bad – she just wasn't feeling anything. She didn't feel, feel real, feel human, anything... Everything had become so surreal and so detached. Her time in hospital, she felt, was quite a negative experience. *"When you're 18, about as mature as a 15 year old – surrounded by very ill adults, it was very intimidating. This looked like my future."*

In her mind, Emma began to believe that this was what she deserved. Could her class- mates have been right about her all along? She vividly recalls watching many of the people in the hospital in green pyjamas shuffling around, their eyes sunken, and their expressions, to her mind, soulless. *"Souls that had been frosted over to stop them feeling any pain of what they had experienced in the past."* Hers, like so many, was a Catholic school and too many things, Emma felt, had been shovelled under the carpet. Reflecting back, she sums up her time in hospital. *"The whole place was anesthetised. We were all so numb as if the very life had been sucked from our souls."*

In Emma's head, the whole period was just emphasising in her mind how different she felt. The day she came out of hospital, came the clanger... One of her teachers approached her and incredibly announced "*We really weren't surprised you ended up there Emma. I always knew you were different.*"

Despite not being able to finish a number of her papers, she got 335 points but no offers. She had planned to repeat that September and worked in her dad's business during the summer period. She tried to switch schools to the Vocational in Enniscorthy but her mind couldn't focus on the task in hand. Instead, she began working in the local factory Clearstream in Enniscorthy – "*It was something to be able to do while still at home*".

She worked there diligently from 8am till 4pm each day doing the same task every day. "*We made coronary catheters. We had to test the balloons to make sure they wouldn't burst in the water.*" Looking back she says smiling, "*There was a real touch of the Corrie knickers factory about it all!*" She enjoyed the company the work afforded her. For three months it gave her some routine back in her life and provided her with some much needed structure. She decided to leave and go and do a Diploma in Office Skills. "*It was my first time living outside the family home.*" She got her first car, a little green Fiat, known affectionately and simply as '*Punto*'. She received a distinction and for the first time, for as long as she could remember, she felt good about herself. "*I wasn't failing at something. I was meeting new people.*" Her past was finally her own to own. She no longer had to apologise for who she was or what she was about. One day, she was sitting quietly, reading the '*Enniscorthy Echo*' when she noticed a picture of a group of Gaisce Bronze Award holders.

Her eyes were firmly fixed on the copy below. "*It was the chance to prove to myself and to others that I wasn't a failure, and an opportunity to do the things that I'd always dreamed of doing, the things that I knew I could do.*"

To earn Gold you must set and achieve your goals arranged in advance with your Award Leader. There are four distinct areas: community involvement, physical recreation, venture activity and personal skill development. Emma had always wanted to run a marathon. She decided to ignore the common thinking that you shouldn't run a marathon till you're at least 25 and so at the tender age of 22, she set her sights on the Dublin marathon. Her parents came up to support her and watched her as she proudly crossed the line in a modest time of 5 hours. She'd no idea just what she was really capable of at that point, but the fuse had been lit. "*It was the best fun I'd had in ages. I felt euphoric crossing the line. Not bad for a girl who had been given day release from the hospital to do the run in the first place,*" she says, smiling at me. October the 2nd was her chance to show two fingers to those who had questioned her resolve, doubted her commitment. Emma Farrell wasn't as the world was about to discover, a quitter...

She wasn't sure about what to do for her Community Involvement section, other than knowing that she wanted to help a charitable cause, to give something back... The Marianne Finucane show was on in the background one Saturday morning in early February 2006. Her sister was moving flat, helped by her dad who was supplying the furniture, naturally! Dr Tony Bates was on the show talking about setting up a national centre for youth mental health. Compelled by something inside her, she looked up the RTE website later that day for more information. There was a number to call. The next morning she anxiously paced the floor, rehearsing the speech in her mind. Finally she picked up the phone and dialled the number.

She remembers blurting her details out to Debbie Byrne who took her details, thanked her for her time and indicated that she would have Tony call her. Next day, to her sheer disbelief, the phone rang. It was Dr Tony Bates. "*He told me he didn't want my money.*" For Emma it felt thoroughly positive. Dr Bates was simply interested in the contribution that she could make as a person and, in so doing, continue to grow as a person...

That phone call would change Emma Farrell's world forever and she became '*Headstrong's*' first ever youth adviser. In '*Headstrong*', which was being set up in response to a clearly identified need to better support the mental health and wellbeing of those between the ages of 12 and 25 in this country, she learned to become strong and was reminded that she was strong, and so she now believed, finally, that she was indeed stronger than she had ever imagined.

Interestingly '*Headstrong*' through Dr Tony Bates' vision of empowerment, sees mental health as being much more than the simple absence of perceived mental illness, but rather sees mental health as being along a continuum spanning from general wellbeing to distress to mental health disorders that require specialised care. As with the World Health Organisation, '*Headstrong*' emphasised the importance of understanding mental health issues in the broader context of a younger person's environment, their family, their friends and wider community. Key to Emma being able to be involved, was the *modus operandi* of including young people in all aspects of its growth and development, from its initial inception through to engaging with local communities. As Dr Tony Bates stresses, "*Without youth participation we cannot effectively shape service planning and development*". Rather than working directly with young people *per se*, the non profit NGO acts as an expert partner with those who do such work as the Health Service Executive and others concerned with providing mental health and well-being supports to young people in this country.

Before joining '*Headstrong*', it would be fair to say that Emma was carrying varying degrees of weight; both physical and mental which were getting her down enormously. *"I just wasn't comfortable in any aspect of myself. I had to learn to take back ownership of my own thoughts and feelings. Now that I have, I'll never give them away again!"*

****

"Just breathe, Emma. That's it, deep breaths..." Her Gold Award acceptance speech was going remarkably well... *"In conclusion, the difference, Ladies and Gentlemen..."*. Her attentive audience were completely silent. You could hear a pin drop...

"The difference was - The Gaisce award ignited a burning fire within my life. But the fire needed to be set beforehand. Within everybody lies the motivation to change their predicament. That motivation is unique to each individual. Even more so, the decision to act on that desire for change and turn it into reality. This takes courage. Not the 'fighting a tiger' type of courage, but the courage to challenge your own personal beliefs and structures; not just to step out of your comfort zone, but to leap out of it, arms flying.

They say never test the water with both feet, but sometimes jumping in can be the most rewarding – scary, but rewarding. Challenging yourself, whatever way you choose to do it, whether it be a Gaisce award or learning to swim later in life, not only challenges you yourself, but everyone around you. By choosing to alter your own life, your own existence, your own self, you are a living demonstration of the human capacity for change and the depth of untapped opportunities in the world.

This probably sounds far-fetched but by pushing, even nudging yourself just that little bit, you are moving down a path that leads down many other paths. That's one thing the Gaisce award has really taught me.

Walk through one door and you are faced with many windows of opportunity. Keep walking and you never know where you will end up. The path you choose to walk down should be because you want to, not because you should or could or because it's the easier route or because it's the one your mates are taking. Herein lies the laying of the fire – you've got to step back, strip away all preconceptions about yourself – those constructed by your community, family, school, work, socio-economic status or by you yourself – and think. Who am I? Who do I want to be? When it comes to my old age, will I be satisfied that I have squeezed out every last drop of my potential? Answering these questions sets the fire. The ignition is easy and the warmth generated by its flames will stay with you and warm you, and those around you, for life!"

Emma Farrell is currently in her fourth and final year at Waterford Institute of Technology. She is undertaking a thesis study in resilience.

She is a member of the Irish Race Walking squad, despite taking up the Olympic sport of race walking just last November. Earlier this year, she came

3rd in the 5km race walking event at the Senior Track and Field Championships at the National Athletics Stadium, Santry. No doubt with the application of the dedication and determination she has displayed throughout her Gaisce award, she will grace many podiums in the future and do her country proud...

****

In one word, President McAleese had summed it all up; this remarkable lady is truly *"powerful"*.

13

Just Getting Started

Richard Morgan

*'Before you write, think; before you spend, earn; before you invest, investigate;
before you criticise, wait; before you pray, forgive; before you quit, try;
before you retire, save; before you die, give.'*

William Arthur Ward

They say good things come to those who wait...

When we're younger, the trouble is we are often in such a rush to do
everything. Of course, we rarely stop to enjoy the actual experiences along
the way; savouring the moment and being in the 'now' of it all... With age
or at least experience comes a certain brand of wisdom, a realisation that we
don't always have control of when these special moments may occur in our
lives, but that when we do, we must indeed seize the moment and take full
advantage... Nathan Birnbaum was one such character who understood the
precious opportunities that life presented, perfectly. It was in his earlier years
when he took the name *"Burns"* from the Burns Brothers Coal Company,
whose trucks he'd stolen lumps from, growing up, to help heat the family
home. *'George'* was a sobriquet his brother occasionally used. The man who
often joked that they had to eat his sister because his family was so poor
growing up, was better known to all of us as George Burns, one of the most
versatile and gifted comic geniuses to ever come out of the United States of
America. His comic timing was impeccable and his *'one liners'* are as
memorable and entertaining as any that have gone before or subsequently...
*"Actually, it only takes one drink to get me loaded. Trouble is, I can't remember if it's
the thirteenth or fourteenth!"* to cite just one of hundreds of shining examples...

Burns had been many things including a movie actor all his life, but was little known as such. He was in his eighties when he got the opportunity to play the lead role in a movie after one of his best friends, Jack Benny, who was initially to play the role, died. That role in the *'Sunshine Boys'* released in 1975 is relevant to this story for these reasons. Firstly, he hadn't done anything in film for 35 years and the movie producers were on edge and more than a little nervous. At the auditions he didn't show up with any scripts, making the crew feel that age must have finally caught up with poor George. When reciting his lines, however, he didn't just quote his own impeccably, but also all the lines of his leading co actors as well! He remains, to this day, the oldest actor to ever win an Oscar for Best Supporting Actor for his memorable portrayal as the laconic half of the pair of vaudevillians, playing opposite Walter Matthau in the screen interpretation of Neil Simon's Broadway play *'The Sunshine Boys'*. It was also one of the rare occasions when George didn't wear a hairpiece or a wig...

So how old is too old? Should age ever be a barrier to our success in life? Indeed, who are we to decide it should be in the first place? A great many of you reading this are no doubt, fans of the popular TV Series, *'Strictly Come Dancing'* and therefore, some of you may have been a little dismayed over the row concerning the removal of one of the shows judges, Arlene Phillips, who at 66 was being replaced by a younger presenter, a ploy which in certain quarters has fuelled suspicions that women of a certain age are simply not encouraged to strut their stuff...

The BBC vigorously denied at the time, that its decision had anything to do with Arlene's date of birth, but there are those who believe we all have a sell by date, most especially women... Recent figures from Age Concern and Help the Aged reveal that 65% of older people believe age discrimination still exists in the workplace, and over the past year, unemployment in the 50-plus age bracket has risen by nearly 50% across the water in the UK.

So it's heartening when we hear of older women who are refusing to let their age dictate their lives. One example that caught my eye was the inspiring story of Bridget Sojourner who refuses to play the numbers game. Last year, I believe it was, this sprightly 71 year old decided to give modelling a shot, spurred on by the positive comments she received about her striking street style.

She got some professional photos taken, put a portfolio together, and set about pounding the pavements, knocking on the doors of the agencies. Then Bridget had the idea of phoning a fashion designer by the name of Fanny Karst, whose label *'Old Ladies Rebellion'* produces high quality cutting-edge clothes for mature women with attitude. Fanny loved Bridget's look, and contacted The Guardian. Within just a few weeks, Bridget was appearing in the glossy pages of the paper's Weekend magazine...

As I tried to find a parking space as close to Dublin's St Stephen's Green as I could, I thought a little more about Bridget, the late great George Burns and others too, like Michelangelo who did some of his finest work in St Peter's Basilica well into his 70s. I thought about all of them and smiled, wondering what Richard Morgan, the person I was about to interview, would make of them all. Here was a true *'Renaissance Man'* whose own life at 79 was well and truly just beginning...

****

Everything must begin somewhere and so it was with the massively popular World Indoor Rowing Championships... The origins lie with the C.R.A.S.H. -B.s (Charles River All Star Has Beens) which broadly consisted of a group of rowers comprising guys who rowed as a group and had previously either competed in the world Team Games or Olympic Games between the period 1976 and 1980. They would gather, lurking on the Charles River seeking competition which usually came in the form of friendly rivalry from the top rowers at neighbouring Harvard University. The C.R.A.S.H.-B.s were notorious for never practising before a race and for always jumping the start against their illustrious colleagues.

With the dawn of a new decade, came the news that the US would not be competing in Moscow in protest at the Russian advances into Afghanistan. The guys (and a few of the ladies too) of C.R.A.S.H.-B., led by the likes of Tiff Wood, Dick Cashin, Jake Everett and Holly Hatton, formed a fun little regatta of about twenty rowers in Harvard's Newell Boathouse, to break up the monotony of winter training. Coincidentally at about the same time, *'Concept2'* who were to the fore in rowing machine development, invented their later-named Model A rowing *'ergometer'*. For anyone who's ever sat on a rowing machine, the *'erogmeter'* is the machine with the bicycle wheel, a wooden handle and an odometer.

And so it wasn't long before the crew left the water for the comfort of the indoors, keen to take advantage of the latest rowing technology on offer. Within a few short years C.R.A.S.H.-B. metamorphosed into the International World Indoor Rowing Championships that it's known as now. In 1995, the Championships moved to Harvard's Indoor Track Facility, almost three times the size of the previously used MIT Rockwell Cage. In 1997, they moved to an even larger and ultra-modern facility, the Reggie Lewis Track and Athletic Center, at Roxbury Community College and now today proudly it has finally settled in its new home at Boston University's

Agganis Arena, a-state-of-the-art facility just downstream of the original C.R.A.S.H.-B. site... In the very beginning, the race was originally five miles long and rowed on the old Concept2 Model A ergometer. With further advancements including the introduction of a digital display, the race was shortened to 2,500 metres (from the 1980s through to 1995), because the times were comparable even with the equipment change. To meet the specific training demands of international rowing coaches who stress 6km and 2km races in the winter, starting with the 1996 World Indoor Rowing Championships, the distance was then changed to 2km. The 2km race is today rowed on the latest Concept2 Model D ergometers, which are used by athletes, by universities, clubs, schools and national teams across the globe. As of last year, there were as many as 58 different categories and nearly 2000 competitors... These include lightweight and heavyweight, juniors and masters. The current world record holder for the fastest ever time recorded is New Zealand's Rob Waddell with a time of 5:36.6 (2008).

In 2007, over the tannoy system, organisers announced that for the first time ever, a grandson and grandfather were competing at the same time in the same meeting. The grandfather had just won the gold medal in the over 70s category.

****

We agree to meet in the Westbury Hotel. Running late as usual, I ask Richard Morgan if he'd like to join me for a bite to eat. He hesitates. *"I won't Ian, if you don't mind, I'm watching the weight, - at 10 stone 6lbs I need to lose another 7lbs off the rowing tummy."* I strain my neck across the table to see evidence of this slim, extremely fit, slight gentleman carrying any excess baggage... I can find nothing! He smiles across at me. With typical Cork humour he replies *"Don't be put off by the gaunt face. It's deceptive – all I need to do is look at food and I'm in trouble."* Lord help the rest of us, I think to myself. Incredibly he informs me that the last time he'd had a fitness test done, they found 23% body fat. I joke that he must have declared it all at the US customs, the last time he was competing in the World Indoor Rowing Championships. I smile inwardly to myself wondering how many *'seventy somethings'* would be concerning themselves with such hassles. But Richard Morgan is no ordinary seventy something. At 79, he's busy preparing for his next major challenge; to win a gold medal in the over eighties category and he's as committed as any sports athlete of any age. This man means business! In fact, when we meet I consider myself privileged that he's taken the time out of his busy diary. It would be rare, if ever, that Richard Morgan didn't train intensely two days in a row. This is his first rest day in weeks, in fact, and he's fully aware of the task that lies ahead.

His weight concerns stem in part from a genetic disposition. His mother, when she was 68, had a heart attack and had been overweight. Rowing at this incredible level at the ripe young age of 79 is one thing, doing so, minus a disc in your back and a leaking heart valve is quite another...

Richard is philosophical about such things. *"I ruptured lumber disk no.5 in my lower back,"* he explains. *"It's a trade-off... limited flexibility in the back for a pain free existence."* The last time I had met this man was in Cork, in November 2008, when I was training on the River Lee in preparation for the South Atlantic crossing. He was writhing in pain. The fact then, that he went on in February of this year to take the silver medal at the World Championships in Boston, beggar's utter belief.

Since taking up the sport of rowing at the tender age of 73, Richard has won six medals, two bronze, two silver and one gold medal - quite remarkable. I ask about the leaking valve in the heart. *"Yes,"* he says smiling. *"That causes funny things to happen!"* As the intensity of Richard's exercise increases, you would expect the blood pressure to naturally rise. Incredibly the opposite happens in his case. His blood pressure drops after exercise and his heart rate is up markedly, requiring him to have to lie down for anything up to four hours. *"I usually train before lunch and it's down by six o' clock in time for the news."* His resting heart rate is an impressive 52 beats a minute. *"It used to be as low as 47 – the year I won the gold medal in 2007,"* he recalls modestly. When he rows, he rows with a great deal of pain in his chest – not caused by the strain on his heart, but rather it has something to do with the Agganis arena in which the World Championships are held. People walk around and spray the ground before the start of the races with water, to discharge the static electricity which builds up on the rubber floor and prevent it from interfering with the ergometer computer network. Richard has discussed it at length with his son-in-law, a Respiratory Consultant in Newcastle. Richard used to be an asthmatic when he was younger. To compensate as such, he starts the race slower than his competitors because he knows he could be in trouble as the race develops. Sure enough by the final 300 metres, he can sense this burning sensation that moves rapidly into his lungs, all the while he's rowing with his eyes closed to help focus the pain. *"Feels like you're dying."* He grimaces at the memories. Two years ago when he won the gold, he thought he could hear this voice in his head urging him on. *"Come on, you can do it Richard!"* He was losing the race right up until the last five metres. As he collapsed over the machine at the very end, he could feel this hand on his shoulder. It was Linda Muri, one of the Harvard coaches.

But how did it all begin for this remarkably modest man from Cloyne in East Cork? A man who smoked 45 - 60 cigarettes a day until the age of 45. This same man who has arthritis in his right knee and was bedridden for nearly two months at the end of 2008, waiting for the leaked disc material to dissipate and finally dissolve away in his lower back, so that one day he might wake up pain free and be happy in the knowledge that he could row again...

When Richard Morgan grew up there, the village of Cloyne had a modest population of roughly five hundred people. For those unfamiliar, it is situated about five miles from Ballycotten, along the coast and six miles from Middleton – it is an old village, as Richard describes it, with plenty of local history. It's instantly recognisable for the round tower located in the middle as you drive through. *"It was a very quiet and peaceful place to grow up."* Richard's father was a baker by trade and interestingly, in the Morgan household there's a tradition of naming the first sons *'Richard'*. His own son is called Richard Victor (although they call him Victor), and his grandson is called Richard Breffny Morgan.

His mother came from Cloyne and his father from Youghal. The Morgan family first appeared on the Irish landscape with the arrival of Cromwell onto these shores. *"They settled in places like Waterford, Youghal and Tramore."* Richard is interested in history and enjoys researching facts and dates. Growing up he had two older sisters, Kathleen (who passed away ten years ago with cancer) and Rita who practises today as a barrister. She had been in the civil service, but like many at the time, had to leave the public sector when she got married. Having had three children of her own, she went back to school and qualified. He speaks very fondly and admiringly of her. *"She's very outgoing unlike me,"* he says rather modestly. *"On the bus she'd have three conversations struck up with various groups before her journey's end. She absolutely loves people!"* Richard tells me that she thrives in the law world and adores the pace and the craic of it all. *"She has no inhibitions – it's really no wonder she remains so very positive,"* he says.

Perhaps somewhat unusually, growing up as a kid, if anything ever went wrong, it was always his father he ran to for refuge and cover. *"Mum was very strict on us – she had high standards for us and expected us to behave. Dad was easier to go and beg from!* He laughs and says *"He'd a much softer side."*

His memories of his early days were very pleasant. His sister Rita played the violin very well and he laughs when re recalls the heated debates that used to take place between her and his father who had this uncanny knack of being able to play any instrument simply by ear, though he had no training whatsoever. *"That's not the right way to play,"* she would insist to him. She was no more than ten at the time. Richard says he wasn't particularly sporty at all and showed little or no promise on the football pitch. "*Even though we came from a small parish, sometimes I got selected for the junior hurling team and sometimes even when they were short of players, I didn't!*" he recounts. I simply can't help but wonder what he might have been like, had he started to row back then.

In school Richard excelled. He was bright and applied himself well. He went to secondary school in Middleton (the CBS). He was bright enough, in fact, that they put him straight into his Inter Cert year after 1st year, though it pains him to admit as much to me. He had a real '*Grá*' for drawing, art and science. He always managed to avoid the leather strap by staying on top of everything. However, witnessing those who did suffer through corporal punishment, had a profound effect on him. "*I decided after the Inter Cert that I had had enough and asked my father could I join the bakery and do an apprenticeship instead.*" Though his parents hated to see him leaving school, his father supported his decision and so he began to serve his time for his three year apprenticeship. I suppose as someone who has to watch what they eat and would be diet-conscious, I'm curious about good quality brown bread.

"*The science is very simple,*" he informs me, as he outlines the basic ingredients: the flour, the yeast, the salt and the water. "*The art,*" he says smiling "*is in handling the dough.*" Richard patiently explains the delicate process of handling the dough in sections, how it was kneaded and shaped back then. "*You need to know how to handle it without dropping it or putting your hands through it.*" With time, as he explains to me, one acquires what can be best described as a '*tactile sense*', ensuring that the hands don't stick to the dough. Of course, today with the advent of modern technology, the mix is hardly touched by the human hand… I do my best to get a bread recommendation from him, but he's none too happy with most of what's on offer at the moment. "*Too much salt used,*" he tells me. According to Richard, the best bread is made from coarse brown flour and should be made without any seeds, as it ruins the bread, he believes - an observation that comes as a bitter blow to my hopes of ever finding a bread that lives in harmony with pumpkin and various other flaxseeds. After he qualified, he did the equivalent of '*GP locum*', covering for neighbouring bakeries, providing holiday cover. He did this for a few years, enjoying the freedom it afforded and the money was good too. One day he received a call from a bakery in Ballincurra, from a man whose arm was in a sling. "*He'd cut himself cleaning out the machines,*" he continued. Eventually the baker announced that he wouldn't be returning and so Richard decided to stay on, where he remained happily for the next four years. At first he was living at home. He didn't socialise too much back then. "*I was a bit of a loner,*" he admits.

Instead, he fed his voracious appetite for reading. It turns out that one of his favourite works is the very one that I most despised with a passion, but was forced to read and critique in my first year in college in UCD. Perhaps my failure to critique it well, simply fuelled my disdain…

Niccolò di Bernardo dei Machiavelli to give him his full name (3 May 1469 – 21 June 1527), among other things was an Italian philosopher and writer. His fame today is denoted for two things in particular… He wrote a short political treatise entitled '*The Prince*', written in 1513 but not, in fact, published till 5 years after his death in 1532, although it was circulated among his peers and friends during his lifetime.

This remarkable work provides various theories as to how exactly an aspiring Prince might acquire and hold onto his throne and then govern his principality. This in-depth study of power in acquisition, its expansion and its use, earned the writer the accolade of being a '*founding father of political science*'. Moreover the book led to the term '*Machiavellian*' coming into wide usage in the English language as a pejorative term; denoting crafty, sneaky or deceitful in one's actions, be they political or otherwise … Since the sixteenth century, generations of politicians and students of history alike, remain attracted and repelled by the cynical approach to power posited in '*The Prince*' and his other works. Whatever his personal intentions were, which Richard feels were wholly misunderstood at the time, the debate nevertheless rages on today…

Richard found someone to share his passion of books and indeed most other things in life when he was 27. He met his wife Rita and "*From the start we were happy and comfortable in each other's company.*" As Richard himself says rather humorously, "*Our silences never became pregnant ones!*" Among their shared interests – was a love of music and the Arts. Richard joined a choir in Cork city when they began going out together. "*The marvellous thing about a choir*" he says, *is that it can accommodate a nondescript voice like mine!*" He used to head in on his motorbike to his choir practice. Eventually as the relationship blossomed, he felt he needed to make a choice between the choir and his time with Rita. He chose wisely and so their relationship grew. Rita was a ballet dancer and a member of the Cork Ballet Company and Richard used to often enjoy seeing her perform. They travelled a great deal, mostly on the motorbike as Richard had something of an aversion to cars at the time. Having just recently celebrated their 50th anniversary, I ask him the secret to a good relationship. He smiles back at me and says "*Thankfully Rita's a very good listener as I tend to mouth off a bit!*"

They have five children, all grown up, of course. Ger is the eldest and teaches in Russia. Aedeen is also a teacher, an art teacher, in fact, in Kiltemach in Co Mayo, where she met her Japanese husband. One of his other daughters, Evelyn, lives in Newcastle and the baby of the family, Gwen, also lives in Mayo where she works as a doctor. A keen marathon runner herself, she continues to proudly encourage her father to stay as fit and healthy as he can be. "*When she was a baby we called her Gwendolyn because the name Gwen in Welsh, is a boy's name.*" Their son Victor is the General Manager of a successful hurling helmet making factory called Mycro, located in Ballincollig, Cork. Their main customer not surprisingly is the GAA.

Richard eventually left the bakery world and went to work for '*NET*' (formerly Nitrogen Eireann Teoranta) as a production supervisor before moving on to '*Quigley Magnetite*'. His boss Johnny Mulcahy also owned Ashford Castle at the time. He remembers his German boss at the time, taking him aside and asking him what they were there for. He was duly informed that they were all there to make money! As the production superintendent, he got to make all the decisions except those that were forbidden by the company and the list of protocols was clearly posted up for all to see. "*You had a great deal of responsibility and freedom to do your work.*"

He left the company to return to Cork to work with Mitsui (meaning '*three wells*') a Japanese chemical company which was opening up in Little Island. Here remained for sixteen years until he took early retirement at 61 resulting from tinnitus, (an aggravating booming sensation that develops in the ear) resulting from high noise levels in the plant, which in turn led to high blood pressure… He enjoyed his time with the company. "*They were wonderful people to work for, very fair and most honourable in their ways.*"

Interestingly when he joined, he underwent a health check which clearly showed his diminished lung capacity from years of smoking up to 60 cigarettes a day. That, however, was not what made him stop. "*When we joined the company, we did a three month induction programme in Japan, where I rapidly discovered that their cigarettes were not very nice!*" He and his work colleagues made a bet to stay off them till they returned to Ireland. And so at 45, Richard finally quit smoking. His doctor did a graph comparison from being off the fags over the sixteen years. Not surprisingly, at 61 he was told that his lungs were still recovering. His capacity to take in oxygen was measured at 2.4 litres, less than half the capacity of a typical healthy normal male. In addition to his hearing issues he was also diagnosed on holidays with another condition in his face called Trigeminal Neuralgia, an incredibly painful thing to have, which effectively locks the jaw. "*It only occurs in males, but the pain can be controlled,*" Richard says, "*through medication*". For the next twelve years, Richard and Rita enjoyed their retirement years. At first, they used to holiday abroad but soon discovered that, in fact, they were happier at home nearer to the family and their eleven grandchildren.

Years later when he had just turned 73, his grandson Breffny had become a keen and talented rower in school and Richard often used to bring him down to the local Shandon boat club, where he rowed single sculling with the Presentation Brothers. To pass the time when his grandson was on the water, Richard would sometimes go upstairs to the gym and try to lift the odd weight. "*They were too heavy for me!*" he says laughing. One day for the hell of it, he decided to sit on one of the rowing machines with his back turned – he didn't notice Breffny standing behind him. A few minutes later, his grandson announced that he should try to row a little more and that it would, in fact, be good for him.

It was November and Breffny informed his grandfather that the National Championships were taking place the following month – "*Why not enter?*" he suggested. Richard was understandably sceptical having never rowed before. Nevertheless, Richard was curious. He asked Breffny to do up a programme. He was to train every day for twenty minutes following the pace and direction his grandson had laid out for him to do. He decided to check out the times for his age category. "*The last thing I wanted to do was make a fool out of myself. I didn't mind so long as I wouldn't be too far behind everyone else*"... He discovered that the Irish record for his age category in the lightweights was 8 minutes 30 seconds. "*If I can just get under 9, that would be a very good effort*", he thought to himself. To his astonishment, the week before the championship he did 8min 56sec. He couldn't believe it! He kept training away diligently. Rita wasn't sure what to make of it all, but she continued to be as supportive as possible, keeping him properly hydrated and fed. His appetite was increasing and he was starting to feel like he had more and more energy to burn.

When he arrived for the Nationals that December, Richard Morgan had no idea about the protocols involved in competing... He duly weighed in and received a stamp on the arm to make sure that he was in the right weight category. He couldn't recall the last time he had exposed his white legs to the world, so had arrived in tracksuit bottoms and felt self-conscious about taking them off. Rather memorably, there was a comment card which the participants were asked to fill in for the organisers. On it he wrote considerately "*I've never rowed on the water before, but promise to do better and train harder for the next number of years*".

There were 20 machines side by side in the University College Dublin sports centre with competitors rowing simultaneously on each of them. He rowed the race of his life clocking 8min 49sec and won the gold medal. The only trouble was that when the medal was being presented, he was informed that there was nobody else competing in the lightweight over 70s! He felt terrible and somewhat cheated. It turned out that the actual record for his category was, in fact, 8min 22sec. He joked that if nobody came the following year, he would try to beat that time.

In 2004, Richard Morgan returned and took 16 seconds off the national record. He did it in 8min 06sec, once again the only lightweight competitor in the over 70s. In 2005, he had decided at 75 years of age, now that he was getting the hang of the rowing, his goal would be to go under 8 minutes. True to his word he became the first Irish man over the age of 70 to ever go under 8 minutes in a wonderful time of 7min 59sec. From there, Richard Morgan moved onto the biggest stage of all to compete - the World Championships; having come a very respectable fourth in his first time of asking in 2005, he would go on over the next five years to collect a bronze, two silver and, of course, the coveted gold medal in 2007.

As we sit and finish our wonderful chat, I know that competing in the over 80s category represents this man's next big challenge. I ask of the competition facing him. *"Dean Smith, the American, is a legend in rowing circles and remains my greatest adversary."* It turns out that Dean didn't show up at the last championships in February. After each of the races, it's customary that the international competitors gather for a post race chat in the locker rooms. *"The view held in the 75 - 80 category is that if you're missing for two years in a row, it's presumed you're not coming back..."*

Before we leave I ask him about his grandson, Breffny, who has been appearing in this year's Apprentice series on TV3. He smiles across and says *"That boy's pure gold entertainment for sure – he brightens that show up."*

As we walk out of the hotel, we chat a little more about training, diet, motivations and staying determined to achieve our goals, come what may, in life. As he leaves me to make his way to get a connecting bus to his sister Rita's home, I feel very inspired and reassured at the same time.

Inspired to know that so much is possible in life at any age, reassured in the realisation that so much of what we would like to achieve in our lives, comes down to attitude.

14

Machine Gun Baby

Gary Keegan

'Improvement begins with I.'

Arnold H Glasgow

Boxing is one of our oldest sports, whose history extends all the way back to Ancient Greece. In modern Olympic Boxing, the competition between boxers is to anticipate your opponent's moves and strike them using padded gloves. The winner is decided either by knockout or by the number of blows landed as determined by a judge(s). For many of us, in truth, boxing is something of a euphemism for life's daily struggles...

As I drove on the M50 *'en route'* to Bettystown to meet one of our last heroes, I thought about how this person's character had been moulded with time, how he handled the *'knocks and the blows'*, and what motivated him to stay in the *'ring'* and keep going the distance throughout his life, regardless of the odds or the size of the opponents he faced...There were so many things about which I was curious - like so many people, I guess, particularly those who followed the sport of boxing.

My thoughts escaped back to an article that Vincent Hogan had written in the Irish Independent, from Beijing in 2008, just before the Irish fighters were due to step into the ring and fight for their coveted medals. In the article, Vincent cited the fact that on the eve of one of the biggest boxing days in Irish history, Gary Keegan, the Director of the High Performance Programme, hadn't been accredited to the Olympic Village, having been overlooked for the position of Irish manager. I recalled the comments that followed from Head Coach Billy Walsh, who had expressed his understandable frustration (and that of his boxers) at what was unfolding before their very eyes... *"He's the main reason"* Billy had said for all of their pending success. "*This programme would not have been in operation or existence without Gary Keegan. He has guided us every day in our work, pushed us and challenged us in our work and in our training.*" Four years previously, Keegan had also been left out of the accredited party in Athens at the previous Olympics...

I remembered too, the offers that followed the Olympic Games, offers that Gary himself played down massively in the press. The man who had '*strategically and painstakingly masterminded Ireland's boxing successes in 2008*' turned down in the end what must have been a tempting offer - to prepare the cream of British fighters for the 2012 Games in London. He had been approached by British boxing chiefs after the Beijing Games and subsequently offered a contract. They wanted him. In the press Gary said this: "*I had the contract before me to sign. It is flattering when your work is recognised elsewhere. But I thought about it long and hard and I realised my heart would always be with Ireland in the lead up to the London Olympics. I also had to consider my family and, in the end, I did not sign the contract.*"

Instead Gary would go on to become the Director of Performance Management with the Institute of Sport; not bad for a kid who had left school at 14. At the time he accepted the position, he was fully aware in 2008 that he - and the organisation - faced very challenging and tough times ahead in the current economic climate.

The '*Big Picture*' man sensed, I suspect, as I continued my drive along the N1, that the Institute could and would play a huge role in the development of all Irish sport in the future... challenge enough perhaps, to accept the role in the first place, knowing that success would require keeping one eye firmly on an ever changing future and the countless possibilities that it can hold good and bad...

As I passed through Laytown nearing my journey's end, two final scenarios struck me...

I thought about Kenny Egan earlier this year, preparing for the World Boxing championships in Milan in Italy, who as the papers put it "*was back in town, ready to pick up the pieces of his life again, ready to be the old Kenny Egan that those closest to him knew and loved*". Curiously enough, one of the very first steps Kenny would take on his road to new future glories, would be to visit his old mentor and friend Gary Keegan at the Institute of Sport in whose company he would spend '*several long hours putting the pieces back in place*'.

My final thoughts as I pulled into the driveway of Gary's family home were of one boxer in particular, that Gary and his team had helped guide and prepare for his Olympic Bronze medal, Darren Sutherland. I knew that he and Gary were very close. I simply couldn't begin to imagine just how tough the last few weeks had been for Gary or more especially Darren's immediate family.

****

As I entered his family home, I was met with a firm but friendly handshake, the trademark I guessed of a man who had boxed modestly for much of his earlier life. Waking in the doorway, I was greeted by one of Gary's daughters, Kate his youngest - on her way out the door with a rather big dog in tow. This was no ordinary canine however; it was in fact a rare example of a 'Leonberger', a massive but truly elegant dog whose breed hail originally from the German town of Leonberger. Kate informed me that she was only ten weeks old but growing rapidly, easily distinguished by her kind eyes and black marking on her face. For such a massive dog she was remarkably agile, and it was obvious to see the growing attachment forming between her and her young adoring owner. Kate tells me that she was preparing her for a special guest appearance at 'Pet Expo' in the RDS, the following weekend – the first time the organisers had ever managed to track down a puppy example of this incredible animal. "*Normally they grow far too quickly*" Kate laughs, as she is pulled enthusiastically by her new friend, down the steps...

Entering the living room, Gary hands me a picture as if anticipating the many thoughts that had been circling my mind... On the front there is a wonderful moment caught on camera and frozen rather appropriately in time; three Olympians celebrating their proud moments of glory. Darren, who took bronze in the middle weight 75kg division was pictured beside Kenny holding his silver medal, won in the light heavy 81kg division, and to his right Paddy Barnes of course, who claimed a brilliant bronze in the light flyweight 48kg class. I notice there's a note on the back of the framed picture. Curiously, I turn it around to investigate... The attached note comes from Dr Jim Ryan, the same doctor who had joined and supported Gary's fifteen strong, high performance team, and a man who had been a key and integral part of their remarkable collective five year journey together. At the interview for the medical role back in 2003, he had asked Gary what the impending journey to the Olympics were really all about. Gary looked him in the eye and replied "*It's about people*". Six roller coaster years later, Jim had hand written this message he'd received from Gary by text on the eve of the Olympic final on the back of the picture Gary had just handed me. He sent it to Gary 11 months after the Olympics was over...

"Dear Johnson, Jim, Sharon, Orlagh, Giles and Alan,

On the eve of the Olympic final in the city of Beijing, I find sleeping a little difficult. My thoughts are of the journey and not of the destination and the people I have had the privilege of sharing this 5 year experience with.

I want you all to know that although you are not here to witness our arrival at the Olympic dream in person, you are very much in my apartment room with me this morning. I can't find words (because I left my dictionary at home!) to describe what all your contributions have meant to me personally and our boxers, contributions equal and as valuable as the rest of our great support team who are here right now.

Thank you all for staying the distance on what has sometimes been a difficult journey for all of us. I am honoured to say I was part of your team."

At this point I expected Gary to naturally vent feelings or express possible frustration about watching 'from the outside in' as these sporting heroes were about to perform on the greatest stage of them all. He did neither. *"I was in the apartment reflecting on how every morning it felt like I was a parent leaving my children at the school gates."* He had to part company with his boxers and team four days before the games began and though the boxers came to visit him in his hotel room from time to time, the experience must have felt wholly surreal. But then as he points out to me *"the journey was about the people, all of the people who had made it possible in the first place and their impact on the overall experience was just as important as those who were contributing equally inside the village".*

Eight of the original fifteen were in Beijing while seven remained at home. In wondering why Gary is not bitter or even the slightest bit negative, I was about to get my answer, *"I was lucky. I had come to the realisation that sometimes we take things very personally on our respective journeys in life and therefore, sometimes fail to maintain any context for our emotional reactions and behaviours."* What Gary rapidly discovered was, in essence, that he was simply part of the bigger story; *"but I wasn't the actual story"* he observes astutely. His time to reflect in that hotel room also gave Gary Keegan a chance to contemplate the things that made him happiest in life, his family and three children. He had paid a high price over the past five years, no question. This man entered all of his relationships new or established in the same, uncompromising fashion; take me as you find me – I will trust you until you lose my trust… Anyone who has ever committed themselves to any quest or goal in life knows that at times there are prices to be paid…

It was in those moments of epiphany that Gary Keegan's pennies dropped mercifully before his very eyes. Before Egan's big fight, Gary accepted that being in the village wasn't actually important and what really mattered was what was unfolding before his eyes, *"had I been in the ring I might have gotten caught up in my ego and failed to truly appreciate how the head coach Billy Walsh and Zaur Antia were about to step up brilliantly to the plate and how the team of boxers would take full responsibility for themselves and their actions. In my eyes these boys were champions outside the ring."*

****

Miyamoto Musashi, a legendary Japanese Samurai warrior, was born in 1584, in a Japan struggling to recover from more than four centuries of internal strife. *'Kendo'*, the Way of the sword, had always been synonymous with nobility in Japan.

Since the founding of the Samurai Class in the eighth century, the military arts had become the highest form of study, inspired by the teachings of Zen, a Buddhist school of thought purporting that enlightenment comes through meditation and intuition rather than necessarily through faith. Many in Japan, in the aftermath of the devastation of a country ravaged by the effects of the Second World War, turned for inspiration to the teachings contained in a book written by Musashi called the *'5 Rings'*.

Apart from providing a blue print for life, the book contained strong reference to the importance of *'Kaizen'*. The word literally means *'continuous improvement'*, (the word *Kai* means change; *Zen* in this case referring to *making better)* reflecting the slow accumulation of many small developments in either a process and or in terms of quality output.

Post Second Word War in Japan, this resulted over a 50 year period, in many companies becoming world leaders – companies like Toyota for example, the lowest cost and highest quality automobile company in the world. In short, the Japanese went back to their basic core values, something Gary believes we are also going to have to do in this country to pull ourselves back from the brink.

Ask anyone who really knows this man, and they will give you three words they associate with Gary Keegan: people, systems and trust... Dr Johnston McEvoy, his head of physio in the lead up to the Olympics, is convinced that Gary still sleeps with the Toyota blue print under his pillow at night!

"With Kaizen, the central component", Gary tells me, (you can sense his passion building) *"is that you must continuously improve your processes to keep a 'quality product' in production. Not just because you can always get better, but because 'better' is a moving target"*. He challenges me to consider what's better? It's a fair question because the answer depends surely on the perception of what quality is: McDonalds for example is *'quality'* to a kid, who would find a fancy restaurant unsatisfying. Quality therefore is really about the perceptions of

the 'customer' – their wants, their needs or in Gary's world, the boxer, the athlete, those who compete at the very highest level; those who are continuously striving to raise their bar in life – those like Gary Keegan. It strikes me that any great leader will never ask something of his people that he or she is not prepared to strive for first. Gary and his colleagues have developed what they refer to as, their '*Warrior Model*' for developing the key strengths that an athlete needs to perform at the very highest levels, most importantly, as Gary points out, not just on the track, but in life itself. As he puts it, *"if there are critical pieces missing, the performer will suffer"*. In the workplace, it's a bit like closing the sale perhaps – it's often not the sale we are struggling to close but rather putting closure on various peripheral issues around us that can affect sales performance. So for Gary, it's always been about the person first, then the systems required to make it happen second; *"unfortunately we do not win in life or on the track by being defensive"*, he points out. In his world, the Institute of Sport's mantra for success is simple: *'believe – perform – achieve'*. Gary believes that talent is in fact only a small piece of the equation and is too often overrated! *"Talent often walks out the back door at the first sign of trouble and you are left unable to grind out results and handle the disappointments."*

He goes on to make the point that *"high performers take risk high. They make mistakes and lots of them"*. But as we can all appreciate in life, they, like anyone who wants to succeed at anything in this world, have to have the resilience to bounce back and accept feedback and are always willing to learn. *"Ego - we all face in this world, all of the time – the only one who deserves to have one is the athlete themselves; we all have an ego and we all have to manage it because it can be blinding."*

After the 1992 games, Ireland had to suddenly qualify for the Olympics. While we were coming to terms with same, other nations had begun to professionalise their preparation, training and coaching techniques. We now had to qualify. The bar had been raised but we didn't move with it and get better, Gary reflects back, *"our training was still essentially based around the old 3x3 minute rounds, training long and slow – the sport was now fast, explosive, intervals of higher intensity as opposed to the endurance based training we were undertaking"*.

In short, Gary Keegan was making the point that Irish boxers at the very top level simply didn't have the engine to compete and the fights were more often than not over before they had begun because were weren't quick enough to adapt to what was happening in the ring.

****

In 2003, having been a boxing coach for 21 years, Gary became the Secretary of the National Coaching Committee and also chaired the Coaching Educational Committee. He had plenty of time to assess in his own mind what was needed to take the next quantum steps to go forward... He was fortunate too to have great mentors around him; guys like Austin Carruth (who trained his son Michael on route to his gold medal in Barcelona) and Gerry Storey MBE from Belfast, two of the most decorated coaches Ireland had. Gerry Storey was an interesting character. Apart from training guys like Barry McGuigan through to his Olympic and Commonwealth bids, he was asked in 1981 during the Maize hunger strikes by Republicans and Loyalists alike to train prisoners in the Maize gymnasium. His outstanding contribution to bridging divides in sport made him the first Irish person to ever win the prestigious 'Laureus' World Sports Award in 2005, fittingly presented to him on the podium by two of the sports greats, Barry McGuigan and 'Marvellous' Marvin Hagler.

It was while presenting a report that same year as a volunteer coach to the Irish Sports Council that Gary asked the Irish Amateur Boxing Association's President, Dominic O' Rourke for a chance to see how a *'high performance plan'* might be best implemented to give Irish boxers the best chance of future success. He was given five days to come up with a better way – a blue print for high performance returns, a model that could help to ensure that Ireland would go to the Beijing Olympics ready and capable of winning medals. And so like any glass half full kind of guy, Gary Keegan chose to see the reality thus: finite resources; infinite possibilities... (finite resources, infinite possibilities shared by his friend Padraig O'Cadiegh CEO, Aer Aran)

****

Gary Keegan's inherent sense of pride stemmed in part, from his coming from the heart of the inner city in Dublin; he grew up in Ballybough, in the flats on Sackville Avenue. Here, certain basic, core values were instilled early. It was a strong vibrant community, a place where people looked out for each other, the place that he and his four brothers and baby sister Rose grew up. The eldest was Paul then Raymond. Gary was next, with Matthew and Frances propping up the rear. *"We fought like cat and dog! – Like any healthy family does,"* he laughs. Like so many other families, his mum Rose was the matriarch of the house. The love he feels towards his mother, (the other key contributor to his inherent sense of self-pride and worth) is apparent; *"she never had to dish out punishment once, but still somehow managed to keep us all in our place"*.

From the get-go, Gary Keegan sensed he was on a great journey. The freedom he enjoyed to explore the world around him sometimes got him into trouble and caused his mother more than a little anxiety at times. He attended St Cannice's school on Dublin's North Circular Road. He never missed a day. *"I loved school but school didn't always love me!"* he freely admits. When he was 14, he went to see the guidance councillor and she advised him that he might make an excellent jockey, given his height and love of sport. So off to the Curragh he went to spend six happy months as an apprentice, *"problem was as soon as they fed me I grew!"* He's now 5'9.5" but still only weights 67kgs – which he puts down to not eating enough in his crazy work days.

At 16 Gary Keegan went off to see the world in the Merchant Navy with Irish Shipping. He had been working in the *'Long Bar'* on North Earl Street, as an apprentice bar man where he would sometimes stand fascinated, listening to all the seamen regaling their adventures and travels across the world. Our intrepid young explorer felt the need to do the same and so travelled to Sandymount to sign up. *"I'd never been on the south side of Dublin before,"* he says, smiling at me.

He took the No. 3 bus to meet a man called John Davis who observed looking at this slight figure before him, *"you have a pigeon's chest son, you'll never make it at sea!"* Perhaps he saw something in Keegan's keen brown eyes that made up for his lack of physical stature. Either way young Keegan was bound for Antwerp, cases packed, completely unprepared for the massive berthed 26,000 tonne, steel structure that towered over him in the water, as if mocking his teenage naivety. He spent three great years on the water, where he learned a strong work ethic and the importance of being a team player. *"I boarded as a non drinker,"* he recalls, *"I used to order a coke on the ship's makeshift bar, to which a voice would reply back in response 'don't use bad language on this vessel Sonny!' "*. But despite their best efforts they never changed him. He remains a teetotaller to this day.

When he left the Navy, he got married at 19 to his childhood sweetheart, Susan. He'd known her since their days growing up together. She came from Coolock. Within a year he was a father. His daughter Kellie, the apple of his eye, had entered his world. Life suddenly had new meaning for Gary Keegan. He joined the army soon after and trained initially in the Cathal Brugha Street barracks. *"I moved around a lot during the six years I was there. I learned a great deal from my colleagues and even got to serve time in the Lebanon."* But the explorer in him was challenging him once more and he found himself needing to express himself in new ways once more.

He had always wanted to have his own business so he bought a van and a contract working initially for a local bakery called Manning's. The transport business was tough and it took a long time before he was able to feel like he was making reasonable inroads. *"It began with forty pounds then fifty, then sixty. Eventually you have enough to call it a salary".* Small hard steps were needed. *"There was something looking back that was very engaging about those early days – all the striving, the appreciation, the honest toil."* What Gary found out as he progressed slowly over the years was that he had an innate ability to solve problems. In those days, they were transportation and logistical solutions he was being called to solve for clients. *"When I think back to it"*, his thoughts drifting back to his childhood, *"my mum was like that really, always having to come up with solutions and provide for us in hard times, whether that was putting food in the trolley or just making sure that we had something for Christmas."*

Along the way he up-skilled every chance he was afforded. He went back at 23 to take his Inter Cert when in the army, taking twelve subjects. But that was just the beginning of this man's thirst and quest for knowledge. Whether it was in the army taking every course he could or sitting years later in the Irish Management Institute, debating the merits of good leadership, his learning journey was ever evolving.... Twelve years after setting up his own business, Gary Keegan was ready to take on even bigger challenges and Dominic O'Rourke, the IABA (Irish Amateur Boxing Association) President knew they had found their man to lead them to future boxing glories.

Gary Keegan had an instinctive feeling for what boxing gave to a person in their broader development and conversely what the person could bring to the sport of boxing. He had begun to box at the age of 12, though by his own admission he wasn't particularly good, but he always carried a skipping rope and he always trained. He would go on to become a coach at nineteen in the Glin Club in Coolock. In 1987, he set up his own club with John Domican in Blanchardstown called the St Mochta's Club (which eventually became St Bridget's and is run today by Ger McDaid). When he started to operate the high performance programme, he insisted that all three of the head coaches coming on board left their respective clubs behind – Billy Walsh, seven times Irish Senior Champion, Jim Moore (whose son James had won a bronze medal in the World Championships in Belfast in 2001) and even his world class addition, Zaur Antia, who hailed from Poti in Georgia, a man who had worked previously with the old Soviet Union team. All three of these men, like Gary himself, shared a passion for life, and for their children. *"It was important that Billy would become the head coach – to leave an Irish legacy behind"...* Gary is quick to point out to me that, as he rushed to complete the initial 15 page application for the high performance programme that was hurriedly delivered into the offices of the Irish Sports

Council at 4.55pm on a Tuesday afternoon, none of this would have been possible without a team of mentors that helped Gary over those crazy five days – people like Dr Giles Warrington and Sheila Quinn from the National Coaching and Training Centre, the NCTC. It wasn't long interestingly, before Pete Taylor, Katie's father was on board the programme, he correctly wanted his daughter Katie in the programme too. *"As soon as Billy and I saw her, she stood out like a burning ray of light."* Although managing a father and daughter relationship might at first have seemed potentially difficult, in truth it wasn't; *"they travelled together and Pete was on board as a volunteer high performance coach, dedicated to the core to support Katie to her goals and he would bleed Zaur for information, hungry to learn..."* The bond between them was amazing.

Others to be recruited on board the high performance bus included nutritionist, Sharon Madigan from Donegal who had a *'high performance'* baby along the way.

"The baby used to bounce up and down on the boxers' knees – it became a part of our growing family" – Gary's eyes lit up thinking back to the fun they used to have. He also remembers Sharon bursting into tears with delight from her home kitchen, with her high performance babies crying in the background during a phone call to him in Italy, just after Kenny Egan achieved qualification for the Olympic Games – he was the last to qualify on to the high performance programme.

John Cleary looked after strength and conditioning, Gerry Hussey was the Psychologist, Alan Swanton the Performance Analyst, Dr Jim Ryan was the medic, Dr Giles Warrington and Caroline McManus advised on specialist physiological testing and training, while Emira Pacarada and Angelena Rea advised on Logistics. Dr Johnston McEvoy was the head physio and he brought other physios on board too – Orlagh Sampson, Conor Murphy and Scott Murphy who exemplified what this team was really all about. *"We learned on the job fast, self-development was critical to each and every one of us. What made this team special was the fact that everyone was prepared to roll up their sleeves and cross over skillsets. When Scott joined, he was not only an excellent professional like all the rest. He was prepared to do anything – such was his enthusiasm to contribute".*

The team of five boxers travelled to Vladivostok for their final camp before launching into Beijing. The word Vladivostok translates as 'Conquering the East'. The place itself is located deep in Siberia and is where the Trans Siberian railway ends. It was ceded by the Chinese to the Russians in 1860 following the *'Treaty of Peking'.* All in all, a daunting place for a travelling team of boxers who traditionally had feared the Russians and their training techniques. Just before the Athens Olympics, Keegan led six of his most experienced charges there to learn. They were amazed to see the Russians rising at 6am, running on snow and ice-filled roads, training three times a day. These guys sparred with anger in their punches; "*the lessons were brutal for the lads to take on board*". Unfortunately Athens came too soon – more time was needed, more information gathering required. Gary was determined that they would return again. He needed his boxers fighting the best of the best. He scoured every opportunity in Europe and pestered every boxing authority in his pursuit of knowledge.

Two years later, they would return to Moscow on invitation – just four boxers this time, preparing for the European Championships. This time the Irish were tougher, fitter, faster and stronger. Things had changed somewhat. Three members of the Irish team would make the last eight of those Championships and Kenny Egan would win a medal. In Moscow, strength and conditioning coach, John Cleary, taped heart monitors onto the Irish during sparring. Gary described the Russians' reactions. "*They were intrigued. They asked what we were doing and why and we explained and offered to test their fighters too*". Happy to oblige and foster better relations, before leaving Moscow, Gary Keegan gave a '*PowerPoint*' presentation to the Russians on what the monitors revealed about those tested. He then flew home with the data. A little Russian espionage had ensured that the Irish were in business – "*Until then we had nothing to benchmark what we were doing against,*" he recalls. For the first time he now had international data from the best team in the world. They were on their way ready to mix it with the very best in the world.

****

Before leaving Gary's, we chatted a little more about coaching on the ground here in Ireland in all sports – "*We need to put higher value in everyones' contributions*", he points out "*and give equal recognition to all who contribute in all areas and all aspects of the sport, from the volunteer parent coaches to those who contribute at the very highest levels*". Beside me is a stunning picture of Gary with his two daughters, Kate aged 17 and Kellie aged 24, who is working in Australia. "*We all miss her – she's out there on a 2 year sponsorship working as a building surveyor*". When she was younger, he taught her to always weigh up the pros and cons. She hopes to be able to return in better economic times and better up-skilled.

Before we finish, Kate arrives back with a very thirsty dog. "*What I love about her is that she's not afraid to speak her mind!*" It's obvious he adores his kids and is wholly determined to get the work-life balance thing right going forward. "The next three years are huge for us as we get ready for London. But my kids are my number one priority and always will be," he says. Before I go I get invited in to hear his talented son Stewart's band, 'Machine Gun Baby' – They're jamming in the neighbouring room. They generously offer to play me their up-and-coming song soon to be released as a single. It's damn good too – U2 meets Kings of Leon. Watch this space...

The three or so hours spent in Gary Keegan's company have been rewarding, enlightening and in truth, quite humbling. The future of sports people reaching their full potential at the very highest levels in this country is in the right hands, the hands of Gary and his talented team in the Institute of Sport. Whatever they may lack perhaps in financial resources compared to some other countries, they more than make up for in the most important resource of all, people, quality people.

Irish sport owes much to this unsung hero.

15

Running on Empty

Dave Campbell

'Never give in! Never give in! Never, never, never. Never – in anything great or small, large or petty – never give in except to convictions of honor and good sense.'

Sir Winston Churchill

In truth, if we are really honest, we possibly envy them; people, that is, who know exactly what they want to do with their lives from an early age. Me? I hadn't a clue, and so therefore took the circuitous or 'scenic' route in life. I knew that whatever it was going to involve, it had to centre on people, which was all I really knew for sure...

It's taken me all of my thirty-nine years on this planet to finally discover ways in which work can be truly meaningful for all concerned, the people I work with and most importantly, I guess, for myself.

Driving home one day, earlier this year, just before the Lisbon Treaty Referendum took place, I was listening intently to an interesting debate on the radio. The debate concerned the fact that many of our politicians come from a teaching background and, in essence, this was one of the reasons being put forward by some detractors as to why we don't have real leaders!

Some of the greatest leaders this country has are, in fact, teachers; whether they may or may not be running the country as politicians, is another matter entirely.

When we find the time to stop and consider the importance of a teacher's role in the future development of any young person, their potential power to inspire, to empower and ultimately lead, is wholly underestimated and possibly even undervalued by society at large.

Some of us are born to be teachers, born with an innate ability to impart information, to inspire others and to bring out the best in people, making us as a result, want to learn in the classroom and from life itself.

Johnny Nevin was one of those people. In May 2008, he proudly took over the role of full-time Principal of Maynooth Post Primary School. This was the school he had attended in his youth, the place he had spent many wonderful hours in the classroom and on the playing field... He was appointed full-time Principal, having acted as Principal since the retirement of Senan Griffin.

When he was appointed, Johnny was just 38 years of age, one of the youngest principals in the country, having served as the Deputy Principal since 2005. It was refreshing to think that sometimes in life, people have the courage to make the right decisions when it comes to making crucial appointments based on fairness and quality, as opposed to politics and seniority, not that Johnny didn't earn his stripes, to be fair. Having completed the Hdip in 1992, he continued to teach in the school up until his appointment as Vice Principal. During that period, he taught Geography, History and English and was also the LCVP Co-Ordinator (Leaving Certificate Vocational Programme Support Service) during this time. He also completed a Higher Diploma in Pastoral Care studies and a further Higher Diploma in Educational Management, both taken through the neighbouring University of NUI, Maynooth. That second qualification would prove invaluable in helping him to cope with the often underestimated demands of being a school principal.

A principal's job is varied and involves having to make many, many decisions each and every day, usually on the spot! For Johnny Nevin, overall it's been a very enjoyable and rewarding role, but there is always a great onus of responsibility on one's shoulders and that can be a hard weight to bear on such young shoulders. However, as all good leaders strive to do, his decision making centres on those he serves first, namely his students. His ethos is that if it's good for the kids, then, in the end, it is the right decision to make.

He happily makes the daily 120km journey to work each day from his home just outside Templemore, where he is married to a beautiful and loving wife Sandra, who is a PE teacher in the neighbouring Garda College. Sandra may be four inches taller than him, (Johnny is 5' 7") but their compatibility as a couple is unquestionable. They have three gorgeous kids, Jack, 6, Molly aged 4 and then there's baby Kate, just 6 months old.

Of the journey's 240km, three hour round trip distance, he simply believes that the distance, in fact, gives him the time to clear his head, formulate and plan for the day that is to come or an opportunity to reflect on the day that has just been. Most importantly, it means that by the time he comes home, his head is generally emptied of such concerns and he is able to switch his focus onto the things that really matter most in his life, his wife and three children.

The Post Primary is, in fact, a co-educational multi-denominational school, run under the auspices of the Kildare Vocational Educational Committee. The current enrolment of 870 students is roughly 50:50 male to female, with most of them coming from the local catchment area of Maynooth, Kilcloon, Mulhussey, Straffan and Rathcoffey.

Commenting on the teaching ethos that exists in the school, Johnny Nevin says *"We aim to create a warm, caring learning environment in which all our students can reach their full educational potential. Respect and responsibility are core to our school and the welfare and positive atmosphere are very important. This is a caring school in which student care and concern are central to all we do."* He is lucky, undoubtedly, to have a committed, hard working and professional teaching staff who each and every day are prepared to go beyond the call of duty and provide for this in the form of sports, musicals, dramas, young scientists etc. His Deputy Principal, Andrew Dunne, a very affable man and as a Maths teacher, is famed for telling his students *"All you need in this world is love and Maths - though not necessarily in that order!"* When you walk down the long and inviting corridors of the Maynooth Post Primary School, you cannot but be struck by two things. Firstly, there are numerous messages of positivity usually captured in highly visual terms - large stunningly framed photographs, with inspiring messages for the kids to take on board. One such message from Peter A Cohen reads – *"Persistence: There is no giant step that does it. It's a lot of little steps."*

The second thing that strikes you is the number of kids who have represented this school at county level across a whole range of sports. There cannot be too many schools in this country which have as many Inter County representatives; from gaelic football to camogie, soccer to karate. This is a school which can excel equally well in sport and academics. In sixth year, they currently have two young talented females both representing Kildare at Minor Ladies Level; Aisling Hughes and Jenny Moore. Anyone who watched the final of the recent All Ireland Ladies Senior Football Championships between Dublin and Cork, will testify as to the incredible skill and fitness levels these talented female athletes possess. In fifth year, they have the *'goalie'* for the Kildare Minors, Mark Donnellan. Another 5th year, Suzi Farrell came top of Europe (80,000 competed) and 5th in the world in the recent Microsoft Word Global Competition which tests proficiencies across a range of

Microsoft packages. Post Primary was the first school to boast the first student getting nine straight As in the Leaving Cert, Fergus Denman in 2001. They have a Transition Year student, Aisling Chathain, who got 12 A1s in her Junior Cert.

Post Primary are the Gael Linn national debating champions. They have a 6th year representative, Robert Holt on the Irish under 18 youth rugby team. The list of achievers, to be fair, is endless.

There is one person, however, who all of these students and indeed, the entire collective of teachers look up to, whose own determination in life and eternal will to achieve, shines as a constant beacon of hope to students past and present, and serves as a source of continued inspiration. This unsung hero, passed through the school some years ago, but his influence is still felt today. He's a young 27-year-old who exemplifies the dictum that if, at first, you don't succeed, then keep trying until you find a way to achieve your goal in life. Many in the school today, feel that they can relate to such difficult journeys with this person because his own personal goal remains, as yet, unfulfilled.

****

It's a story that has been played out many times in sport and in the media before... an intense rivalry between two athletes, where everything is at stake – winner takes all.

In this case, the two athletes going head to head were competing for the ultimate prize – the chance to represent their country on the grandest of stages, a chance to go to the World Athletic Championships in Berlin... What added a little extra punch to this battle for a precious place in the 800m was the intensity of the rivalry. In Irish Athletics terms, this was a modern day version of Coe versus Ovett. This time, the victor who took the spoils, hailed from Dublin – the loser was from Maynooth in Co Kildare.

Two years ago, Dave Campbell had won the 800m title to deny Thomas Chamney a place in the World Championships. Last year, the roles were reversed, and in October 2009, there was once again nothing between them, but after jogging the first lap and a half, when it came down to the home stretch, Chamney was just that bit stronger on the day, winning in a time of 1:49.87 to Campbell's 1:50.20 – and with that, had booked his ticket to Berlin.

Later, Thomas was quoted as saying in the press *"When it comes down to that passion and emotion, both of us are really going to go at each other, hammer and tongs. Any time we race, I don't want to lose to him. And he doesn't want to lose to me. It's great for the sport, but I don't always look forward to racing him. It's nerve-wracking. He's a great competitor. I've a lot of respect for him as an athlete."*

Although both athletes had the B-standard for Berlin, only one is permitted to go under IAAF rules. Chamney also had the B-standard over 1,500m and was therefore set for selection for both events in Berlin. To Chamney's credit, he was just one hundredth of a second outside the A standard qualifying time in the 800m (achieved in a race both he and Dave had run over the summer in the famous Bislett Stadium, which had seen many great battles over the years in Norway). Indeed he came agonisingly close to that 1:45.40 mark when he ran 1:45.41 – a race in which Campbell also ran his breakthrough best of 1:45.59.

To appreciate Dave Campbell's capacity to see the bigger picture in difficult moments, just after he had lost to Chamney in Santry stadium and with his chance to compete on the world stage gone for another year, he went for a '*warm down*' jog with his father, John, outside the stadium. There was very little conversation, each reflecting on their own personal thoughts. The normal post race scrutiny would come later. On their jog through the neighbouring forest, Dave ran past a wheelchair user who was coming towards him. He turned to his father and smiled. "*I'm the lucky one here,*" he said to him. Suddenly the notion of having to now run the 1,500m didn't seem so hard to face, a race he would go on to win, incidentally.

****

Sport is filled with inspiring stories of courage and determination. You could pick any sport really and the results would be equally impressive. There's a wonderful story of a Dublin athlete, currently living in Kildare, which caught my attention some time ago. It is the story of Shane Healy, who moved to the States having grown up in an orphanage. It was there, living in a beat-up Volkswagen camper that, one day, Healy observed a coach training his athletes on a track, and the athletes were all middle-distance runners. The coach noticed Healy watching and asked him if he had ever run before. So he then asked Healy to run a mile. Asking the coach how many laps it took, having never run a mile before, he then proceeded to run an untrained time of 4min 52sec at the age of 22. The coach promised him weekly groceries if he would continue with the team, and Healy gladly accepted. He would go on one day to make the semi-final of the Olympics in Atlanta, coached, at that stage, by Eamonn Coghlan. Every

Kildare athlete who has ever come since, recognises the marker which Healy laid down for others to follow.

****

Bernie Campbell has a framed message that sits on her desk at work. In tough times, she turns to its meaning for the strength to keep fighting the proverbial *'good fight'*. The message was given to her by her son. It's a message that fuels his own deep passion and drives him on. It reads: *"Pain is temporary. It may last a minute, or an hour, or a day, or a year, but eventually it will subside and something else will take its place. If I quit, however, it lasts forever."*

These words were spoken famously by Lance Armstrong in deference to his cancer, and so has become the creed by which Bernie's son, Dave Campbell, lives his life each and every day. Dave Campbell serves to inspire his former school teachers and pupils, past and present, not because of what he had achieved or may achieve in the future but, moreover, because through it all, on his journey to excel as a middle distance athlete, he has never quit once, though there have been many times when he might as well have thrown in the towel. *"He's a born fighter,"* his mother acknowledges proudly. *"He was born prematurely at 27 weeks and lived in an incubator for five weeks."* His father John remembers that rocky road from Cavan to Dublin filled with numerous potholes. *"They had baptised him in the hospital in Cavan. The nurse was the godmother and the priest the godfather. They didn't really expect him to live through the night."* Both his mother and father knew and believed that if he made it to Dublin, this little boy would continue on his path as he was meant to go on – a born fighter ready to fight for everything he got in life.

Johnny Nevin will never forget a certain cold dark November afternoon in 1995. He was teaching in the Post Primary at the time, taking the students for English and Geography. The school had just reached its first ever Dublin Colleges final in Croke Park. The team taking to the pitch, that day, was the under 14s. *"What a team we had too!"* Johnny recalls. In the front line, they had Paddy Keane at right corner, William *'the Chilly'* Farmer (nicknamed *'Chilly'* because he was *'cool'* - he would go on to play at under 18 level for Ireland in soccer) and Dave Campbell at left corner. In the end, according to Johnny, it came down to a kick of the ball. *"Dave Campbell took all the frees, and at just 13 years of age, slotted them all coolly over the bar to give us the win. Pressure never phased this kid. He was born to perform on the big stage,"* said Johnny and indeed, most of the teaching staff believe that had he not chosen to run the following year, he could and would have played Inter County football for Kildare.

As to just what made him choose running over football, well that might have come down to his father's influence, in part. His father, John, was quite a respectable club runner in his day, or perhaps, maybe it was the knowledge that in that same year, 1996, a certain Shane Healy was busy putting Kildare on the map, running in the Olympics. Either way, Dave made his decision – he would run 800m and 1,500m.

His love of sport was fuelled from an early age, like many kids born in the early eighties or late seventies, by the success of the Irish soccer team under Jack Charlton. As a young lad he sat and watched, enthralled at the World Cup in 1990, hoping like the rest of the country that Ireland's dream could go on forever… He would go on to play for Bohemians.

His father John instilled a sense of giving only your best on the track or indeed, any surface you are competing on. He grew up believing that you only get one shot at the thing you want in life. His fiercely competitive spirit and will and determination to win weren't lost on his PE teacher, John Holt, who has taught and trained teams in the school for the past 30 years. *"I've never really met any kid who was more keenly focussed on a prize than Dave Campbell. He was meticulous in his planning in everything he did, from studying the opposition to preparing for a race. He hated to lose and would often sit and analyse proceedings on the way home on the school bus."*

What was interesting, John reckoned, was the support that Dave got from those around him, his father who accompanied him to all of the race meets, his family at home and his local running club in Maynooth, who supported him all of the way. John believes that too often, talented kids appear on the scene with all the skills but burn out by 16 because they either can't handle the pressure or aren't properly supported by the key people around them.

Being a good runner had its advantages as Bernie, his mother, recalls. *"When he was younger, he had a strict curfew of 9pm to be home by during school hours. He was seeing a girl on the other side of Maynooth at the time, which was a distance of about two to three miles. He used to maximise his time with her, so that he could run the couple of miles and be home by 9!"*

His first medals came in cross country running with his running club, Maynooth AC, where he was member of the cross country team that won the Under 12s. According to his PE Teacher, John Holt, he never really looked like losing from a young age. His quiet confidence helping him to stay on track. With his father being from Meath, Donncarney, in fact, just outside Bettystown, it was inevitable that he would go to all of the big Inter County football matches involving Meath with his dad. The 90s, as if the Dubs need reminding, were kind to Meath and they flourished in Leinster.

"His pragmatic approach to training would have been moulded to some extent by guys like Sean Boylan, who taught his teams to play the whistle and not the clock," his dad said reflectively.

Interestingly, although Dave promised so much, and displayed a wonderfully positive attitude to both running and to life, behaving like a real team player in what was effectively an individual sport, he never actually won a national title in school.

His best performance came in 1997 when he won the silver medal in the 800 metres at the National Senior under 17s. The same year he ran on the Irish team. At first glance, given what he would go on to achieve, this might seem rather odd, but the trouble was, he was running against the very best guys in the country, exceptional talents and gifted athletes like Mark Carroll (who would go on to win an indoor European 3000m title) and James Nolan, and while he was always there or thereabouts, he couldn't quite make the breakthrough he was so desperately looking for.

Nevertheless, he did an excellent Leaving Cert and continued to flourish as an individual. *"With every year that passed in school, he became more and more outgoing, friendlier and more helpful to his fellow students and teachers alike. He was a pleasure to teach and a wonderful role model to his fellow students,"* Johnny surmises about Dave's final years at Post Primary, Maynooth.

His first real setback came post Leaving Cert... Marcus O' Sullivan, one of Ireland's greatest ever middle distance runners (a former three time World Indoor Champion over 1,500m) who had taken over as Head Track and Field Coach at Villanova in the US, had initially expressed interest in Dave coming over on a scholarship. He tracked his results with interest, but in the end, the forthcoming results just weren't good enough and the offer didn't come. It was a tough break and despite other American offers, Dave decided, in the end, to take a year out before going on to do a Degree in Finance in Maynooth. He focused, in his year out, on his running and most winter evenings this 5' 8", 8 stone athlete now running for Kilcock (St Coca's AC) would cut a rather lonely figure on the canal banks of Maynooth. There's nowhere to hide as a middle distance runner, no place to take solace from your team mates, no one to motivate yourself but you.

DCU established an *'Elite Athletics'* scholarship programme in 2002 with the aim of providing talented young Irish athletes with a viable alternative to going to the US. Dr. Niall Moyna, Head of the Centre for Sport Science and Health, was instrumental in setting up the programme, believing that it was long overdue, that it was time for Third Level institutions to play a much *'greater role in the development of elite sport in Ireland'.* Enda Fitzpatrick, a former teacher at Coolmine in Dublin, was appointed head of track and field. It was he who suggested Dave come to DCU to take a Masters option in Finance and run for the College. Despite coming on board, he almost quit the sport in 2004 at the tender age of 22, as he just couldn't seem to find a way to break through. In the spring of that year, his pal James Nolan asked him to go to a training camp in Cyprus just before the Athens Olympics – he even got approval from Athletics Ireland for Dave to join the training camp. Perhaps, for the first time in his short career, Dave came home realising that all athletes are humans first. They suffer the same fears and confidence issues as everyone else. Maybe he just needed a jolt, a shot of confidence in the arm. Either way, his thirst to succeed had returned.

Sbygniew Orywall, who hailed from Poland, was a pal of Dave's father and a top athletics coach. He missed the opportunity to race our own Ronnie Delaney in the 1956 Melbourne Olympics, having beaten him previously (at one point, Orywall held the world record for the 1,000m), because the Polish Government didn't fund athletes, back then, to travel to the games. His knowledge of coaching and physiology was primed from years of working behind the *'Iron Curtain'* with top athletes. He had known and respected Dave's potential from his early teenage years and suggested to him that he train at altitude in South Africa. Orywall believed *'you must live with the athlete to coach the athlete'.* Determined to give it one last almighty throw of the dice, in 2005, Dave qualified for the European Championships. He started working with Coach Nic Bideau (Sonia O' Sullivan's husband who had trained Cathy Freeman to her brilliant gold on home soil at the Sydney Olympics) in the autumn of 2006 after competing at the Europeans in Gothenberg. After his first spell with the group that autumn in London, and Nic carefully scanning his training diaries, it was clear that he had an awful lot of work to do for improvement on the aerobic side of things. Nic explained to him that in order for him to improve as an athlete, and ultimately improve his 800m and 1500m times, where his potential lay, he needed to improve aerobically as he was limited anaerobically. He based himself in Australia for a few months a year because that's where Nic and Sonia lived. *"It's fun to be down there and train with the sun on your back and be around some really positive and talented runners,"* he noted.

On his return to Ireland in 2007 at the age of 25, he finally began to show his true potential, winning both the 800m and 1500m at the 2007 National Championships - a rare double.

The flamboyant good-looking kid with his dyed hair, ear-rings and tattoos was coming good. His historic double at the National Senior Track & Field Championships in Santry that year, was significant because he had become the first man to win both the 800m and 1500m titles since Eamonn Coghlan achieved the same feat in 1981.

Campbell beat defending champion Thomas Chamney into second in an ultra-competitive 800m final. He was showing great form ahead of the World Championships, and the Osaka-destined Campbell then dethroned Liam Reale of his 1500m crown with a superb finish. It was all looking good for the man who would also win the 1500m in the prestigious Cork City Sports meeting.

Despite being sick in hospital before the start of the games in Osaka, having been struck down with a mystery bug, Dave Campbell got out of his bed against medical advice to run the 1st round of the 800m. Though he didn't qualify, he still managed to somehow run his second ever best time - quite remarkable, missing the semis by 0.2 of a second. Dave was discovering that running can be a cruel game. You never know what way the cards are going to fall, but although he left that track feeling utterly disappointed at not progressing, he felt proud of how he had dealt with that situation and left Osaka hungry to be a better runner.

The lessons he learned in Osaka would serve him well for what was to prove to be the toughest year of his life. The year 2008 had begun promisingly for the man from Kildare. The winter was going great but by February it had all gone pear-shaped. He felt pains in his left shin that progressively got worse. Unfortunately, it wasn't diagnosed correctly by an MRI scan and he continued to race and train on a stress fracture and did more and more damage to it. A bone scan confirmed it was a stress fracture and he didn't run a step for the guts of 10 weeks. Although he cross-trained hard every day for those 10 weeks, when he finally stepped onto the track in May, it felt like he had never run a step before. But you keep faith that it will eventually turn. After all, it had for guys like Mark Carroll who missed a lot of training before he won a medal at the Europeans, and Sonia herself had bounced back from similar problems in the past.

Dave tried to rush himself to become race fit, sacrificing strength training to get the body to run the A Standard from '*body memory*'. He got himself into shape to have a real go at the 800m but came up short with a time of 1.47.

What followed was unfortunate in the extreme. His old rival Thomas Chamney would beat him in the National Championships and claim a place in the Beijing Olympics. It would be easy to get caught up writing about the surprise late reversal by the Olympic Council of their stance against allowing 'B' standards to compete in the Olympics. It would be easy to focus on the fact that Dave Campbell didn't know that it had come down to a straight shootout for a place in the games, but, in truth, either way it doesn't really matter; Chamney went to the Olympics and Campbell didn't. It's at moments like these that you make your most important decisions in life – '*better or bitter*' - you choose. Perhaps you don't like what's just unfolded, but you always have the power to decide how you react. Campbell, after much soul-searching, considered the bigger picture. He would come back stronger.

****

When I finally catch up with him in South Africa by Skype phone, Dave and his new bride, fellow top athlete Zoë Brown, are busy training. Zöe, a former top gymnast, is Ireland's top ranked pole vaulter. Just before they got married, Dave came home to see his mum Bernie to ask for her '*blessing*' of sorts before he proposed. Every time they were in Paris, he attempted to get down on one knee to propose. Zoe would pull him back up, thinking that he was injured!

Dave's times are ranking him in the top eight in Europe and he's currently preparing for the European Championships in Barcelona in 2010. After base training finishes in South Africa, Dave Campbell will join Bideau and Sonia O'Sullivan in Melbourne from next January. Zoe will remain in South Africa with a group of other pole vaulters including Polish world champion, Anna Rogowska.

Both will then return to Ireland next March, before Dave Campbell joins Bideau's group in London. Perhaps it's a good omen - London beckoning... the Olympics just around the corner, this courageous athlete intends to keep the home fires burning back in the Post Primary in Maynooth.